T0319822

Business Ethics and Corporate Sustainability

STUDIES IN TRANSATLANTIC BUSINESS ETHICS

Series Editors: Laszlo Zsolnai, *Corvinus University, Hungary* and George Brenkert, *Georgetown University, USA*

Over the past several decades the importance of ethical issues in business has become widely acknowledged. Business scandals, globalization, the Internet, outsourcing of production, environmental concerns, a growing appreciation for business responsibilities for human rights, and numerous other developments have raised the level of attention paid to business ethics and corporate social responsibility. At the same time, it has become apparent that there is a pressing need for more refined studies of business ethics as informed by an international perspective. Though American and European business ethics have developed differently, many problems are similar on both sides of the Atlantic. Having this insight we established the TransAtlantic Business Ethics Conferences (TABEC) in 2000 for promoting exchange and collaboration between American and European scholars and practitioners.

The first TABEC was held in Budapest in 2000 at the Budapest University of Economic Sciences. The second one was organized in Washington, DC in 2002 at Georgetown University. Subsequent conferences have been held at such prominent locations as the ESADE Business School (Barcelona), the Wharton School (Philadelphia) and the SDA Bocconi School of Management (Milan). The intention in each case was to bring together a group of distinguished business ethicists from Europe and North America to address current and central problems of business ethics.

The purpose of the *Studies in TransAtlantic Business Ethics* series is to publish some of the best thinking on business ethics that is currently available on either side of the Atlantic. Though the main engine behind the series is TABEC, the series is not limited to papers presented at one of the TABEC conferences. Other contributions from prominent business ethicists are welcome too. It is our hope that our series can catalyze fresh and innovative thinking and practices in America, Europe and beyond.

Business Ethics and Corporate Sustainability

Edited by

Antonio Tencati *and* Francesco Perrini

Università Bocconi, Italy

STUDIES IN TRANSATLANTIC BUSINESS ETHICS

Edward Elgar

Cheltenham, UK • Northampton, MA, USA

Published by
Edward Elgar Publishing Limited
The Lypiatts
15 Lansdown Road
Cheltenham
Glos GL50 2JA
UK

Edward Elgar Publishing, Inc.
William Pratt House
9 Dewey Court
Northampton
Massachusetts 01060
USA

A catalogue record for this book
is available from the British Library

Library of Congress Control Number: 2010939276

ISBN 978 1 84980 371 7

Typeset by Servis Filmsetting Ltd, Stockport, Cheshire
Printed and bound by MPG Books Group, UK

This book is dedicated to the memories of
Thomas W. Dunfee and Henk van Luijk

Contents

Figures

Tables

Contributors

Daniel Arenas is associate professor for the Department of Social Sciences at ESADE Business School, where he is also the head of research for the Institute for Social Innovation. He holds a PhD and an MA from the Committee on Social Thought at the University of Chicago, a degree in philosophy from the University of Barcelona and a diploma from the Program of Executive Development at ESADE. He teaches courses in sociology, business ethics and corporate social responsibility. His research interests focus in the areas of business ethics and corporate social responsibility, and he has also published in the fields of political theory and aesthetics. He has been professor at ESADE since 2002.

Arenas' recent publications include: 'Healthcare provision of a multinational company operating in emerging markets: ethical motivation, benefits of healthcare investment and impact on socially responsible investors', in C. Louche, S. Idowu, and W. Filho (eds), *Innovative CSR: From Risk Management to Value Creation* (2010), Sheffield: Greenleaf Publishing (co-authors K. van Cranenburgh and L. Albareda), pp. 241–63. 'Societal ethos and economic development organizations in Nicaragua', *Journal of Business Ethics* (2009), **88** (Supplement 2), 231–44 (co-author J.F. Mària); and 'The role of NGOs in CSR: mutual perceptions among stakeholders', *Journal of Business Ethics* (2009), **88** (1), 175–97 (co-authors J.M. Lozano and L. Albareda).

Michael Bourlakis is professor in marketing at Kent Business School. He graduated with a BSc in business administration from Athens University of Economics and Business (1990) and completed MBA (1995) and PhD (2001) at the University of Edinburgh. He previously held academic positions at Brunel University, Newcastle University, Oxford Institute of Retail Management at Templeton College, Oxford University and Leicester University Management Centre. He also worked as a sales and distribution manager for the leading Greek food manufacturer Delta. Bourlakis has published over 130 papers in numerous journals, books, conference proceedings and other academic and professional outlets and he has co-edited a book called *Food Supply Chain Management* (2004), published by Blackwell.

George Brenkert is professor of business ethics at the McDonough School of Business at Georgetown University, USA. He is former editor-in-chief of the *Business Ethics Quarterly* and past president of the Society for Business Ethics. He is an academic member of the Ethics Resource Center and chair of the Business Ethics Committee of the Association for Professional and Practical Ethics. Together with Laszlo Zsolnai, he is a co-founder of the TransAtlantic Business Ethics Conference. His research areas include business ethics, corporate social responsibility, marketing ethics, ethics and entrepreneurship, and social and political philosophy.

Brenkert's recent publications include: 'Corporate control of information: business and the freedom of expression', *Business and Society Review* (2010), **115** (1), 121–45; 'ISCT, hypernorms, and business: a reinterpretation', *Journal of Business Ethics* (2009), **88** (Supplement 4), 645–58; and *Oxford Handbook of Business Ethics* (2009), New York: Oxford University Press (co-edited with T.L. Beauchamp).

Jane Collier holds a BSc from the London School of Economics, an MA from Cambridge University and a PhD (theology) from Birmingham University. She holds the honorary title of senior fellow at the Judge Business School at Cambridge University. She is also emeritus fellow at Luck Cavendish College in Cambridge, where she was director of studies in economics and management. Her research interests are in the fields of business ethics, corporate accountability, corporate social responsibility, governance and socially responsible investment. She sits on the board of CIS (socially responsible investors), and is a trustee of the Institute of Business Ethics in London.

Collier's recent publications include: 'Nurturing society from the bottom up: the state and social enterprise', in A. Tencati and L. Zsolnai (eds), *The Collaborative Enterprise: Creating Values for a Sustainable World* (2010), Oxford and Bern: Peter Lang AG – International Academic Publishers, pp. 335–50; 'Corporate social responsibility and employee commitment', *Business Ethics: A European Review* (2007), **16** (1), 19–33 (co-author R. Esteban); and 'The art of moral imagination: ethics in the practice of architecture', *Journal of Business Ethics* (2006), **66** (2–3), 307–17.

Christopher J. Cowton is dean of the University of Huddersfield Business School and professor of accounting there, having assumed the latter post in 1996 after ten years lecturing at the University of Oxford. He holds a BA with first class honours in Accounting and Financial Management from the University of Sheffield, an MA (by special resolution) from the University of Oxford, an MSc Econ. from the University of Wales, a PhD from the University of Sheffield and a graduate diploma in philosophy from the University of York. He is a chartered secretary (ACIS) and a fellow of the Royal Society of Arts (FRSA).

Cowton has published in fields as diverse as philosophy, biblical studies, production engineering and operations management, but his principal interests are in business ethics, especially in relation to accounting and finance. In addition to authoring many journal articles, he has edited books for Oxford University Press (*Business Ethics: Perspectives on the Practice of Theory*, 1998, with Roger Crisp) and Springer (*Trends in Business and Economic Ethics*, 2008, with Michaela Haase).

A frequently invited speaker on business ethics, Cowton is editor of the international journal *Business Ethics: A European Review*. He gave the P.D. Leake Lecture in 2007 ('Meeting the ethics challenge: prospects and proposals for promoting professional integrity') and is a member of the Ethics Standards Committee of the Institute of Chartered Accountants in England and Wales. He was chairman of EBEN-UK, the UK Association of the European Business Ethics Network from 1998 to 2001 and has been a member of the ethics advisory committee of one of the UK's first socially responsible investment funds.

Wesley Cragg is a professor emeritus and a senior scholar in the Department of Philosophy and the Schulich School of Business at York University in Toronto, Canada. He has published widely in Canadian and international journals and written and edited books on topics in business ethics, corporate citizenship, bribery and corruption, occupational ethics, moral education, applied ethics, moral, political and social philosophy, philosophy of law and philosophy of punishment. He is currently project director for the Canadian Business Ethics Research Network (CBERN). Funded by the Canadian Social Science and Humanities Research Council and other donors, CBERN's goal is to encourage, support and raise the profile of business ethics research in Canada.

Cragg's recent publications include: 'Being virtuous and prosperous: SRI's conflicting goals' (2010), *Journal of Business Ethics*, **92** (Supplement 1), 21–39 (co-author B.J. Richardson); *Corporate Social Responsibility* (2009), Farnham: Ashgate (co-edited with M. Schwartz and D. Weitzner); and 'Business and human rights: a principle and value-based analysis', in G. Brenkert and T. Beauchamp (eds), *Oxford Handbook of Business Ethics* (2009), New York: Oxford University Press, pp. 267–304.

Antonello Di Giulio has several years of management consulting experience in the fields of corporate strategy, sustainability, multi-channel strategies and business development. He has been instrumental in establishing Accenture's Italian Sustainability Strategy Practice. He has led numerous

Business ethics and corporate sustainability

research activities internationally and has conducted executive training on sustainable development topics. His work aims at integrating sustainability issues into corporate strategies and operations and enhancing overall corporate social responsibility performance.

Di Giulio is also a market information system specialist with deep field experience across African countries, devising business solutions embedding technology for social change. His areas of interests and expertise include social entrepreneurship, green technologies, social networking, strategy, corporate social responsibility and cocoa sector development. He is also the winner of an International Accenture Strategy Competition with two innovative concepts: 'Sustainability for banks: an unexplored way to rebuild trust and reputation' and 'M2M: when machines become Smart'.

Georges Enderle is the John T. Ryan Jr Professor of International Business Ethics at the Mendoza College of Business, University of Notre Dame (Indiana, USA), and former president of the International Society of Business, Economics, and Ethics (ISBEE; 2000–04). Educated in philosophy (Munich), theology (Lyon), economics (Fribourg) and business ethics (St Gallen), he has extensive research and teaching experiences in Europe (1983–92), the USA (since 1992) and China (since 1994). He serves on the board of advisors of several academic journals and centres for business ethics in various countries and has authored and edited 18 books and over 120 articles. He conducts research on the ethics of globalization, wealth creation, business and human rights, and corporate responsibilities of large and small companies, with a view on developments in China.

Enderle's recent publications include: 'A rich concept of wealth creation beyond profit maximization and adding value', *Journal of Business Ethics* (2009), **84** (Supplement 3), 281–95; also in G. Moore (ed.), *Fairness in International Trade* (2010), Dordrecht, the Netherlands: Springer, pp. 9–26; 'Rediscovering the golden rule in a globalizing world', in K. Tzewan (ed.), *Responsibility and Commitment: Eighteen Essays in Honor of Gerhold K. Becker* (2008), Waldkirch, Germany: Edition Gorz, pp. 1–15; and 'Corporate responsibility in the CSR debate', in J. Wieland et al., *Unternehmensethik im Spannungsfeld der Kulturen und Religionen* (2006), Stuttgart, Germany: Kohlhammer, pp. 108–24.

Knut J. Ims is professor in business ethics at the Norwegian School of Economics and Business Administration (NHH), Bergen, Norway. He received his PhD from the School of Economics and Legal Sciences, Gothenburg University, Sweden. He has taught courses in ethics (Ethical Action – Individual, Organization and Society; and Business Strategy and Business Ethics) for more than a decade. He has also taught PhD courses in systems development and information and management. He is a member of the Business Ethics Interfaculty Group of the Community of European Management Schools – The Global Alliance in Management Education (CEMS), and is chairman of the board of the Centre of Ethics and Economics at NHH.

Ims' recent publications include: 'Quality of life – the golden mean between materialistic consumerism and spiritual ascetism', in L. Zsolnai (ed.), *Europe-Asia Dialogue on Business Spirituality* (2008), European SPES Cahiers no. 2, Antwerp, Belgium: Garant, pp. 119–33 (co-author O.D. Jakobsen); 'Partnership in the market – Max Havelaar as an example of moral consumers, vulnerable producers and Fair Trade', in S. Ingebrigtsen and O.D. Jakobsen (eds), *Circulation Economics: Theory and Practice* (2007), Oxford: Peter Lang AG – International Academic Publishers, pp. 93–108; and 'Consumerism and frugality: contradictory principles in economics?', in L. Bouckaert, H. Opdebeeck and L. Zsolnai (eds), *Frugality: Rebalancing Material and Spiritual Values in Economic Life* (2007), Oxford: Peter Lang AG – International Academic Publishers, pp. 169–84 (co-author O.D. Jakobsen).

Kevin T. Jackson is professor of law and ethics at Fordham University Graduate School of Business in New York City. Formerly on the faculties of Princeton University, Georgetown University and Peking University (China), he is a senior fellow and director of the Program in Ethics and Business at The Witherspoon Institute in Princeton, NJ.

Jackson's recent publications include: 'The scandal beneath the financial crisis: getting a view from a moral-cultural mental model', *Harvard Journal of Law and Public Policy* (2010), **33** (2), 735–78; 'Global corporate governance: soft law and reputational accountability', *Brooklyn Journal of International Law* (2010), **35** (1), 41–106; and 'Cultivating the ethics-economics interface', in S. Gregg and J. Stoner (eds), *Profit, Prudence and Virtue: Essays in Ethics, Business and Management* (2009), Exeter, and Charlottesville, VA: Imprint Academic, pp. 128–54.

Ove D. Jakobsen was born in Bodø, Norway, in 1952. He is professor at Bodø Graduate School of Business (HHB). He is co-founder of The Centre for Ecological Economics and Ethics in HHB. He is also a member of the National Committee for Research Ethics in the Social Sciences and the Humanities (NESH). He has masters' degrees in philosophy (University of Bergen), management (Norwegian School of Economics and Business Administration) and marketing (Buskerud University College). He received his Dr Oec. from the Norwegian School of Economics and Business Administration in Bergen.

Jakobsen's recent publications include: 'Moral development of the economic actor', *Ecological Economics* (2009), **68** (11), 2777–84 (co-author S. Ingebrigtsen); 'Quality of life – the golden mean between materialistic consumerism and spiritual ascetism', in L. Zsolnai (ed.), *Europe-Asia Dialogue on Business Spirituality* (2008), European SPES Cahiers no. 2, Antwerp, Belgium: Garant, pp. 119–33 (co-author K.J. Ims); and *Circulation Economics – Theory and Practice* (2007), Oxford: Peter Lang AG – International Academic Publishers (co-author S. Ingebrigtsen).

Josep M. Lozano was awarded a PhD in philosophy by the University of Barcelona and a degree in theology by the Theology Faculty of Catalonia. He also holds a degree in executive management from ESADE Business School. He is currently full professor at the Department of Social Sciences at ESADE and senior researcher in corporate social responsibility at the Institute for Social Innovation (ESADE). His academic and professional activity focuses on the fields of business ethics, corporate social responsibility, and values, leadership and spirituality.

Lozano's recent publications include: *The Relational Company: Responsibility, Sustainability, Citizenship* (2009), Oxford: Peter Lang AG – International Academic Publishers; 'From risk management to citizenship corporate social responsibility: analysis of strategic drivers of change', *Corporate Governance: The International Journal of Business in Society* (2009), **9** (4), 373–85 (co-author I. Castelló); and 'The role of NGOs in CSR: mutual perceptions among stakeholders', *Journal of Business Ethics* (2009), **88** (1), 175–97 (co-authors D. Arenas and L. Albareda).

Paolo Migliavacca is lecturer of management at Università Bocconi, Milan, Italy, and at the University of Turin, Turin, Italy. He received his PhD in management at Catholic University, Milan. He is research fellow of the CSR Unit and CReSV Research Center, Università Bocconi. He serves as an independent director in some public and private institutions. He is vice chairman of Lucos Alternative Energies and CEO of Vita Content Group, the leading European publishing and consulting group for the non-profit sector. His research interests are merger and acquisitions, strategic alliances, innovation finance, renewable energies, sustainability and social venture capital.

Eleanor O'Higgins is on the faculty of the School of Business at University College Dublin (UCD) and a visiting fellow at the London School of Economics and Political Science. She specializes in teaching, research and publications in business ethics, corporate social responsibility, corporate governance and strategic management. She is a member of the Business

Ethics and the Public Management & Governance Interfaculty Groups of the Community of European Management Schools – the Global Alliance in Management Education (CEMS) and serves on the editorial boards of a number of international management journals. She has held a range of leadership positions in the US Academy of Management. She is a member of the Press Council of Ireland, and director of Transparency International Ireland and the Marine Institute, where she also serves on the Audit Committee. O'Higgins is the author of numerous papers in academic and professional journals, newspaper articles, book chapters and case studies.

Francesco Perrini is professor of management and CSR at the Institute of Strategy, Department of Management and Technology, Università Bocconi, Milan, Italy. He is also SIF chair of Social Entrepreneurship and senior professor of corporate finance at the Corporate and Real Estate Finance Department, SDA Bocconi School of Management. He is director of the Center of Università Bocconi for Research on Sustainability and Value (CReSV), head of Bocconi CSR Unit, Department of Management and Technology, Università Bocconi, and coordinator of CSR Activities Group at SDA Bocconi. His research areas are management of corporate development processes, from strategy implementation (acquisitions and strategic alliances) to financial strategies and valuation; small- and medium-sized enterprises; and social issues in management: corporate governance, corporate social responsibility, sustainability, social entrepreneurship, social innovation and socially responsible investing.

Perrini's recent publications include: 'Collaborative social entrepreneurship', in A. Tencati and L. Zsolnai (eds), *The Collaborative Enterprise: Creating Values for a Sustainable World* (2010), Oxford and Bern: Peter Lang AG – International Academic Publishers, pp. 351–71 (co-author C. Vurro); 'The missing link between corporate social responsibility and consumer trust: the case of Fair Trade products', *Journal of Business Ethics* (2009), **84** (1), 1–15 (co-authors S. Castaldo, N. Misani and A. Tencati), and 'CSR strategies of SMEs and large firms. Evidence from Italy', *Journal of Business Ethics* (2007), **74** (3), 285–300 (co-authors A. Russo and A. Tencati).

Yvon Pesqueux is professor at Conservatoire National des Arts et Métiers (CNAM), and head of the chair 'Développement des Systèmes d'Organisation'. He is also editor of *Society and Business Review* and member of the Société Française de Management (SFM). He has a PhD in economics from the University of Paris 1 Panthéon-Sorbonne (1975). His special interests are management, philosophy and ethics, business and society, and corporate social responsibility. He has published several scientific articles.

Pesqueux's recent books link organization and politics: *La 'société du risque' – analyse et critique* (2010), Paris: Economica (co-authors Jérôme Meric and Andreu Sole); *L' 'école japonaise d'organisation'* (2010), Paris: AFNOR (co-author Jean-Pierre Tyberghen); and *Filosofia e organizaçoes* (2008), São Paulo: Cencage Learning.

Laura J. Spence is director of the Centre for Research into Sustainability (CRIS) at Royal Holloway, University of London, UK, where she is also a reader in business ethics. She is vice president of the International Society of Business, Economics, and Ethics and was formerly an Executive Committee member of the European Business Ethics Network. She is co-editor of the ISBEE book series with Springer and section editor of the *Journal of Business Ethics* for 'small business, entrepreneurship and social enterprise'. Her research interests cover a wide range of issues relating to business ethics, corporate social responsibility and sustainability. She has published on these topics particularly in relation to small- and medium-sized enterprises, supply chains, social capital and accounting for sustainability in multiple food retailers.

Spence's recent publications include: *Ethics in Small and Medium Sized Enterprises: A Global Commentary* (2010), Dordrecht, the Netherlands: International Society of Business, Economics, and Ethics Book Series, Springer (co-edited with M. Painter-Morland); 'Practice as a members' phenomenon', *Organization Studies*, Special Issue, Return to Practice (2009), **30** (12), 1419–39 (co-author N. Llewellyn); and 'The nature of reciprocity in family firm succession', *International Small Business Journal* (2009), **27** (6), 702–19 (co-author S. Janjuha-Jivraj).

Antonio Tencati is assistant professor of management and corporate social responsibility at the Institute of Technology and Innovation Management, Department of Management and Technology, Università Bocconi, Milan, Italy. He is a senior researcher at the Center of Università Bocconi for Research on Sustainability and Value (CReSV), and a member of the CSR Unit, Department of Management and Technology, Università Bocconi. He is also a member of the Business Ethics Faculty Group of the Community of European Management Schools – The Global Alliance in Management Education (CEMS). His research areas comprise business management, management of sustainability and corporate social responsibility, environmental management, innovation and operations management.

Tencati's recent publications include: *The Collaborative Enterprise: Creating Values for a Sustainable World* (2010), Oxford and Bern: Peter

Lang AG – International Academic Publishers (co-edited with L. Zsolnai); 'The collaborative enterprise', *Journal of Business Ethics* (2009), **85** (3), 367–76 (co-author L. Zsolnai); and *The Future International Manager: A Vision of the Roles and Duties of Management* (2009), Houndmills and New York: Palgrave Macmillan (co-edited with L. Zsolnai).

Clodia Vurro is postdoctoral fellow of strategy and member of the CSR Unit at the Department of Management and Technology, Università Bocconi, Milan, Italy. She is assistant to the Bocconi SIF chair of Social Entrepreneurship and research fellow at the Center of Università Bocconi for Research on Sustainability and Value (CReSV). Her research areas comprise management of corporate development processes, learning dynamics of sustainability strategy implementation, corporate social responsibility and social entrepreneurship.

Vurro's recent publications include:

'Institutional antecedents of partnering for social change: how institutional logics shape cross-sector social partnerships', *Journal of Business Ethics* (2010), (co-authors T. Dacin and F. Perrini) available online at www.springerlink.com/content/p3073r13770n5818/; 'Collaborative social entrepreneurship', in A. Tencati and L. Zsolnai (eds), *The Collaborative Enterprise: Creating Values for a Sustainable World* (2010), Oxford and Bern: Peter Lang AG – International Academic Publishers, pp. 351–71 (co-author F. Perrini); and 'Shaping sustainable value chains: network determinants of supply chain governance models', *Journal of Business Ethics* (2009), **90** (Supplement 4), 607–21 (co-authors A. Russo and F. Perrini).

Johan Wempe holds a chair in governance at Saxion University, the Netherlands. As a professor at Erasmus University, he supervises a number of PhD projects in the area of business ethics. He previously held a chair in business ethics and sustainability management at Rotterdam School of Management at Erasmus University. He was the founder and first director of CSR Netherlands. He was also the founder and a director/partner of KPMG Sustainability. He has published several books on business ethics, including *The Balanced Company. A Theory of Corporate Integrity* (Oxford: Oxford University Press, 2002), as well as a large number of articles in this field.

Laszlo Zsolnai is professor and director of the Business Ethics Center at the Corvinus University of Budapest. He is chairman of the Business Ethics Faculty Group of the Community of European Management Schools – The Global Alliance in Management Education (CEMS). He is also fellow associate at Judge Business School, University of Cambridge. He is editor-in-chief of *Ethical Prospects* published by Springer. He serves as editor of the 'Frontier of Business Ethics' book series at Peter Lang Publishers in Oxford. He was born in 1958, in Szentes, Hungary. He has a master's degree in finance and a doctorate in sociology from the Budapest University of Economic Sciences. He received his PhD and DSc degrees in economics from the Hungarian Academy of Sciences.

Zsolnai's recent books in English include: *The Collaborative Enterprise: Creating Values for a Sustainable World* (2010), Oxford and Bern: Peter Lang AG International Academic Publishers (co-edited with A. Tencati); *The Future International Manager: A Vision of the Roles and Duties of Management* (2009), Houndmills and New York: Palgrave Macmillan (co-edited with A. Tencati); and *Responsible Decision Making* (2008), New Brunswick, NJ and London: Transaction Publishers.

Preface

The legitimacy of all firms is at stake. The mainstream business model –
still prevailing even after the heavy financial downturn – is characterized
by a narrow focus on monetary results, short-termism and a competitive,
disruptive approach for the benefit of specific groups of interest, such
as main shareholders and top managers, at the expense of society as a
whole, human beings, ecosystems and future generations. But, as the
current systems crisis clearly shows, this model is self-defeating, ethically
questionable and, after all, unsustainable. So, a critical and imagina-
tive perspective is needed to identify, develop and advance innovative
solutions and new interpretations. In many cases there are already existing and well-functioning alternatives to addressing the sustainability
challenge.

This volume collects a set of cutting-edge contributions from prominent
European and North American scholars who reflect upon business ethics
foundations, firms, markets and stakeholders in order to envisage more
sustainable patterns of development for business and society.

The first part of the book, which addresses the role of business in
society, begins from the concept of corporate legitimacy, defining the real
conditions that make a company activity system morally justifiable and
socially acceptable (Laszlo Zsolnai).

Rethinking the mainstream models also calls for rethinking the concept
of corporate responsibility. Thus, if the aim is to intervene to modify
actions and outcomes, it is crucial to determine, beyond generic collective liabilities, specific personal responsibilities within the organizations
(Christopher J. Cowton). Furthermore, the introduction of the related
notions of prospective responsibility and role responsibility is essential
to better address the needed change for the better in corporate behaviour
(Johan Wempe).

The same idea of corporate social responsibility (CSR) should be deeply
revised and reframed to face the intertwined economic, energy, climate,
food and social crises (Yvon Pesqueux).

The market, which is at the centre of the analyses of the second part,
should also be rethought in terms of its functioning mechanisms, its purposes and its acting players' orientations and dispositions. For example,
the new breed of philanthropy-centred enterprises involves the rediscovery

of principles like mutual assistance, cooperation and collaboration, and compassion and generosity, which were substantially denied by the dominant competitive paradigm (Kevin T. Jackson).

But even the more conventional financial players, with their increasing weight and role in the market, could contribute to the sustainability goal: in the case of private equity they could operate under the alternative premise of adding value for the benefit of all stakeholders (including workers and society) in their leveraged buyouts of public companies (Eleanor O'Higgins); in the case of sovereign wealth funds they could adopt appropriate principles for responsible investment and integrate environmental, social and governance (ESG) criteria into their investment processes (Jane Collier).

This means that firms and investors should assume more comprehensive and reliable, long-term wealth-creation goals: that calls for new metrics capable of integrating the financial ones, to assess the genuine success of a firm or an investment (Georges Enderle). That also calls for the introduction of different, more operational approaches – beyond the traditional studies on the relationship between corporate social performance (CSP) and corporate financial performance (CFP) – to understanding how companies create value by engaging, involving and partnering with stakeholders. In particular, evidence suggests that advanced and strategic CSR policies can reduce the overall risk profile of a firm as perceived by stakeholders, and especially the financial ones, and measured by the weighted average cost of capital (WACC) (Antonello Di Giulio, Paolo Migliavacca and Antonio Tencati).

Therefore, relationships with stakeholders, on which the third part of the volume is focused, are crucial and go beyond the market and its financial dimension.

In more detail, because of their power and impact, companies, within their sphere of influence, also have an ethical obligation to foster the protection of human rights through collaboration with public institutions and civil society organizations. This effort is part of a broader commitment to building an equitable and sustainable society where freedom, equality and dignity are respected (Wesley Cragg).

A critical area where companies are required to meet this kind of commitment is along the supply chain. Normally, large customers set the rules, including CSR requirements, that all suppliers have to comply with; however, this approach, called corporate social watchdog (CSW), is far from satisfactory or effective in terms of results and reliability. Therefore, a more appropriate situation would be a wider supply chain responsibility (SCR) where all the actors involved are engaged (Laura J. Spence and Michael Bourlakis).

The crucial idea of shared responsibility is not easy to implement and calls for collaboration and mutual understanding with and among stakeholders. But for a multistakeholder dialogue to foster consensus, legitimacy and best practices in the CSR field is not always possible, especially when the mindsets and role interpretations of participants differ. A clear example of this point is seen in the different perceptions between non-governmental organizations (NGOs) and trade unions (Josep M. Lozano and Daniel Arenas). Thus, an effective dialogue requires renewed efforts in the accountability area to make disclosure a fruitful lever for managing the stakeholder network in which a company is embedded (Clodia Vurro and Francesco Perrini).

Finally, to foster higher levels of responsibility and sustainability a change of paradigm is needed: we should abandon a mechanic worldview to embrace an organic worldview, where the individual is part of an interconnected and interdependent web of life. Such a radical change in the interpretative frameworks can lead to a deep authenticity and a better comprehension of the genuine purposes of a firm. In particular, this implies the shift from partial and wrong goals (like maximizing shareholder value) to systemic objectives such as increasing the enjoyment of life for all stakeholders according to a coherent stakeholder value perspective (Knut J. Ims and Ove D. Jakobsen).

Previous versions of these chapters were presented during the Fifth TransAtlantic Business Ethics Conference on Business Ethics and Corporate Sustainability held on 3 and 4 October 2008 at SDA Bocconi School of Management in Milan, Italy.

This conference was a continuation of the Transatlantic Business Ethics Summit, which Laszlo Zsolnai held in Budapest (September 2000); the second TransAtlantic Business Ethics Conference (TABEC), which George Brenkert organized in Washington, DC (September 2002); the third TABEC, which Josep M. Lozano hosted in Barcelona (October 2004); and the fourth TABEC, which Thomas W. Dunfee held in Wharton (October 2006).

TABEC objectives are

- to bring together academic leaders in business ethics from North America and Europe, as well as representatives from businesses and NGOs committed to business ethics, in order to explore ideas and research the subject of the conference;
- to create an ongoing framework to continue these conferences and the related dialogue on a biennial basis; and
- to produce academic outputs based on the papers presented at every conference.

The present book is the first in the *Studies in TransAtlantic Business Ethics Series* edited by Laszlo Zsolnai and George Brenkert and published by Edward Elgar Publishing.

Antonio Tencati and **Francesco Perrini**
Milan, August 2010

Acknowledgements

First of all we would like to thank Laszlo Zsolnai and George Brenkert, founders of the TABEC initiative and editors of this book series: without their passion, personal involvement and generosity all of this would not be possible.

Furthermore we express our gratitude to Alberto Grando, dean of SDA Bocconi School of Management; Sergio Pivato, former director of SPACE, the European Research Centre of Università Bocconi on Risk, Security, Occupational Health and Safety, Environment and Crisis Management, and current president of CReSV, the new, enlarged Centre of Università Bocconi for Research on Sustainability and Value that has since June 2010 embodied SPACE; and Carlo Secchi, former rector of Università Bocconi and current director of ISLA, the Università Bocconi's Center for Latin American Studies and Transition Economies, who encouraged and supported us in the organization of the conference and realization of this volume.

We are also grateful to Paolo Nazzaro, head of the Group Sustainability Department in Telecom Italia, and Silvio de Girolamo, head of the Internal Auditing and CSR Department in Autogrill, for their participation in and financial support of the conference.

Clearly, we thank all the participants in the TABEC in Milan and all the contributors to this volume: their friendship and trust is one of the main reasons our work is so involving and stimulating.

Finally, we would like to acknowledge Ben Booth, our commissioning editor at Edward Elgar Publishing, and Doug Shokes, our language editor, for their engagement and commitment.

The book is dedicated to the memories of Thomas W. Dunfee (1941–2008) and Henk van Luijk (1929–2010), masters and friends.

Antonio Tencati and **Francesco Perrini**

PART 1

The role of business in society

1. Corporate legitimacy

Laszlo Zsolnai*

1.1 INTRODUCTION

In his famous book *The Economy of Love and Fear*, Kenneth Boulding suggests that business is a peaceful alternative to war (Boulding, 1973). This might be true in principle, but today business seems to be at war with society and nature. Striving for profit and competitiveness, mainstream businesses produce monetary results at the expense of nature, society and future generations.

In his influential book *When Corporations Rule the World*, social critic David Korten argues that today's global economy has become like a malignant cancer, advancing the colonization of the planet's living spaces for the benefit of powerful corporations and financial institutions. It has turned these once useful institutions into instruments of a market tyranny that is destroying livelihoods, displacing people, and feeding on life in an insatiable quest for money. It forces us all to act in ways destructive of our selves, our families, our communities and nature (Korten, 1995).

Conventional legitimizing arguments for business do not work anymore. Referring to efficiency or job creation is not enough for stakeholders who are angry with corporate bosses and their insensitive policies. New arguments and performances are needed for corporations to gain legitimacy in the twenty-first century.

1.2 JUST WAR THEORY

I suggest that the Just War theory provides an excellent methodological device for determining the conditions of legitimacy of companies.

The Just War theory promotes the view that a specific war is just if satisfactory conditions are met. The Just War tradition addresses the morality of the use of force in two parts: when it is right to resort to armed force (the concern of '*jus ad bellum*') and what is acceptable in using such force (the concern of '*jus in bello*'). In more recent years, a third category – '*jus post bellum'* – has been added, which governs the justice of war termination and peace agreements, as well as the trying of war criminals.

Just War theory has different sets of criteria. The first establishes the right to go to war (*'jus as bellum'*); the second establishes the right conduct within war (*'jus in bello'*), while the third establishes justice concerning the results of war (*'jus post bellum'*).

In business ethics we can make analogous distinctions. A company activity system can be considered morally justifiable if the company's activities are substantively right, procedurally fair and bring justice to the company's ecosystem.

1.3   SUBSTANTIVELY RIGHT

Being substantively right implies that the company activity system is ecological, future respecting and prosocial (Zsolnai, 2009).

This means that

1. The company activity system does not harm nature or allow others to come to harm.
2. The company activity system does not violate the interests of future generations.
3. The company activity system serves to enable people.

1.3.1   Not Harming Nature

From the perspective nature integrity is a central value. The notion of ecological integrity was introduced by American environmentalist Aldo Leopold in his classic *A Sand County Almanac*. He writes, '[A] thing is right when it tends to preserve the integrity, stability, and beauty of the biotic community. It is wrong when it tends otherwise' (Leopold, 1984, p. 262).

Company activity systems might be evaluated against environmental indicators that operationalize the notion of ecological integrity.

Let A be the company activity system. Let $E1, \ldots, Ej, \ldots, En$ be environmental indicators ($n > 1$).

$Ei(\ )$ is an ecological value function defined as follows:

$$Ej(A) = \begin{cases} 1 & \text{if company activity system } A \text{ is good regarding environmental indicator } Ej; \\ 0 & \text{if company activity system } A \text{ is neutral regarding environmental indicator } Ej; \end{cases} \quad (1.1)$$

−2 if company activity system *A* is bad regarding environmental indicator *Ej*.

Ei(A) reflects the ecological value of company activity system *A* regarding environmental indicator *Ej*.

The following vector represents the ecological value of company activity system *A* regarding all environmental indicators *E*1, . . ., *Ej*, . . ., *En*.

$$\underline{E}(A) = [E1(A), \ldots, Ej(A), \ldots, En(A)] \tag{1.2}$$

To get an aggregate picture of the ecological value of the company activity system we should define weights that show the importance of environmental indicators. Let *a*1, . . ., *aj*, . . ., *an* be such importance weights.

It is required that

$$\sum aj = 1 \tag{1.3}$$

The aggregate ecological value of company activity system *A* can be calculated as follows:

$$E(A) = \sum aj \, Ej(A) \tag{1.4}$$

E(A) shows the aggregate ecological value of company activity system *A* $(1 \geq E(A) \geq -2)$.

The company activity system is considered ecological if and only if its aggregate ecological value is positive. That is

$$E(A) > 0 \tag{1.5}$$

1.3.2 Respecting Future Generations

How can we evaluate a company activity system from the perspective of future generations? We cannot know a great deal about the interests of future generations, but freedom is a central value here.

According to Edith Brown Weiss the freedom of future generations is ensured by satisfying the following principles (Brown Weiss, 1989):

1. conservation of options;
2. conservation of quality;
3. conservation of access.

Considering principles (1), (2) and (3), future-generations indicators can be created. Let $F1, \ldots, Fj, \ldots, Fn$ be such indicators against which company activity systems can be evaluated ($n > 1$).

Future-generations value function $Fj(\ )$ is defined as follows:

$$Fj(A) = \begin{cases} 1 & \text{if company activity system } A \text{ is good regarding future-generations indicator } Fj; \\ 0 & \text{if company activity system } A \text{ is neutral regarding future-generations indicator } Fj; \\ -2 & \text{if company activity system } A \text{ is bad regarding future-generations indicator } Fj. \end{cases} \quad (1.6)$$

$Fj(A)$ reflects the future-generations value of company activity system A regarding indicator Fj.

The following vector represents the future-generations value of company activity system A regarding future-generations indicators $F1, \ldots, Fj, \ldots, Fn$.

$$\underline{F}(A) = [F1(A), \ldots, Fj(A), \ldots, Fn(A)] \quad (1.7)$$

To get an aggregate picture of the future-generations value of company activity system A we should introduce weights that show the importance of indicators $F1, \ldots, Fj, \ldots, Fn$. Let $b1, \ldots, bj, \ldots, bn$ be such importance weights.

It is required that

$$\sum bj = 1 \quad (1.8)$$

The aggregate future-generations value of company activity system A can be calculated as follows:

$$\sum bj\, Fj(A) \quad (1.9)$$

$F(A)$ shows the aggregate future-generations value of company activity system A. ($1 \geq F(A) \geq -2$).

The company activity system can be considered future respecting if its aggregate future-generations value is positive. That is

$$F(A) > 0 \quad (1.10)$$

1.3.3 Enabling People

Amartya Sen proposed to understand people's wellbeing in terms of capabilities. Capability is a reflection of the freedom of a person to achieve valuable functioning. Therefore capabilities can be interpreted as substantive freedom that people enjoy (Sen, 1992).

Let $G1, \ldots, Gj, \ldots, Gn$ be capability indicators against which the company activity system can be evaluated ($j > 1$).

Let $Gj(\ )$ social-value function be defined as follows:

$$Gj(A) = \begin{array}{ll} 1 & \text{if company activity system } A \text{ is good regarding} \\ & \text{capability indicator } Gj; \\ 0 & \text{if company activity system } A \text{ is neutral regarding} \\ & \text{capability indicator } Gj; \\ -2 & \text{if company activity system } A \text{ is bad regarding} \\ & \text{capability indicator } Gj. \end{array} \qquad (1.11)$$

$Gj(A)$ shows the social value of company activity system A regarding capability indicator Gj.

The following vector represents the social value of company activity system A regarding all the capability indicators $G1, \ldots, Gj, \ldots, Gn$.

$$\underline{G}(A) = [G1(A), \ldots, Gj(A), \ldots, Gn(A)] \qquad (1.12)$$

To get an aggregate picture of the social value of company activity system A we should introduce weights that show the importance of the capability indicators. Let $c1, \ldots, cj, \ldots, cn$ be such importance weights.

It is required that

$$\sum cj = 1 \qquad (1.13)$$

The aggregate social value of company activity system A can be calculated as follows:

$$G(A) = \sum cj\, Gj(A) \qquad (1.14)$$

$G(A)$ shows the aggregate social value of the company activity system A ($1 \geq C(A) \geq -2$).

The company activity system is considered prosocial if its aggregate social value is positive. That is

$$G(A) > 0 \qquad (1.15)$$

1.4   PROCEDURALLY FAIR

Being procedurally fair implies that the company should treat all the important stakeholders in a fair way.
   This includes that

1.   The company provides the owners with a fair return of investment.
2.   The company ensures a decent livelihood for its employees.
3.   The company deals with its customers properly.
4.   The company adheres to fair trade with suppliers.
5.   The company establishes collaboration with local communities.

1.4.1   Fair Return on Investment

Let $P1, \ldots, Pj, \ldots, Pn$ be indicators of return on investment against which the company activity system can be evaluated ($n > 1$).
   Let $Pj\,(\,)$ value function be defined as follows:

$$Pj(A) = \begin{cases} 1 & \text{if company activity system } A \text{ is good regarding} \\ & \text{return-on-investment indicator } Pj; \\ 0 & \text{if company activity system } A \text{ is neutral regarding} \\ & \text{return-on-investment indicator } Pj; \\ -2 & \text{if company activity system } A \text{ is bad regarding} \\ & \text{return-on-investment indicator } Pj. \end{cases} \quad (1.16)$$

$Pj(A)$ shows the value of company activity system A regarding return-on-investment indicator Pj.
   The following vector represents the value of company activity system A regarding all the return-on-investment indicators $P1, \ldots, Pj, \ldots, Pn$.

$$\underline{P}(A) = [P1(A), \ldots, Pj(A), \ldots, Pn(A)] \quad (1.17)$$

To get an aggregate picture of the value of company activity system A we should introduce weights that show the importance of the return-on-investment indicators. Let $d1, \ldots, dj, \ldots, dn$ be such importance weights.
   It is required that

$$\sum dj = 1 \quad (1.18)$$

The aggregate value of company activity system A regarding the owners can be calculated as follows:

$$P(A) = \sum dj \; Pj(A) \tag{1.19}$$

$P(A)$ shows the aggregate value of the company activity system A regarding the owners ($1 \geq P(A) \geq -2$).

The company provides fair return of investment if its aggregate value regarding the owners is positive. That is

$$P(A) > 0 \tag{1.20}$$

1.4.2 Quality of Working Life

Let $Q1, \ldots, Qj, \ldots, Qn$ be quality-of-working-life indicators against which the company activity system can be evaluated ($n > 1$).

Let $Qj\,(\,)$ value function be defined as follows:

$$Qj(A) = \begin{cases} 1 & \text{if company activity system } A \text{ is good regarding} \\ & \text{quality-of-working-life indicator } Qj; \\ 0 & \text{if company activity system } A \text{ is neutral regarding} \\ & \text{quality-of-working-life indicator } Qj; \\ -2 & \text{if company activity system } A \text{ is bad regarding} \\ & \text{quality-of-working-life indicator } Qj. \end{cases} \tag{1.21}$$

$Qj(A)$ shows the value of company activity system A regarding quality-of-working-life indicator Qj.

The following vector represents the value of company activity system A regarding all the quality-of-working-life indicators $Q1, \ldots, Qj, \ldots, Qn$.

$$\underline{Q}(A) = [Q1(A), \ldots, Qj(A), \ldots, Qn(A)] \tag{1.22}$$

To get an aggregate picture of the value of company activity system A we should introduce weights that show the importance of the quality-of-working-life indicators. Let $e1, \ldots, ej, \ldots, en$ be such importance weights. It is required that

$$\sum ej = 1 \tag{1.23}$$

The aggregate social value of company activity system A can be calculated as follows:

$$Q(A) = \sum ej \, Qj(A) \tag{1.24}$$

$Q(A)$ shows the aggregate value of company activity system A ($1 \geq Q(A) \geq -2$).

The company ensures decent livelihood for its employees if its aggregate quality-of-working-life value is positive. That is

$$Q(A) > 0 \qquad (1.25)$$

1.4.3 Dealing With Customers Properly

Let $R1, \ldots, Rj, \ldots, Rn$ be customer-relationships indicators against which the company activity system can be evaluated ($j > 1$).

Let $Rj(\ )$ customer-relationships value function be defined as follows:

$$
Rj(A) =
\begin{cases}
1 & \text{if company activity system } A \text{ is good regarding} \\
& \text{customer-relationships indicator } Rj; \\
0 & \text{if company activity system } A \text{ is neutral regarding} \\
& \text{customer-relationships indicator } Rj; \\
-2 & \text{if company activity system } A \text{ is bad regarding} \\
& \text{customer-relationships indicator } Rj.
\end{cases}
\qquad (1.26)
$$

$Rj(A)$ shows the value of company activity system A regarding customer-relationships indicator Rj.

The following vector represents the value of the company activity system A regarding all the customer-relationships indicators $R1, \ldots, Rj, \ldots, Rn$.

$$\underline{R}(A) = [R1(A), \ldots, Rj(A), \ldots, Rn(A)] \qquad (1.27)$$

To get an aggregate picture of the customer-relationships value of company activity system A we should introduce weights that show the importance of the customer-relationships indicators. Let $f1, \ldots, fj, \ldots, fn$ be such importance weights.

It is required that

$$\sum f_j = 1 \qquad (1.28)$$

The aggregate customer-relationships value of company activity system A can be calculated as follows:

$$R(A) = \sum f_j \, Rj(A) \qquad (1.29)$$

$R(A)$ shows the aggregate customer-relationships value of company activity system A ($1 \geq R(A) \geq -2$).

The company appropriately deals with its customers if its aggregate customer-relationships value is positive. That is

$$R(A) > 0 \tag{1.30}$$

1.4.4 Making Fair Trade With Suppliers

Let $S1, \ldots, Sj, \ldots, Sn$ be supplier-relationships indicators against which the company activity system can be evaluated ($j > 1$).

Let $Sj(\ )$ supplier-relationships value function be defined as follows:

$$Sj(A) = \begin{cases} 1 & \text{if company activity system } A \text{ is good regarding supplier-relationships indicator } Sj; \\ 0 & \text{if company activity system } A \text{ is neutral regarding supplier-relationships indicator } Sj; \\ -2 & \text{if company activity system } A \text{ is bad regarding supplier-relationships indicator } Sj. \end{cases} \tag{1.31}$$

$Sj(A)$ shows the value of company activity system A regarding supplier-relationships indicator Sj.

The following vector represents the value of company activity system A regarding all the supplier-relationships indicators $S1, \ldots, Sj, \ldots, Sn$.

$$\underline{S}(A) = [S1(A), \ldots, Sj(A), \ldots, Sn(A)] \tag{1.32}$$

To get an aggregate picture of the supplier-relationships value of company activity system A we should introduce weights that show the importance of the supplier-relationships indicators. Let $g1, \ldots, gj, \ldots, gn$ be such importance weights.

It is required that

$$\sum gj = 1 \tag{1.33}$$

The aggregate supplier-relationships value of company activity system A can be calculated as follows:

$$S(A) = \sum gj \, Sj(A) \tag{1.34}$$

$S(A)$ shows the aggregate supplier-relationships value of company activity system A ($1 \geq S(A) \geq -2$).

The company adheres to fair trade with its suppliers if its aggregate supplier-relationships value is positive. That is

$$S(A) > 0 \qquad (1.35)$$

1.4.5 Collaborating With Local Communities

Let $T1, \ldots, Tj, \ldots, Tn$ be community-relationships indicators against which the company activity system can be evaluated ($j > 1$).

Let $Tj(\ )$ community-relationships value function be defined as follows:

$$Tj(A) = \begin{cases} 1 & \text{if company activity system } A \text{ is good regarding} \\ & \text{community-relationships indicator } Tj; \\ 0 & \text{if company activity system } A \text{ is neutral regarding} \\ & \text{community-relationships indicator } Tj; \\ -2 & \text{if company activity system } A \text{ is bad regarding} \\ & \text{community-relationships indicator } Tj. \end{cases} \qquad (1.36)$$

$Tj(A)$ shows the value of company activity system A regarding community-relationships indicator Tj.

The following vector represents the value of company activity system A regarding all the community-relationships indicators $T1, \ldots, Tj, \ldots, Tn$.

$$\underline{T}(A) = [T1(A), \ldots, Tj(A), \ldots, Tn(A)] \qquad (1.37)$$

To get an aggregate picture of the community-relationships value of company activity system A we should introduce weights that show the importance of the community-relationships indicators. Let $h1, \ldots, hj, \ldots, hn$ be such importance weights.

It is required that

$$\sum hj = 1 \qquad (1.38)$$

The aggregate community-relationships value of company activity system A can be calculated as follows:

$$T(A) = \sum hj\, Tj(A) \qquad (1.39)$$

$T(A)$ shows the aggregate community-relationships value of company activity system A ($1 \geq T(A) \geq -2$).

The company collaborates with the local community if its aggregate community-relationships value is positive. That is

$$T(A) > 0 \qquad (1.40)$$

1.5 BRINGING JUSTICE TO THE COMPANY'S ECOSYSTEM

Bringing justice to the company's ecosystem means that

1. The company pays its necessary contribution to the public good.
2. The company activities provide transparency.
3. The fruits of the company activities are distributed equitably.

The crux of the literature about corporate citizenship can be reduced to this.

1.5.1 Contributing to the Public Good

Let $U1, \ldots, Uj, \ldots, Un$ be public-good-contribution indicators against which the company activity system can be evaluated $(j > 1)$.

Let $Uj(\,)$ public-good-contribution value function be defined as follows:

$$Uj(A) = \begin{cases} 1 & \text{if company activity system } A \text{ is good regarding} \\ & \text{public-good-contribution indicator } Uj; \\ 0 & \text{if company activity system } A \text{ is neutral regarding} \\ & \text{public-good-contribution indicator } Uj; \\ -2 & \text{if company activity system } A \text{ is bad regarding} \\ & \text{public-good-contribution indicator } Uj. \end{cases} \qquad (1.41)$$

$Uj(A)$ shows the value of company activity system A regarding public-good-contribution indicator Uj.

The following vector represents the value of company activity system A regarding all the public-good-contribution indicators $U1, \ldots, Uj, \ldots, Un$.

$$\underline{U}(A) = [U1(A), \ldots, Uj(A), \ldots, Un(A)] \qquad (1.42)$$

To get an aggregate picture of the public-good contribution of company activity system A we should introduce weights that show the importance of the public-good-contribution indicators. Let $i1, \ldots, ij, \ldots, in$ be such importance weights.

It is required that

$$\sum ij = 1 \qquad (1.43)$$

The aggregate public-good-contribution value of company activity system A can be calculated as follows:

$$U(A) = \sum ij\, Uj(A) \qquad (1.44)$$

$U(A)$ shows the aggregate public-good-contribution value of the company activity system A $(1 \geq U(A) \geq -2)$.

The company pays its necessary contribution to the public good if its aggregate public-good contribution is positive. That is

$$U(A) > 0 \qquad (1.45)$$

1.5.2 Providing Transparency

Let $V1, \ldots, Vj, \ldots, Vn$ be transparency indicators against which the company activity system can be evaluated $(j > 1)$.

Let $Vj(\ )$ transparency value function be defined as follows:

$$Vj(A) = \begin{cases} 1 & \text{if company activity system } A \text{ is good regarding transparency indicator } Vj; \\ 0 & \text{if company activity system } A \text{ is neutral regarding transparency indicator } Vj; \\ -2 & \text{if company activity system } A \text{ is bad regarding transparency indicator } Vj. \end{cases} \qquad (1.46)$$

$Vj(A)$ shows the value of company activity system A regarding transparency indicator Vj.

The following vector represents the value of company activity system A regarding all the transparency indicators $V1, \ldots, Vj, \ldots, Vn$.

$$\underline{V}(A) = [V1(A), \ldots, Vj(A), \ldots, Vn(A)] \qquad (1.47)$$

To get an aggregate picture of the transparency of company activity system A we should introduce weights that show the importance of the transparency indicators. Let $k1, \ldots, kj, \ldots, kn$ be such importance weights.

It is required that

$$\sum kj = 1 \qquad (1.48)$$

The aggregate transparency value of company activity system A can be calculated as follows:

$$V(A) = \sum kj \, Vj(A) \tag{1.49}$$

$V(A)$ shows the aggregate transparency value of company activity system A ($1 \geq V(A) \geq -2$).

The company provides transparency about its activity system if its aggregate transparency value is positive. That is

$$V(A) > 0 \tag{1.50}$$

1.5.3 Distributing the Fruits of Activities Equitably

Let $W1, \ldots, Wj, \ldots, Wn$ be distribution indicators against which the company activity system can be evaluated ($j > 1$).

Let $Wj(\ )$ distribution value function be defined as follows:

$$Wj(A) = \begin{cases} 1 & \text{if company activity system } A \text{ is good regarding distribution indicator } Wj; \\ 0 & \text{if company activity system } A \text{ is neutral regarding distribution indicator } Wj; \\ -2 & \text{if company activity system } A \text{ is bad regarding distribution indicator } Wj. \end{cases} \tag{1.51}$$

$Wj(A)$ shows the value of company activity system A regarding distribution indicator Wj.

The following vector represents the value of company activity system A regarding all the distribution indicators $W1, \ldots, Wj, \ldots, Wn$.

$$\underline{W}(A) = [W1(A), \ldots, Wj(A), \ldots, Wn(A)] \tag{1.52}$$

To get an aggregate picture of the distribution value of company activity system A we should introduce weights that show the importance of the distribution indicators. Let $l1, \ldots, lj, \ldots, ln$ be such importance weights.

It is required that

$$\sum lj = 1 \tag{1.53}$$

The aggregate distribution value of company activity system A can be calculated as follows:

$$W(A) = \sum lj \, Wj(A) \tag{1.54}$$

$W(A)$ shows the aggregate distribution value of company activity system A ($1 \geq T(A) \geq -2$).

The fruits of the company's activities are distributed equitably if its aggregate distribution value is positive. That is

$$W(A) > 0 \tag{1.55}$$

1.6   GAINING LEGITIMACY

The company activity system is substantively right if

$$E(A) > 0 \text{ and } F(A) > 0 \text{ and } G(A) > 0 \tag{1.56}$$

This means that the company activity system is sustainable, future respecting and prosocial.

The company activity system is procedurally fair if

$$P(A) > 0 \text{ and } Q(A) > 0 \text{ and } R(A) > 0 \text{ and } S(A) > 0 \text{ and } T(A) > 0 \tag{1.57}$$

This means that the company creates fair return on investment, ensures decent livelihood for its employees, deals with its customers properly, adheres to fair trade with its suppliers and collaborates with the local community.

The company activity system brings justice to the company's ecosystem if

$$U(A) > 0 \text{ and } V(A) > 0 \text{ and } W(A) > 0 \tag{1.58}$$

This means that the company pays its necessary contribution to the public good, provides transparency about its functioning and distributes the fruits of the company's activities equitably.

If the company activity system is substantively right, procedurally fair and brings justice to the company's ecosystem then the company can achieve full legitimacy. This means that the company's *raison d'être*, the company's functioning as well as the company's end results are morally justifiable.

NOTE

* The chapter was written as part of the research project of the Corvinus University of Budapest 'Társadalmi Megújulás Operatív Program' TÁMOP-4-2.1.B-09/1/KMR-2010-0005.

REFERENCES

Boulding, K. (1973), *The Economy of Love and Fear: A Preface to Grants Economics*, Belmont, CA: Wadsworth.

Brown Weiss, E. (1989), *In Fairness to Future Generations: International Law, Common Patrimony, and Intergeneration Equity,* New York: The United Nations University, Tokyo and Transnational Publishers.

Korten, D. (1995), *When Corporations Rule the World*, Bloomfield, CT: Kumarian Press.

Leopold, A. (1984), *A Sand County Almanac*, Oxford: Oxford University Press.

Sen, A. (1992), *Inequality Reexamined,* New York: Russell Sage Foundation and Oxford, UK: Clarendon Press.

Zsolnai, L. (2009), 'Nature, society and future generations', in H.-C. de Bettignies and F. Lépineux (eds), *Business, Globalization and the Common Good*, Oxford: Peter Lang AG – International Academic Publishers, pp. 139–52.

2. The moral status of the corporation, collective responsibility and the distribution of blame

Christopher J. Cowton

2.1 INTRODUCTION

The moral status of the corporation is a foundational issue in business ethics. A long-running debate has considered whether a corporation can be considered a moral agent in its own right, akin to an individual human agent. As Moore (1999, p. 330) comments, the views are 'essentially twofold and diametrically opposed'. Some think corporations[1] are moral agents, while others disagree.

As befits such a long-running and important debate,[2] several review articles have been produced (for example, Danley, 1999), in addition to the literature reviews that precede any attempts at novel analysis. Moore's (1999) review covers most, if not all, of the many significant papers on this topic over the years,[3] considering the principal arguments on both sides of the debate. As he notes, the debate on the moral status of the corporation can be seen as a particular case regarding collective responsibility – an issue that has been extensively discussed in the general philosophy literature, where concerns have included attribution of blame to particular races or nation states.

In this chapter, rather than revisiting the business ethics literature and reviewing it anew, I take a step back and undertake a review of the philosophical literature on collective responsibility. This is not to imply that previous business ethicists have not also referred to the philosophical literature. However, in reviewing that literature I wish to bring out a particular issue that I regard as having been ignored or under-played by previous authors – namely, the distribution of blame. I pay particular attention to the work of Sverdlik (1987) who, like most other protagonists in the debate within the philosophical literature, is concerned with the general nature of collective responsibility rather than its particular application in relation to business corporations.

The term 'collective responsibility' clearly involves two elements. As in the literature on collective responsibility, the element on which I wish to focus in this chapter is 'collective'. However, I will first make a few points about 'responsibility', with the principal aim not of finding some essentialist definition but of ensuring that it is sufficiently clear for the purposes of this chapter how I am using the term.[4] Given the tenor of the debate on corporations, I am particularly interested in blame and its relationship to responsibility and obligation.

2.2   ON RESPONSIBILITY AND BLAME

'Responsibility' and 'obligation' are closely related terms in everyday discourse. Thus, for example, if I fail in my legal obligation to drive with due care and attention, I am liable to be held legally responsible for the consequences. This reflects the etymological roots of the word; Lucas (1993) notes the origins of the word 'responsibility' in the Latin *respondeo*, I answer,[5] and an important element in the meaning of the term is the idea of being answerable for one's actions. In everyday speech, we are accustomed to speaking of being responsible for something before the event (often some form of obligation), but such usage nevertheless carries with it an implication of being answerable or accountable after the event. The philosophical literature seems to concentrate on this *ex post* aspect of responsibility. Thus, Eshleman (2004), for example, summarizes the notion of being morally responsible for something, such as an action, as being 'worthy of a particular kind of reaction – praise, blame, or something akin to these – for having performed it'. I suggest that both academic literature (for example, textbooks and case studies) and popular discourse (for example, newspapers) tend to focus on *ex post* blame when it comes to the putative responsibilities of business corporations – especially in the case of 'scandals', which do so much to raise the profile of business ethics as an issue (Cowton, 2008).

An 'action' considered blameworthy may include the failure to do something that was demanded of me, an obligation (Dent, 2005). Whether I should be praised for something I was obliged to do is a moot point, but in the literature on collective responsibility, the focus is very much on blaming (Smiley, 2005); and Sverdlik (1987), whose paper I examine in greater depth below, for the purposes of his analysis treats responsibility as meaning, roughly, blameworthiness.

Thus, although the work of authors such as H.L.A. Hart (see Finnis, 2005) demonstrates that responsibility is a rich and complex concept, in the literature on collective responsibility it can be characterized as being concerned with blameworthiness for failure to meet some obligation, where that obligation is here taken to be a moral one in some sense.[6] And it is the 'collective' aspect of 'collective responsibility' that attracts the most debate. In the following section, I review the principal strands of the debate in the philosophical literature.

2.3   ON 'COLLECTIVE' RESPONSIBILITY

The construal of groups as moral agents in their own right is controversial; as Sverdlik (1987, p. 61) comments, talk of collective responsibility is 'apt to excite deeply-conflicting sentiments'. On the one hand, it engenders hostility because of association with thinking, such as heredity guilt and racism, which treats an individual on the basis of their membership of some group rather than on the basis of what they themselves have done. On the other hand, 'it is said that the notion of individual responsibility is to some degree outmoded in an era when much human activity is organized collectively and cooperatively' (Sverdlik, 1987, p. 61), for example, nation states declaring and conducting war – to which, one might add, corporations playing a central role in modern economies and societies. One fear is that the ability to attribute moral blame in relation to some of the most morally troubling events might be lost.[7]

Some of those who are in favour of attributing moral blame to 'collectives', as moral agents in their own right, point out that this is the way we talk – a common sense move, reflecting ordinary language. Others, cognizant of how language can mislead, do not necessarily rely on this but nevertheless point to the fact that collectives can and do perform actions (Copp, 1979).

Not surprisingly, such a view has come under attack. Normative individualists argue that the notion of collective responsibility is unfair and violates principles of individual responsibility. They see undesirable echoes of 'taint' (see Appiah, 1986–87) or 'tribalism' (see McGary, 1986) when collective responsibility is being advocated. At a basic level, to blame an individual for an action they have not done is unfair. I work for a particular university; indeed, I hold a senior position within it. Yet to hold me responsible for any and all morally blameworthy actions carried out in the name of the University of Huddersfield would, I suggest, be unfair.[8] I might have no knowledge of all or some of those actions; nor might I be expected to have knowledge of such actions. I might disapprove of those actions if and when they come to my attention. Or I might have disagreed with those actions when decided upon and I might even have attempted, unsuccessfully, to prevent their occurrence. Alternatively, it might be the case that I am to blame, wholly or partially, for an action perceived by, say, an external critic as morally blameworthy on the part of the University; but the final apportionment of blame surely requires a more careful and extended analysis of what happened, who did (or did not do) what, and my own position, actions and obligations in relation to what happened. In other words, while 'the University' might be a reasonable starting point for identifying blame, in either case (whether it is in some sense my fault or not) further analysis of the actions and obligations of individuals needs to occur before blame can be said to finally come to rest somewhere. And to blame me, or any other individual, with any degree of finality, before such work has been undertaken is, I would suggest, unfair. To do otherwise is, in effect, to impose guilt merely by association. Normative individualism therefore seems to be the appropriate stance to take. This is not to say that all members of a group cannot be blameworthy, but it is what they have or have not done in relation to their responsibilities that matters, not their membership of the group as such.

Methodological individualists, on the other hand, take a slightly different route, in arguing that it is not possible to associate moral agency with groups as distinct from individual members. Milton Friedman (1970) famously takes this position, when he states that corporations cannot have responsibilities; only individuals, or individual executives, can. An early example in the collective responsibility literature is Lewis (1948), who – apparently motivated by concerns over 'war guilt' – begins by asserting that responsibility belongs essentially to the individual, though he does surprisingly little in the remainder of the paper to argue his case.[9] Stronger arguments have been made around the issues of intention and agency; groups, it is claimed, cannot form an intention and so cannot be blamed; they do not engage in '*genuinely* collective actions' (Smiley, 2005, emphasis added).

Possible responses to methodological individualists include: first, that while intention is important, the role of negligence in attributing moral blame suggests that it is not essential (see Appiah, 1986–87); and second, that although groups do not form intentions as such, they have equivalent processes that mean that we can talk of collectives taking decisions and performing deliberate actions. This seems a reasonable point, and to deny it seems little more than to reassert that individuals can be held responsible and groups cannot. French pursues such an approach when focusing on corporations, employing the notion of the 'corporation's internal decision structure'. As later writers have pointed out, there are some problems with his notion, but I do not think it fundamentally undermines the general point that business corporations, at least, amongst collectives could be considered to form intentions.[10]

This latter point has led many defenders of collective responsibility to be careful to identify it only with certain cases, and business corporations are an obvious example – perhaps the classic case, as apparently rational, goal-seeking and organized collectives. Thus, the people on the train in Feinberg's (1968) example, subject to a Jesse James robbery, are not a group; in Held's terms (Held, 1970), they are just a random collection of individuals, where randomness is seen in terms of lacking decision methods beyond those possessed by all persons (cf. Bates, 1971, on this criterion). Thus, according to some writers, some – but not all – groups can have moral responsibility attributed to them. Attributes such as formalization and continuity would seem to play a part in identifying such 'collectively responsible' groups.

However, the identification of a responsible group still raises the issue of what happens to blame when a moral obligation has not been fulfilled. Assuming that membership of the group can be determined,[11] it seems strange to blame the group without blaming members of the group. What, then, would be being blamed? I recognize that there might be questions of legal responsibility and liability. However, I am concerned with the different – if sometimes related – issue of moral responsibility and blame. Furthermore, the argument of this chapter can be seen as pre-legal (Velasquez, 2003); the law differs from time to time, from place to place, and can be changed. It might be argued that all members of the group should be blamed equally, but that raises the unfairness issue mentioned earlier; there seems no a priori reason to view all members as equally culpable, and some might be deemed to have no culpability at all. It might be suggested that the group be redefined to exclude those with no blameworthiness, but in that case individual responsibility (present or absent) is being used to determine apparent collective responsibility, which removes the need for a concept of collective responsibility. Moreover, if a group as such cannot be blamed but individual members of a group can, perhaps to varying degrees, where (again) is the need for a concept of collective responsibility? Furthermore, for those who find it persuasive, Ockham's Razor – the principle that entities are not to be multiplied beyond necessity[12] – might be invoked here; for William of Ockham, 'only particular beings, and in the social sphere only particular human beings, really exist' (Lukes, 1973, p. 47).

This line of reasoning is consistent with a strand of writing on collective responsibility that investigates how moral responsibility can be distributed across members of a group – and which, in a sense, is therefore not really about collective responsibility at all (Smiley, 2005), at least in the sense intended by many writers. In the following paragraphs, I discuss Sverdlik's (1987) paper in order to examine the issues involved more closely.

Although not the most recent analysis of collective responsibility, Sverdlik's paper does take account of most of the earlier literature, which had already identified many of the central issues previously mentioned in this chapter. In summarizing his argument, I will omit the detail of his examples and concentrate on the substantive points.

Having noted the deeply conflicting sentiments that talk of collective responsibility is apt to excite, Sverdlik (1987, p. 61) comments: 'Obviously what is called for is a careful sorting out of the arguments – in other words, analytical philosophy.' His first significant move – a useful one – is to distinguish between 'collective' and 'corporate' responsibility.[13] On his view, collective responsibility is

> the idea that individual persons within a group are responsible for an outcome produced collectively. That is, responsibility is apportioned to individuals and to them alone. (p. 62)

On the other hand, with corporate responsibility,

> the group is treated as a being distinct from its members and responsibility for wrongdoing is attributed to it. If one supposes that corporate responsibility is possible then it is an open question whether the individuals in the group are also responsible for the outcome or whether the group as such is alone responsible. (p. 62)

The distinction between the two is at the heart of the debate, even if the terms are not always employed as Sverdlik uses them. What Sverdlik terms 'collective' responsibility is the sort that Smiley (2005) suggests is really not collective responsibility, in the sense of being a non-distributive phenomenon, at all. What she has in mind is what Sverdlik refers to as 'corporate' responsibility. There is thus some scope for terminological confusion here, but as long as Sverdlik's employment of the terms is borne in mind, his distinction is useful in posing the choice with clarity.[14] The question is: what does he do with that distinction?

Sverdlik remarks that one may accept one and deny the other, but he is correct in remarking that one is more likely to accept collective responsibility than corporate responsibility 'since the latter has many more presuppositions, both ontological and moral' (Sverdlik, 1987, pp. 62–3). For example, he comments that, for corporate responsibility to obtain, it is necessary to establish that groups exist and can act rationally. As I have already indicated, that does not seem unreasonable, at least in some circumstances, even if groups are never exactly like individuals. He also states that for his definition of corporate responsibility to obtain, it is necessary that such groups can be properly blamed if they neglect to do obligatory actions. That is really just a restatement of the problem.

Indeed, his point about which form of responsibility is the more likely to be accepted carries little or no weight as a part of his argument. We know that the controversial issue is whether groups can be blamed. The general philosophical treatment of moral responsibility is rooted in a consideration of individuals, and the underlying issue in the debate being considered here is whether groups, qua groups, are different from individuals in respects which some writers take to be critical. The thought that people are more likely to accept his notion of collective responsibility (based on individuals) than his notion of corporate responsibility because the latter is more problematic is thus the starting point for his argument, not a move in it. It is thus, again, just a restatement of the problem and begs the issue.

The next distinction Sverdlik makes is more important, namely one between responsibility for results or outcomes,[15] on the one hand and responsibility for acts, on the other. He goes on to comment that '[r]esponsibility for outcomes is a matter of being responsible for acts that contribute to the existence of the outcome' (p. 65). Furthermore, he notes that '[w]herever there is responsibility for a result, there is responsibility for an action that causes, at least in part, that outcome, but the converse is not true' (p. 65). There might be no external outcome (of any moral significance) for two possible reasons. First, the nature of some acts means that they need not have external outcomes; Sverdlik cites as examples dance, masturbation and pre-marital sex.[16] Second, an act might fail in its intended outcome; for example, I shoot at someone but the bullet harmlessly misses.[17] On the other hand, it does not seem possible to think of cases where responsibility for an outcome cannot be paraphrased as involving the person's being responsible for an action that at least partly produced the result, leading Sverdlik to conclude that 'responsibility for actions is logically the more fundamental idea' (p. 66). From this, it is possible to infer that 'more than one person can be morally responsible for an outcome even though it is true that every person is only responsible for his or her own actions' (p. 66). These points are fundamental to Sverdlik's argument, and he uses them to provide a telling insight into the debate on collective versus corporate responsibility.

Sverdlik's reading of the debate, with which I tend to concur, is that advocates of collective[18] responsibility hold that more than one person can be responsible for an outcome, whereas their opponents tend to say that a person is responsible only for his or her own actions. He then argues that the latter is the more fundamental idea and summarizes the result of his argument as follows.

I claim, then, that the principles underlying collective responsibility are no different from those underlying the acts of a single individual. If all that people who defend the idea of collective responsibility mean is that more than one person can be responsible for an outcome then there is no argument.[19] But, if proponents of this view mean to suggest that this idea represents some supplementation or modification[20] of the idea that people are only responsible for their own actions then they are radically mistaken. It would be unfair, where we are considering a result produced by more than one person, to blame a person for a result that he or she did not intend[21] to produce. (p. 68)

Thus, while it might make some sense to speak of a group's being responsible for an outcome, perhaps as a first approximation, when it comes to moral blame, analytically it makes sense to proceed by attributing it on the basis of the actions – or inaction – of individuals. This is not an eliminativist move, seeking to 'analyse away' the group, but it is reductionist. In terms of what I might call the 'economy of moral blame', not only are there dangers in referring to collectives in many cases (see the earlier comment on unfairness), but just as important, there seems no need to attribute blame to groups as entities in themselves, since there does not seem to be any blame 'left over' after attribution, in the appropriate manner, to individuals – important though groups and group dynamics might be as features of the social world.

2.4   CONCLUSION

Sverdlik's analysis, which I find broadly persuasive, seems to leave corporations without moral agency, responsibility, blameworthiness and so on. However, I do not want to imply that it makes no sense to speak of corporations having responsibilities or, indeed, of their being blameworthy as a result of what they have or have not done. I am not suggesting that ordinary language is necessarily in need of replacement or significant reform. Thus it might make sense, subject to the facts of the matter, to blame BP for the Gulf of Mexico oil spill in 2010. However, I see this as a first approximation; a perfectly reasonable one for anyone external to BP, but merely a first move in determining blameworthiness nonetheless.[22]

It would be wrong to blame all BP employees, though, not to mention all its many subcontractors and suppliers. It might be practically difficult to carry out, but in principle there are individuals who have responsibilities and, to the extent that they have failed to fulfil them in ways that are causally related to the Gulf of Mexico oil spill, they are to blame – not the other, unconnected employees. To ostracize or disapprove of a person, following the Gulf of Mexico oil spill, simply for being a BP employee is unjust in much the same way as it would have been unjust to blame all Germans for the Second World War (see Lewis, 1948). I would further suggest that simply 'leaving' blame as resting with BP, rather than treating it as a first approximation, risks failing to identify and blame culpable individuals. This should not be taken to imply that those individuals acted alone though; it is of the essence of corporations that they are collaborative endeavours. The point is that individuals have responsibilities in such settings.

My position respects, for certain purposes, ordinary language. I have argued that it is reasonable to talk as if business corporations have moral responsibilities, but at least when it comes to the identification of blame, the process should seek to identify culpable individuals and, in doing so, absolve from blame other individuals. Thus, as explained earlier, my position is not eliminativist (I still talk of business corporations), but when it comes to moral blame it is ultimately reductionist, based on normative individualism.

For the business ethics literature I suggest that this implies at least two things. First, I hope we can move on from the corporate moral agency debate. Corporations cannot, in the final analysis, be subject to moral blame – yet we may continue to speak of them as if they can be as a kind of first approximation or shorthand. I think this gives Moore (1999) what he seems to be seeking when he comments that

> both views have their strong points, although it does seem . . . that the arguments in favour are more convincing than those against.[23] This is partly on the strength of the arguments (and the criticisms of the case against . . .), *but partly also that the acceptance of corporate moral agency seems to be a better reflection of 'reality' in the sense of how most people interpret the world around them.* (p. 339, emphasis added)

Thus, I suggest that we can engage in some talk of apparent corporate moral agency without needing to find a convincing theoretical justification for corporate moral agency as such.[24] Second, there is a need to understand how to distribute blame within business corporations. This will be a practical task contingent upon the circumstances of particular cases. The complexity of particular cases might make this challenging, but the organized nature of business corporations ought to support the tracing of responsibility; and if it is not possible to trace responsibility in detail, this might be taken to be an issue of governance and responsibility allocated accordingly. A focus on the principles and practicalities of the distribution of responsibility and, where circumstances demand it, blame in business corporations seems to me to be a more productive endeavour than seeking (and failing, in my view) to establish that corporations are moral agents in their own right.

NOTES

1. They are generally referring to business corporations.
2. Important to academics, that is; it is doubtful whether the debate is of much perceived significance or interest to managers of those corporations.
3. An important exception is the later paper by Velasquez (2003).
4. Even then, I am less interested in providing a rigorous definition than in providing a broad indication sufficient to get the argument moving. I hope that readers will be able to regard 'responsibility', 'blame' and related terms as placeholders into which they can insert their own definitions without doing damage to the argument.
5. See also Lewis (1948).
6. There is an interesting exchange in which Downie (1969) accuses Cooper (1968) of having failed to identify moral responsibility in his tennis club example (an example that I find unpersuasive in any case), to which Cooper (1969) responds that his papers had the 'escape clause' of stating 'moral or social responsibility'. Downie's error, while perhaps suggesting a lack of close reading, is indicative of the general assumption that collective responsibility means collective moral responsibility.
7. See French's (1972) edited volume on the My Lai massacre, for example.
8. I should note, of course, that I am not suggesting that the University of Huddersfield does engage in morally blameworthy actions. This is merely a thought experiment.
9. Though as Smiley (2005) correctly observes, his paper does contain 'moral outrage', which suggests that his motivation is normative rather than strictly methodological.
10. My position is that I do not find intention to be a crucial issue. I give one reason below, but I note that it cannot be relevant for a normative individualist.
11. Itself not always an easy matter.
12. *Entia non sunt multiplicanda praetor necessitate* (Blackburn, 1994, p. 268).
13. This should not be confused with 'corporate responsibility' as increasingly used by business people when referring to businesses' 'corporate social responsibility' (CSR).
14. I suggest below, though, that later in his paper, he slips into using 'collective responsibility' in the conventional manner, without reference to his distinction.
15. He uses the two terms interchangeably.
16. I leave it to the reader to decide whether these examples are the most appropriate or helpful.
17. See my earlier comments on intention too.
18. Given his chosen terminology, he means corporate responsibility here.
19. That is, his 'narrow' definition of collective responsibility. Smiley (2005) states that almost all of those now writing about it 'agree that collective responsibility would make sense if it were merely an aggregative phenomenon'.
20. Such as 'corporate' responsibility implies.
21. Sverdlik has a broad interpretation of 'intention', with an extended discussion of negligence and recklessness in the context of attributing moral blame.
22. I am assuming that apportioning blame is, in one way or another, a justifiable activity. Exactly how and when it might be justified is not my concern here.
23. I disagree on this point, as indicated earlier.
24. From a theoretical point of view, Moore does not seem to find a convincing case for his preferred position, just a balance in favour, which does not seem altogether satisfactory.

REFERENCES

Appiah, A. (1986–87), 'Racism and moral pollution', *Philosophical Forum*, **18** (2–3), 185–202.

Bates, S. (1971), 'The responsibility of "random collections"', reprinted in L. May and S. Hoffman (eds) (1991), *Collective Responsibility: Five Decades of Debate in Theoretical and Applied Ethics*, Savage, MD: Rowman and Littlefield, pp. 101–8.
Blackburn, S. (1994), *The Oxford Dictionary of Philosophy*, Oxford: Oxford University Press.
Cooper, D.E. (1968), 'Collective responsibility', *Philosophy*, **43**, 258–68.
Cooper, D.E. (1969), 'Collective responsibility – again', *Philosophy*, **44**, 153–5.
Copp, D. (1979), 'Collective actions and secondary actions', *American Philosophical Quarterly*, **16** (3), 177–86.
Cowton, C.J. (2008), 'On setting the agenda for business ethics research', in C. Cowton and M. Haase (eds), *Trends in Business and Economic Ethics*, Berlin: Springer, pp. 11–30.
Danley, J.R. (1999), 'Corporate moral agency', in R.E. Frederick (ed.), *A Companion to Business Ethics*, Malden, MA: Blackwell, pp. 243–56.
Dent, N.J.H. (2005), 'Obligation', in T. Honderich (ed.), *Oxford Companion to Philosophy*, 2nd edn, New York: Oxford University Press, p. 668.
Downie, R.S. (1969), 'Collective responsibility', *Philosophy*, **44**, 66–9.
Eshleman, A. (2004), 'Moral responsibility', in E.N. Zalta (ed.), *Stanford Encyclopedia of Philosophy*, accessed 20 May 2007 at http://plato.stanford.edu/entries/moral-responsibility.
Feinberg, J. (1968), 'Collective responsibility', reprinted in L. May and S. Hoffman (eds) (1991), *Collective Responsibility: Five Decades of Debate in Theoretical and Applied Ethics*, Savage, MD: Rowman and Littlefield, pp. 53–76.
Finnis, J. (2005), 'Hart, H.L.A.', in T. Honderich (ed.), *Oxford Companion to Philosophy*, 2nd edn, New York: Oxford University Press, p. 361.
French, P.A. (ed.) (1972), *Individual and Collective Responsibility: Massacre at My Lai*, Cambridge, MA: Schenkman.
Friedman, M. (1970), 'The social responsibility of business is to increase its profits', reprinted in G.D. Chryssides and J.H. Kaler (eds) (1993), *An Introduction to Business Ethics*, London: Thomson, pp. 249–54.
Held, V. (1970), 'Can a random collection of individuals be morally responsible?', reprinted in L. May and S. Hoffman (eds) (1991), *Collective Responsibility: Five Decades of Debate in Theoretical and Applied Ethics*, Savage, MD: Rowman and Littlefield, pp. 89–100.
Lewis, H.D. (1948), 'Collective responsibility', *Philosophy*, **23** (84), 3–18.
Lucas, J.R. (1993), *Responsibility*, Oxford: Oxford University Press.
Lukes, S. (1973), *Individualism*, Oxford: Basil Blackwell.
McGary, H. (1986), 'Morality and collective liability', reprinted in L. May and S. Hoffman (eds) (1991), *Collective Responsibility: Five Decades of Debate in Theoretical and Applied Ethics*, Savage, MD: Rowman and Littlefield, pp. 77–87.
Moore, G. (1999), 'Corporate moral agency: review and implications', *Journal of Business Ethics*, **21** (4), 329–43.
Smiley, M. (2005), 'Collective responsibility', in E.N. Zalta (ed.), *Stanford Encyclopedia of Philosophy*, accessed 20 May 2007 at http://plato.stanford.edu/entries/moral-responsibility.
Sverdlik, S. (1987), 'Collective responsibility', *Philosophical Studies*, **51** (1), 61–76.
Velasquez, M. (2003), 'Debunking corporate moral responsibility', *Business Ethics Quarterly*, **13** (4), 531–62.

3. From task to role responsibility: towards a prospective business ethics

Johan Wempe

3.1 INTRODUCTION

Recognizing a collective responsibility of a company allows us to visualize the moral role of the culture and structure of the company behind the behaviour of its individual employees. This enables a better analysis of many social issues and helps in finding solutions to these problems. However, recognizing collective responsibility brings new problems. What does collective responsibility mean exactly? A company cannot be punished by putting the organization in prison: 'corporations have neither bodies to be punished, nor souls to be condemned'.[1] In situations where corporate responsibility is an issue, public opinion is inclined to search for concrete individuals that can be held liable for the abuse. Similarly, in court cases, top management is often held accountable for the wrongdoing of the organization. If the management has made demonstrable errors, this is often seen as the cause of the abuse. Removing and punishing the manager is seen as the solution. How is collective responsibility related to the responsibility of the members of the collective? Can you hold specific individuals liable purely based upon this collective responsibility? Is collective responsibility in the final analysis the individual responsibility of the representatives of the collective? If so, is that fair? Are individuals liable for something they themselves have had no part in?

An interesting example in this respect relates to the Dirk Scheringa Bank (DSB) case. The individual responsibilities of some members of the company and the corporate responsibility of DSB are, in this case, complexly entangled. How do these two foci of responsibility relate to each other in this concrete case?

3.2 THE BANKRUPTCY OF DSB

Around the world, governments have rescued banks and helped them avoid bankruptcy. Despite the active role played by governments, the financial crisis has led to the failure of several banks. In many cases, the bankruptcies and/or the rescue operations have uncovered many serious abuses behind the failure of these banks. The bankruptcy of the Dutch bank DSB is a good example of irresponsible behaviour by a company leading to its bankruptcy.[2]

DSB was built up from scratch by its founder Dirk Scheringa. From a small tax consultancy business established in 1975, DSB grew into a small but very prominent bank in the Netherlands. Through the creation of new businesses and by buying up existing companies, a group of companies was created that was engaged in various forms of financial services, from broker services, through the selling of mortgages, to insurance and banking services. In 2007, DSB received its banking licence.

Dirk Scheringa drew in the involvement of several former politicians. For example, former Minister and former Queen's Commissioner for Friesland, Ed Nijpels, and former Deputy Minister Robin Linschoten became members of DSB's Supervisory Board. In 2007, DSB was able to get the internationally well-respected former Minister of Finance, Gerrit Zalm, involved, first as chief economist, and later as financial director. At the beginning of 2009, Gerrit Zalm left DSB. The then Minister of Finance, Wouter Bos, asked him to become chief executive officer (CEO) of ABN Amro, a much larger bank that the government had bought to prevent its possible bankruptcy and, through that, the collapse of the Dutch financial system. In February 2009, another former Minister, Frank de Grave, succeeded Zalm as the chief financial officer (CFO) of DSB.

DSB was able to grow rapidly because it focused on a segment of the market that was seen as unattractive by the other banks. Many customers who were not accepted by other banks were able to get loans from DSB. These customers were granted mortgages that they were unable to afford using the normal criteria. DSB used aggressive marketing methods to attract clients. Mortgages were often combined with insurance policies that had little or no value for the customer. DSB also imposed huge interest payments, sometimes up to 80 per cent of the mortgage value. DSB also used very intimidating methods to collect overdue payments from customers with financial problems. Having chosen its market segment at the bottom of the market, the company was able to attract many customers who did not understand the complex financial products they were buying.

Despite these questionable practices, DSB was successful and, due to this success, acquired a good reputation. This was partly due to the societal activities of Dirk Scheringa. He was the sponsor of the local football club, AZ. With Scheringa's financial support, AZ grew into a football club with an international allure. AZ became the national champion and has some success at the European level. Dirk Scheringa even built an enormous football stadium for AZ. His bank was also a major sponsor of Dutch ice skating and even had its own DSB skating team. Scheringa also established the DSB museum which housed his collection of paintings of the realism tradition.

The supervisor, De Nederlandsche Bank (DNB), the central bank of The Netherlands, perceived the exorbitant interest payments that several financial institutions were now charging as a problem for the entire sector, and urged all banks to make their service charges transparent. According to the Dutch central bank, this transparency requirement created large risks, especially for DSB. The supervisor gave several warnings, but did not intervene. Dirk Scheringa, said former CFO Frank de Grave after the bankruptcy of DSB, had tried to end the criticized practices. The underlying problem was the expensive 'hobbies' of Scheringa. The sponsorship contracts and the museum were dependent on the high interest charges.

From the beginning of 2009, DSB's activities were questioned in several television programmes. DSB customers were realizing that they were paying an unacceptably high interest rate on their mortgages. Former employees started telling about DSB's aggressive sales practices and the coupling of mortgages to useless insurance products. In May, the supervisor of the financial sector, the Netherlands Authority for the Financial Markets (AFM) imposed two penalties on DSB for violating the rules on mortgage interest. The role of the AFM is comparable to the role of the Securities and Exchange Commission (SEC) in the USA. This intervention by the AFM led former Minister and finance director Frank de Grave to resign his position as CFO after only two months. Pieter Lakeman, chairperson of SOBI,[3] a Dutch foundation dedicated to transparency in financial reporting, and well known in the Netherlands for his earlier success in addressing several fraudulent companies, announced in June 2009 that he was going to submit a claim against DSB on behalf of a number of its clients. He mentioned amounts of €1–2 billion. To pursue this claim, he established a special foundation: the Mortgage Suffering Foundation. In reaction to all this negative publicity, DSB became willing to make arrangements with customers who had financial problems. It also appointed special budget advisors to help clients with problems. DSB promoted this arrangement and established a Problem Mortgages Fund. On 1 October, Pieter Lakeman advised DSB customers, in a television interview, to withdraw their money. He wanted to force a bankruptcy since, in his opinion, this was the best way to minimize the damage. Lakeman's message had a huge impact. Customers en masse took their money away from DSB. The DSB customer website became overloaded and the company had to temporarily shut it down. This made it impossible for customers to make transactions. Fear of a run on the bank forced the Dutch central bank (the DNB) to place DSB under court receivership. On television, DSB employees pleaded for the courts and politics to give DSB a chance. However, the trustees appointed by the Dutch central bank asked the court to declare DSB bankrupt. On 18 October 2009 at 09:00 the court agreed to this request.

Many customers were severely affected by DSB's failure. Investors who had savings products with very high interest rates that fell outside the guarantee scheme operated by the Dutch government were seeing their savings disappear. This was also the case for those customers who had larger savings entrusted to DSB than the €100,000 guaranteed by the Dutch state. As with other bankruptcies, employees were also affected. Overnight, 2,000 employees lost their jobs. Suppliers and contractors were also caught up in the fall of the bank. The football team AZ and the DSB skating team also had to find new sponsors. The DSB museum was closed and the construction of a new museum building halted forthwith. The art collection was confiscated by its main creditor: ABN Amro.

However, even before the bankruptcy, customers were already experiencing damage due to the extreme interest rates they were having to pay. In fact, this damage, and the associated social criticism, effectively led to the collapse of DSB. There was clearly serious abuse and it is natural that the public and political debates concentrated on the issue of guilt: there were certainly ample candidates.

The regulators, the Dutch central bank, DNB, and The Netherlands AFM have expressed strong criticism of several DSB directors. Dirk Scheringa was the sole shareholder and also CEO and, with this double function, held too much power. The regulators therefore insisted that Scheringa resign as CEO. There has also been strong criticism by the regulators of other directors, including several former politicians. They had knowledge of the problems, they were also aware of the warnings from the DNB and the criticisms by the AFM, but failed to adequately address the problems.

The case is complicated by the position of the Dutch central bank, the DNB. It knew of DSB's criticized practices and the business model used but, despite this, it gave DSB a banking licence. The Dutch central bank had also warned DSB several times, but no action was taken despite nothing changing and there were no improvements at all.

The call by Pieter Lakeman for customers to take their money away from DSB is seen by many experts as irresponsible: no bank can withstand a run.

Criticism is also targeted at the Ministry of Finance, which had earlier saved two large Dutch banks, ING and ABN Amro, from bankruptcy but was not willing to offer DSB a helping hand. DSB was not seen as part of the financial system: its collapse would pose no danger to the smooth functioning of the Dutch financial system.

3.3 THE POSITION OF THE FORMER CFO

In the aftermath of DSB's bankruptcy, a lot of attention has been paid to the role of former Minister Gerrit Zalm. Shortly before the debacle at DSB, he resigned as its CFO to become CEO at ABN Amro. As long as there was uncertainty over the role of Zalm in DSB's downfall, there would be doubts expressed as to whether he was the right person to lead ABN Amro. The Minister of Finance therefore asked the regulators, the Dutch central bank (DNB) and The Netherlands AFM, to investigate the role of Gerrit Zalm in the DSB affair, so as to remove all uncertainty surrounding him. The result is staggering: an interim report shows that the AFM draws a diametrically opposed conclusion to that of the DNB. According to the central bank, Zalm acted conscientiously throughout, and the failure of DSB has no implications for his position as CEO of ABN Amro. The AFM's harsh judgement would, on the other hand, suggest that Zalm cannot credibly remain as ABN Amro's CEO. Clearly, during his period at DSB, Zalm had failed to end the criticized practices. Formally, having two opposing conclusions is not problematic! The investigation is formally conducted by the DNB, and the views of the AFM are only part of the evidence it considers. It is up to the DNB what it does with the advice offered. However, to the outside world, there are two different conclusions. Can Zalm really stay as CEO of ABN Amro when such a negative opinion has been pronounced by one regulator?

The DSB case is interesting because it is a good example with which to examine how individual and collective responsibilities are connected. What does it mean if a company is held responsible? Does this affect the employees who sold bad products? Does this collective responsibility affect Gerrit Zalm, even after he had moved on to another position?

3.4   TWO STRIKING ASPECTS

Two aspects of the DSB case are interrelated and make a good understanding of the relationship between collective and individual responsibilities difficult. These are factors that also play a central role in the currently dominant paradigm in ethics, and especially in business ethics:

1.   What is striking is that the discussion over these events, as in other debates about the meaning of collective responsibility, focuses on identifying the guilty. There has been an abuse: savers have suffered losses, the financial system has been damaged. The moral debate focuses on the question of who, or what, can we hold liable. The concept of responsibility plays a central role in this debate, but is only used in a retrospective sense. How can one determine who or what can be held responsible afterwards? The bank, the CEO, other top managers, employees, the regulators, the Ministry of Finance or maybe even Pieter Lakeman with his Mortgage Suffering Foundation? Who made a mistake that led to the abuse?
2.   A second aspect in the discussion of the DSB affair, and in other debates about collective responsibility of companies, concerns the need to give responsibility a face. The responsibility of a company is translated into the responsibilities of one or a few individuals. This view is based on the traditional model of companies: we are inclined to think of clearly defined responsibilities within tightly directed hierarchical organizations, where the CEO and the top management give univocal direction to the organization. Within such organizations, it is possible to hold the top management responsible for the abuse: the employees are seen as victims who were forced to participate in the criticized practices. In the case of the CFO Gerrit Zalm, his critics hold him responsible for not acting or for not failing to stop the criticized practices adequately and fast enough; that is, for inaction rather than for action.

These factors are typical of the way in which ethics, and business ethics in particular, are currently practised. In fact, these factors describe a paradigm that is dominant in business ethics and makes understanding the relationship between collective responsibility and the responsibility of the individual members of the collective difficult. This dominant paradigm within business ethics views responsibility in a retrospective sense and sees the company as a hierarchically driven collective action in which the top management turns the actions of individual members of an aggregate into a conglomerate of coherent action.

3.5 THE DOMINANT PARADIGM IN BUSINESS ETHICS

3.5.1 Responsibility

An important cause of the confusion surrounding the responsibility of companies lies in the limited meaning given to the responsibility concept as it is generally used. The common meaning of responsibility assumes that there is an unwanted effect, that there is an act that caused this unwanted effect and that there is an actor who can be held accountable for this unwanted act. In this conceptualization of responsibility, there are four important elements. First, there is an autonomous person: a person who acts. Second, there is an act, and this act is performed knowingly and willingly, that is to say that the actor is aware of the act and its effects, and agrees to these effects. Third, there is an unwanted effect. Finally, there is a causal relationship between that actor, the act and its effect: the actor causes the act, and the act is seen as the cause of the unwanted effect. If all these components are present, then there is responsibility. There is a situation of abuse and it is possible to ascertain who can be held responsible for this. We then look for a causal relationship between the action and the situation of abuse. The person or organization behind that action is held liable for the abuse situation. Here it concerns responsibility after the event. The actor can be held responsible for the effect and, due to that responsibility, can afterwards be assigned praise or blame. Finding the guilty parties dominates in this form of responsibility.

What we see here, as the commonly used meaning of responsibility, is, according to the philosopher Hart, 'liability responsibility'. According to Hart (1978, pp. 136–57), it is possible to distinguish four types of responsibility for natural persons: causal responsibility, liability responsibility, capacity responsibility and role responsibility. Bovens (1990, p. 34) supplements this list with a fifth possibility: responsibility as a virtue.

Causal responsibility involves a morally neutral use of the responsibility concept. An example is viewing the hurricane as responsible for the thousands of people who died or became homeless. This form of responsibility only describes the cause of the situation. Liability responsibility, in comparison, also presupposes a causal relationship between effect and cause, but is also used to hold someone liable for the situation.

Bovens (1990, p. 34) makes a sharp distinction between retrospective responsibility,[4] on the one hand, and prospective responsibility[5] on the other. Causal responsibility and liability responsibility both concern retrospective responsibility, whereas the other three forms of responsibility are, in his opinion, prospective.

Prospective responsibility concerns the present, organizing work in such a way that future abuse situations can be prevented. It is exactly this type of responsibility that is relevant to companies and managers. They want to gain an insight in advance into the requirements of the conducted policy, and how the organization functions. Prospective responsibility covers responsibility based on competence, especially in the sense of being accountable ('a toddler cannot be held accountable for his or her actions'), task responsibility ('this is the responsibility of the sales manager') or responsibility as a virtue ('this is a responsible person'; 'she is someone who takes her responsibilities seriously').

According to Bovens, responsibility is a rich concept and it is undesirable to adopt a responsibility model that allows only one interpretation of the concept: the interpretation of the responsibility concept should be highly dependent on the situation.

By understanding responsibility as liability responsibility, is it possible to hold companies liable? It is also a major reason why understanding the relationship between individual responsibility and corporate responsibility is difficult.

3.5.2 Corporate Responsibility

It is now largely accepted that a company's actions cannot be regarded as only the sum of individual actions. Precisely through collaborating, an advantage is realized, and this means that the responsibility for the effects of the company's actions cannot be distributed among managers or employees without losing some responsibility: the overall responsibility is more than the sum of the individual responsibilities. The moral responsibility of a company rests, according to the business ethicist Peter French, on its moral personhood. To French (1984, p. xii), a company can be seen as a full-fledged moral person because it can act. To identify corporate acting it is necessary to make use of a theoretical construction such as secondary acting. According to French, a company can act in the secondary sense. It is possible to make a distinction between the physical act and the meaning of that act (Copp, 1979, p. 177). A person can sign a contract. Signing the contract is the physical act: it is the act of a natural person. This is acting in a primary sense. When the director, following the correct procedure, signs a contract on behalf of the company, the company is acting in an indirect, or secondary, manner. When actions are guided by formal decision-making procedures, and are in line with the company's culture, there is intentional action by the company, which means that actions are taken willingly and knowingly on behalf of the company. The company is therefore not only a legal agent but also a moral agent. Given this moral agency of a company, it is possible to hold the corporation morally responsible for a undesirable situation caused by its actions (Kaptein and Wempe, 2002, pp. 149–52).

3.6 PROBLEMS WITH THE DOMINANT PARADIGM OF BUSINESS ETHICS

In reality, the concept of corporate responsibility is based upon liability responsibility and, further, upon a hierarchical organization of responsibility within a company. To hold a company liable, the distinction between primary and secondary actions is essential. Having made this distinction, it is possible to recognize a causal link between an actor, the act and the alleged effect in two ways. If there is only a primary act, then the natural person is liable. If the act is caused by the company's culture and structure, then there is acting in a secondary sense, and the company should be held liable.

Applying the dominant paradigm in business ethics in the DSB case is especially difficult when we try to evaluate the actions of the CFO of DSB, Gerrit Zalm. Zalm accepted the role as CFO and had tried to change the culture and structure of the company. It is clear that his actions were not the result of the company's culture and structure and, so, there is no secondary action that can be attributed to the company. You could even say that he showed leadership in this regard by opposing the current practices within the company. The accusations one can level at Zalm are that by linking his name to DSB he prevented intervention by the Dutch central bank, DNB, that he did not publicly criticize the common practices within DSB and even accepted these practices to some extent in fulfilling his role as CFO, that the changes he initiated may have proceeded too slowly and that he did not complete his work by accepting a position at ABN Amro. He also had bad luck: the financial crisis made DSB's problems visible and contributed to a large extent to its downfall.

As already noted, corporate responsibility as used by many business ethicists is based on the concept of liability responsibility. This leads to the following issues:

- How to treat actions by individual employees and directors that violate the company's policy and harm others? For example, fraud by employees or the bribing of officials: are these things for which we can hold the company responsible even when they are contrary to company policy?

- How to respond to the actions of individual employees and directors when they take care of the interests and rights of third parties when this is against the corporate culture or in conflict with corporate procedures and rules? Such actions occur when people try to correct what they see as unacceptable company behaviour, internally and even externally. In the latter case, we call this whistle blowing.

- What to do with a company that wants to care for its stakeholders, but is unable to effect this? This can happen because of competitive market conditions. In some market sectors, it is practically impossible to avoid corrupt payments. Fierce market conditions force you to participate in these immoral practices. Another reason can be that the management of a company fails to stimulate its employees to exercise due care towards the stakeholders.

The fundamental question is whether the actions of individuals who represent the company and act in line with company policy can be regarded as intentional acts of the company. To what extent is it possible to separate the secondary actions of individual managers and employees from the primary actions? Further, if you are able to perceive an action as behaviour on behalf of the company, you can question whether the culture and structure of the company gives a clear direction to the individual on how to act. Unauthorized actions by an employee can also be seen as acts of the company. A care nurse who saves a life by resuscitating an elderly patient is seen as a hero even if so doing breaches the rules that prohibit her giving her clients medical treatment. Was the nurse acting on behalf of the organization? Should we praise the organization for hiring a person with the practical wisdom to know when to follow the rules and when to breach them? Moreover, how would we evaluate the organization, and the nurse, if the nurse had failed to act and the client died?

3.7 PROSPECTIVE RESPONSIBILITY AND HORIZONTAL STEERING

With the introduction of the concept of corporate responsibility, a tension between collective responsibility and the responsibility of the individual members of that collective is created. A major cause of the problem is the restricted concept of corporate responsibility, which is based on retrospective responsibility and a hierarchical model of the organization of a company.

The identification of prospective responsibility, and horizontal steering of organizations, provides a new concept of corporate responsibility. To understand this new concept of corporate responsibility it is useful to make a distinction between task and role responsibilities. In making a distinction, I deviate from the meanings that Hart[6] and Bovens[7] use. I will use an example from the construction industry to clarify the concepts of task and role responsibility and to show the differences I see between the concepts.

In our example, Annemarie L. had decided to build a new building for her veterinary practice. For her, it amounted to a serious investment. She had thoroughly studied the requirements for the new building. One of her ideas was that she wanted to use her existing pharmacy cabinet, but expand it, and locate this cabinet behind the counter. This would save a lot of walking for her assistants. However, the cabinet had a depth of 1.25 m so, together with the architect, she planned a niche in the wall behind the counter. The front of the pharmacy cabinet would then be in line with the other, less deep, cabinets behind the counter because the rear part of the pharmacy cabinet would fit exactly into the niche. The contractor built the building, including the niche, in line with the plans drawn up by the architect. For the furnishing of the practice, two practice furnishers were invited to develop proposals. In both cases, the function of the niche was explained and the requirements for the pharmacy cabinet were discussed. Based on submitted drawings, Annemarie opted for the practice furnisher whose design best fitted the character of the building. The new cabinets and the other furniture required were made in a factory so that a carpenter had only to assemble and install the components in the practice. The installer started with the counter and the cabinets behind the counter. The same evening Annemarie realized that the carpenter had placed the wrong pharmacy cabinet in the niche, one that was only 60 cm deep. Inevitably, this led to a lot of hassle. The installed cabinet had to be replaced with the original deep unit. The work of the other subcontractors was substantially delayed. The discussion centred on who was responsible for all the trouble. Who should bear the extra costs? An interesting question was not asked: how was it possible for the carpenter, a skilled artisan, to put the cabinets together without reflecting on what the function of that purpose-built niche was. The answer was simple: she had a job to do and performed her task without thinking about the way the work would fit in with the work of others. How is it possible that a carpenter can just carry out her task and not think about her role in a larger whole?

The example of the pharmacy cabinet is typical of the construction sector. The entire sector is organized in such a way that all kinds of small specialist companies have emerged: concrete layers, masonry companies, tile companies, roofers, electricians, plumbers, pavement makers and so on. This specialization makes efficient working practices possible. However, each company tries to optimize its own position and part of this involves trying to shift costs and risks onto others. The architect and the contractor have the task of ensuring alignment. Although the above example is still a relatively manageable problem, there have been several examples where misalignments have led to the collapse of recently completed buildings. The construction industry is not unique in this respect and the example is, in fact, a model of developments that have taken place in many sectors of society. Even within care for the elderly, hospital care and the education sector there are examples of similar processes. The work of the carers of elderly people is now elaborated in great detail: four minutes for preparing breakfast, ten minutes for washing and dressing and so on.

In discussions about the example of the carpenter and the pharmacy cabinet, the hierarchical organizational model is often seen as the solution. As such, the carpenter deserves no blame: she had a task to perform and carried this out. The manager who formulated the task might be responsible for issuing unclear instructions. The issue then becomes whether even the ultimate client, Annemarie L., backed by her architect, had been clear enough in formulating her expectations and whether the contractor and the architect had adequately monitored the implementation of the contract. Naturally, the formal aspects play an important role in such a case, especially if it comes down to legal procedures. However, from a responsibility perspective, the interesting question is what you might reasonably expect from a carpenter who assembles the cabinets and fills the niche without considering what its function is – has she fulfilled her wider expectations?

Interestingly, within the theory of the organization, increasing attention is now paid to forms of horizontal, or collegial, steering. Concepts are used such as self-organizing teams and network management. The knowledge that exists within organizations is shared with colleagues within and beyond the organization without direct intervention by the executive. In today's complex society, we require horizontal steering, in addition to the vertical and hierarchical control mechanism, if we are to survive in the market. The phenomenon of corporate governance results from the emergence of horizontal steering within and between organizations. This raises the question of how the top can be held responsible for the actions of employees who act on behalf of the company without direct control. The shift from vertical to horizontal steering within organizations has profound implications for the responsibility of the organization. In understanding this, it is useful to distinguish between task and role responsibilities.

Reasoning from the perspective of the hierarchical model, we cannot hold the carpenter liable. She has done her job. Maybe her manager gave her the wrong instructions. In this way, the hierarchical model makes machines out of employees who only follow instructions. The manager of the carpenter, in turn, has acted in line with the task that was formulated by the architect and the client. What one would like to see is that the carpenter, and also her manager, recognize that they contribute to a greater whole: a well-functioning veterinary practice, a well-functioning business in a well-functioning society. Each functionary plays a role within a larger context.

For the analysis of the behaviour of managers within organizations, or the role of organizations within sectors, branches or chains it is useful to distinguish between task responsibility and role responsibility. Task responsibility rests fully on liability responsibility. People who act in line with their task are afterwards always able to refer to that task. Task responsibility assumes a clear job description, based on which it can be determined whether or not actions were carried out in accordance with the task. When someone has not performed their task well, it is possible that a superior or customer is able to hold them liable. Individuals as well as organizations have tasks.

A role, however, is an open description of the activities. It focuses on the good functioning of a collective, and on the well functioning of the collective in the larger context. Role responsibility refers to the role a person plays within an organization, a segment of society or even within society as a whole. How is a person contributing to the harmonious functioning of the social system? In a similar way, an organization plays a role in a higher-level social system.

What does the notion of role responsibility imply for the responsibility of a company? The company plays a role in the bigger picture. Within the company, its employees contribute to its smooth running. This affects the functioning of the corporation as a social system, but also the adequate functioning of the company as part of the sector within which it operates, and even as part of society as a whole. A realization of the company's responsibility requires the roles within the company to ensure that it, as a social system, is performing adequately internally and that, externally, the company fulfils its role in the wider context. For this, it is necessary that all employees understand how they each contribute to the greater whole and what role the company fulfils in the larger picture.

Within a company, the roles that the various representatives of the company perform vary in their criticality. The expectations placed on the various representatives in contributing to its smooth functioning differ on this basis. Some people are seen as more important in terms of representing the company. They guide the conduct of other employees by their example. They ensure that employees and other stakeholders have confidence in the organization and in its responsible functioning within society. According to MacIntyre certain types of roles characterize a whole societal culture.

> One of the key differences between cultures is the extent to which roles are characters; but what is specific to each culture is in a large and central part what is specific to its stock of characters. So the culture of Victorian England was partially defined by the characters of the Public School Headmaster, the Explorer and the Engineer; and that of Wilhelmine Germany was similarly defined by such characters as those of the Prussian Officer, the Professor and the Social Democrat. (MacIntyre, 1981, pp. 26–7)

In the same way certain people (through their roles) characterize the culture of an organization.

The crucial question is whether someone in a key position is able to credibly fill that role. It is not a question of whether the individual as a natural person deserves blame: the question is whether this person is trusted in his role to represent the corporation. Credibility is about the competence of such a person: it is based upon their history. However, things that are beyond the control of the person such as local involvement and family roots might also be relevant. Coincidence and luck may play a role. If a person fails, in most cases no personal blame can be inferred: the criticism concerns the organization. It is possible that a person is no longer able to credibly fulfil their role within the organization, and even not able to credibly fill a comparable role in another organization. Personal responsibility is only an issue when the role has been abused. Has the individual used their role to favour their own private position?

3.8 SOURCES OF PROSPECTIVE RESPONSIBILITY

Bovens is a fervent advocate of prospective responsibility. According to him, prospective responsibility can be interpreted in three ways: as loyalty to your own conscience, as loyalty to your own organization and superiors and, furthermore, as institutional citizenship. As such, it concerns three levels on which it is possible to contribute to the smooth functioning of the whole: at the level of the natural person, at the level of the organization and at the level of the society. With this, Bovens recognizes three organizational levels that can be sources of responsibility.

What does this mean in concrete terms? In this view, one can reflect upon, at the level of the individual official, what contribution this person can deliver as a citizen. As Bovens observes, a manager of a company is still a citizen (Bovens, 1990, p. 213):

> One of the most important virtues of the responsible official is that he is aware that he is still a citizen in the first place, also within the context of his organisation. That is why he must have an eye for maintaining the political community in his actions and for the protection of a number of important public interests.

In the same way, the manager of a company can ensure that the sector, industry branch or chain functions properly, can contribute to this and can ask other parties to account for their contributions as well.

The moral awareness of a manager within a company thus consists of a number of 'layers'. First of all, managers have to deal with their own consciences, keep a close eye on everything that is required to ensure that their organization functions properly. They also look at the role that the company plays in shaping the sector, industry branch or chain, and furthermore they are all parts of society. If the moral awareness of a manager – which at the same time is part of the moral system at the higher system level – is strongly structured in a formal as well as an informal sense, there will be stronger guidance and, with this, a greater task-oriented responsibility. Given that the structure is less rigidly organized, this reflects more of a role responsibility.

3.9 CONCLUSIONS

In the DSB case, there is a certain ambiguity regarding the responsibility of the CFO, Gerrit Zalm. Despite not making any obvious errors, as CEO at ABN Amro he is still seen, by many people, as a contaminated individual. Due to his role in the DSB affair, he is seen as not able to credibly perform his new role at ABN Amro. Here responsibility gets a new meaning. A CEO is not only held responsible for mistakes in the company that they are leading. Responsibility is also based on a person's credibility to fulfil a certain role.

The differences in the assessments by the two regulators, the Dutch central bank (DNB) and The Netherlands AFM, concerning Gerrit Zalm can be related to the distinction between task and role responsibility described in this chapter. The DNB perceives Gerrit Zalm's responsibility as task responsibility. Zalm had to carry out a list of various duties and, at least according to the DNB, Zalm passes this test. The AFM bases its assessment on the current role responsibility of Zalm as CEO of ABN Amro. Is Gerrit Zalm able to credibly fulfil his leadership role at ABN Amro? The AFM thinks not: Zalm's connection with the DSB affair means that he is not the right person to fulfil the CEO role at ABN Amro.

The issues that companies have to face, from the crisis in the financial system to the climate crisis, require a better understanding of the role responsibility of a company and its directors and employees. We also have to learn how to handle people and organizations that fail in their role. It is desirable that business ethics responds to the new demands that society places on businesses and develops theories about the way companies and their representatives should contribute to solving societal problems, and what new forms of company governance need to be developed. The concept of role responsibility will be crucial in the business ethics of the future.

NOTES

1. A statement from Edward, First Baron Thurlow, Lord Chancellor of England. Cited in Poynder (1844).
2. See http://archief.nrc.nl/index.php/2010/Maart/02/ (accessed 3 March 2010).
3. Stichting Onderzoek Bedrijfs Informatie; see: http://www.sobi.nl (accessed 2 March 2010).
4. Bovens uses the phrase 'passive responsibility'.
5. Bovens uses the phrase 'active responsibility'.
6. Hart uses the term 'role responsibility' as a general term for this type of responsibility. In this chapter, I want to more clearly distinguish between task responsibility and role responsibility. As such, Hart's definition of role responsibility covers what I call task responsibility.
7. Bovens uses the phrase 'responsibility as virtue' for what I term here as role responsibility.

REFERENCES

Bovens, M.A.P. (1990), *Verantwoordelijkheid en organisatie. Beschouwingen over aansprakelijkheid, institutioneel burgerschap en ambtelijke ongehoorzaamheid (Responsibility and organization. Views on liability, institutional citizenship and official disobedience)*, Zwolle, The Netherlands: W.E.J. Tjeenk Willink.Copp, D. (1979),
'Collective actions and secondary actions', *American Philosophical Quarterly*, **16** (3), 177–86.
French, P. (1984), *Collective and Corporate Responsibility*, New York: Columbia University Press.
Hart, H.L.A. (1978), *Punishment and Responsibility: Essays in the Philosophy of Law*, Oxford: Clarendon.

Kaptein, M. and J. Wempe (2002), *The Balanced Company. A Theory of Corporate Integrity*, Oxford: Oxford University Press.
MacIntyre, A. (1981), *After Virtue. A Study in Moral Theory*, London: Gerald Duckworth and Company.
Poynder, J. (1844), *Literary Extracts*, vols 1 and 2, London: John Hatchard & Son.

4. Corporate social responsibility: the exhausting of a management topic

Yvon Pesqueux

4.1 INTRODUCTION

In 2007–08, the correlations among the food crisis, energy crisis, health crisis, economic crisis and climate crisis highlighted a 'crack' in capitalism, a cyclical phenomenon that this political system has tended to produce ever since emerging as a general political system at the end of the fifteenth century. If corporate social responsibility (CSR) marked the discourse of multinational corporations in the first decade of the twenty-first century, then this combined crisis marks the decline and even bankruptcy of the concept. The world is hungry, with 20 per cent of its population lacking the basic necessities. The world faces an energy crisis similar to that at the end of the eighteenth century with waning oil reserves. In fact, it is overheating because of the predatory environmental activity of companies and the consumerist delirium in the 'liberal moment'.[1] The world is also confronting epidemics and threats of plagues related to the increased circulation of both goods and persons. (A case in point is the flu first called Swine, then Mexican and finally H1N1, which spread to over 20 countries in April–May 2009.) Meanwhile, reduced biodiversity has been linked to uncontrolled development in the agricultural sector. Moreover, the foundations of international finance have collapsed. CSR policies were founded with reference to a 'field' for the players, be they multinationals or non-governmental organizations (NGOs). The collapse of their perspectives now forces them to reconsider this field in a radical way. However, on which fields were these 'agents' who did not see one-fifth of the world's population starving, who did not see global warming, who did not see energy resources drying up, who did not see the signs of a health crisis looming, and who did not see how crazy financial logic was already becoming? What CSR policies promoted seems relatively derisory now, even to the point of being ignorant and disdainful of the means applied by the state(s) to confront these various crises.

This chapter outlines the contours of what may be called CSR and then provides a brief conceptual supplement enabling readers to distinguish between an 'organizational model' and a 'management topic'. The 'American' aspect of the model is then treated as well as the stages in the exhaustion of this topic.

4.2 A SKETCH OF CORPORATE SOCIAL RESPONSIBILITY

First of all, one could put forth the hypothesis that the extraordinary development of management studies curricula (a speculative bubble?) corresponds to the equally extraordinary development of various notions. Perhaps the widespread usage of the notion of CSR is just a sign of the times. We could also talk about the jargon striving to qualify corporate economic activity, a lingo that has as a discursive foundation a bourgeois voice raving about CSR and includes a renewal of the fuzziest systemic perspective. This raises the question, what are they trying to hide? Well, perhaps the fact that by stepping forward incognito and in the name of stopping the use of non-renewable natural resources, CSR could just as well go after ever-renewable human resources?

The notion of CSR combines two broad components: first, the taking into account of requests from those now conventionally called 'stakeholders' as the formalization of a response to a social need (which creates confusion between social responsibility and social receptiveness); second, the adopting of practices related to this notion in management. In this respect, the notion remains ambiguous as to whether the company is 'in the marketplace' or 'in society' (Martinet, 1984). CSR is presented as able to meet expectations given trends within those societies experiencing the 'liberal moment'. This would make a management-centred representation of the company unavoidable with respect to the stakeholders in a form of capitalism both utopian and predatory regarding society and the environment. CSR would thus stake the limits of its activity. In this instance, the discourse comes primarily from the general management of multinationals.

As is often the case with popular notions like CSR, it is not brand new. In fact, we can trace its rise through the long history of charitable organizations in the Western world since the Middle Ages. However, CSR could also be considered a revived version of the moralizing paternalism common in the early twentieth century, expressed today by the heads of multinationals. The notion itself cannot be fully described without referring to examples like Henry Ford's five-dollar-a-day policy in the USA, the paternalism of great industrialists in Europe or 'employment for life' in

Japan. These examples reflect how the mechanisms of CSR already existed to a degree. From a conceptual and highly critical perspective, Allouche et al. (2005) speak of a moral illusion and confusion of concepts and practices. It seems the conceptual structure stems from disparate movements, namely, the ethical-religious American current, the ecological movement, communitarianism and neoliberal economics. Actually, the economic and political inspiration may be found along the continuum of the minimalist model of liberal orthodoxy (Chicago School), the intermediary model of positive enlargement (R.E. Freeman) and the maximalist model of social voluntarism. All in all, very different opinions exist on the link between CSR practices and performance, especially as performance remains an equally vague concept defined in part by what is added beyond the financial component.

CSR reveals the potential clash between turning a profit ('begging, borrowing or stealing' to generate a profit margin) and 'doing good'. As such, CSR is the pragmatic (cf. best practices) and proactive response of a company facing pressures linked to environmental, political and social factors. CSR also means there is some change within the company through the integration of these factors and their associated practices. Here one can see both differences and similarities with management by values, because values are dictated, instilled, managed and also modified. Yet in this instance, the values are co-created by management teams and other agents in a corporation or in its milieu.

In *Les métamorphoses de la question sociale* (1995), Castel defends the idea that the Industrial Revolution had placed private property at the core of the social issue because social struggle sought to construct a parallel social property. Today, the metamorphosis of Castel's title would include CSR in a reappropriation of social property through the categories of private property. This would be the way in which a corporation would become institutionalized. Through contracts and through property, a corporation would tend to take shape as a full social fact. CSR would thus be one of the means used in this appropriation of social property through the categories of private property.

The notion of CSR forces us to face down some 'fuzzy' conceptualization based on the idea of expansion, or enlargement, as a company's *raison d'être*. As Noël (2004) points out, referring to the notion of CSR implies identifying companies and society as distinct agents while specifying the links of causality created between them. With CSR, there seems to be an opportunistic effort to gain public sympathy by highlighting a corporation's integration of social concerns related to business activities into its relationship with the stakeholders. At this point the confusion with references to the notion of sustainable development begins. The notion of CSR thus depends upon the proposition that a company may be considered to have its own 'proper' intentions.

CSR actually began in a time of information inflation. It marked the shift from 'advertising-communication' with business ethics during the 1990s and the expression of a commitment, based on a mission statement or declaration of intent (for example, code of conduct), towards the informational perspective, which provides a basis for 'dialogue' with the stakeholders. With quotation marks here, dialogue constitutes an objective in these informational policies. However, it also serves as an example of the impossible because there is actually more 'co-construction' of information (restitution) for 'very special stakeholders' (ratings agencies, agencies measuring social performance, other companies, some NGOs and a demographic of teachers or researchers in the organizational sciences) than any real dialogue. Corporate communications directors more or less choose with whom they wish to dialogue. In fact this situation has raised the issue of interference between CSR and democracy to the point where one could even speak of 'liberal bureaucracy'.

CSR has indeed led to a collective certification of the company along the same lines as the Deming Wheel; that is, stating one's commitment which then leads to the use of measurement tools which provide the basis for an evaluation which constitutes reporting. This process has generated the discursive stakes of CSR. In short, what do we wish to say? And how do we make it credible through reporting? CSR referred to ethical standards and labels, the number of which exploded, possibly signalling saturation or even bulimia, given their quick creation and early expiration. Right away, standards raise the issues of appropriation, integration and assimilation, which lead to different problematics, depending on whether the standards are external (exogenous, often of the macro social type) or internal (endogenous, micro social type). Hence there is a dimension that may be considered strategic, whether involving strategies of conformity, conformism, compromise, avoidance, manipulation, or transgression and deviance.

CSR also relied upon the definition and management of processes suitable to applying the policies drafted by corporate boards of directors, whether as a 'meta-process' regarding values and orientations or as the implementation of a means to measuring the value added of CSR processes.

From a historical perspective, Pasquero (2005) underscores CSR's American origins. First, he describes a CSR 'provoked' by abusive pricing practices, hence market regulation, from 1880 to 1920 and leading to antitrust legislation. Second, from a perspective of economic coordination plus sectorial self-regulation during the New Deal years, and given the association between the state and business, he describes a 'guided' CSR.

Confronted later with societal regulation, CSR became 'obligatory', given quality-of-life issues and the watchful eye of regulatory agencies from the 1960s to the 1980s. And in the face of regulation-promoting efficiency, it became a 'voluntary' CSR, given deregulation during the liberal moment. The dissemination of this concept depends on its institutionalization, as well as the geographic conditions for propaganda, extensiveness in terms of the release of information and adoption of ethical stances in response to the demands of managing diversity, plus the recognition of the increased power of environmental issues. The dynamics of CSR would thus be set in motion with the standard microeconomy, given the legitimacy granted to a doctrinal representation of corporate operations, to a specific sociological approach ('stakeholder theory') and to strategy as an opportunity for deployment.

If CSR is considered as an organizational model, several elements exist, especially regarding the CSR principles defined by commissions reporting to the United Nations, where this concept became institutionalized. What follows is a quick list of these elements:

- certification process, for example, ISO 14001;
- definition and application of codes of conduct;
- creation and application of CSR policies;
- design of corporate activities according to eco-efficiency principles;
- ban on ecological disinformation;
- implementation of an accounting system that includes stakeholders;
- application of the triple-bottom-line policy;
- development of voluntary initiatives;
- application of win-win strategies involving the corporation and society.

Overall the vague and rather uncontrollable nature of these elements does not help answer the question of whether or not an organizational model of CSR exists. A model is conceivable only by hypothesizing that a relatively disparate set of techniques, which cross-fertilized one another, did contribute to creating a technology.

4.3   AN ORGANIZATIONAL MODEL AND A MANAGEMENT TOPIC

The study of organizations belongs to the social sciences, whose social object – in this case, organizations – defines its very nature. The same may be said of sociology (the study of society itself) and anthropology (the study of the 'natural group'). As such, the science or study of organizations is based on a trilogy: organizational techniques, organizational issues and organizational theory. This triad evolved through the cross-fertilization of these different components as seen in the mirror of another social science (not really recognized as such in France); that is, the science of accounting (accounting techniques, accounting issues and accounting theories). In this case, the subject (accounting) has also defined the nature of the science itself since the arrival of the 'great corporate organization' in the early twentieth century. These two 'sciences' founded the managerial categories of corporate administration – the same categories that we find in CSR.

By talking about a CSR organizational model, we are in effect suggesting a model linked to the conditions of one focus and one era; that is, the first decade of the twenty-first century. Again, simply by talking about a CSR organizational model, we are stressing the importance of this issue. However, could we speak of an 'organizational model of quality'? In other words, could we speak of a model born when the issue was on everyone's mind, during the 1980s, when it would be spread throughout the world as made in Japan? Perhaps we could also speak of the American CSR model, a dominant model today. Of course, it is worth recalling that any culturalist perspective works first and foremost in comparisons, and the logic used therein highlights that specificity.

Let us also recall the four criteria used in building an organizational model, as suggested by Hatchuel (2000):

1. A vision that goes beyond organizational techniques.
2. A surpassing of sectorial specificities.
3. A milieu with existing institutions (for example, schools, researchers and professional groups that allow for the creation and dissemination of the model).
4. A few concrete accomplishments.

The actual foundations of an organizational model interest us here. The first characteristic is reduction, which goes hand in hand with simplification; the second is the normative nature of a model. As with any reference to a model, reduction of reality tends to promote the passive side of representation, whereas the active side of identification prevails in normative terms.

This dual process is called modelling, and, in this sense, it is possible to create models ad infinitum. However, what also counts for an organization is the justification of a model. The justification process actually limits the making of models, wears out some and inspires others. It is essential to consider the conditions in which a model is produced and to know why some models appear at a certain time while others disappear, especially as it seems that speaking about things also 'sparks' them. An important distinction must be made between modelling, which is the process of making models, and the models themselves, or the result. Two different stories are going on, given that a model has a performative dimension of self-realization that distinguishes its story from the modelling narrative.

One could, like Sfez (2002), speak of a 'conceptual character' in that a model is neither historical character, nor hero nor myth, but rather a discursive production in sync with a time and place. This hypothetical character acquires substance through the repetition of elements of 'reality' and aligns himself to various reference points. One example that comes to mind is the so-called Japanese organizational model.

Schematization may be conceived as a form of procedural and substantial organizational modelling. Obviously, the notion of a model has a labelling tradition (a demonstrative aspect) but also a conceptual tradition, that of the link between a theoretical ideal type and a practical ideal type (in which, however, the theoretical does pre-exist).

With a model, there is the issue of form blurring distinctive competences. Form is thus both typical and specific, even representative of a 'metabolism'. When reference to a model is made, the organizational forms and the focus on formation become all the more significant. Nonetheless, a model is ahistorical even if following 'old' and 'new' organizational forms using the implicit idea of a 'breakdown', thus making it possible to create chronologies without 'History'. Once established, reference to a model takes place by forgetting the formation process. It is then the model's focus that counts. The institutionalization of the model leads to belief in its legitimacy.

It is important to bear in mind the difference that may exist between an issue, a topic and a fashion. Modelling a situation implies a diachronic dimension while 'model' and 'business model' have a synchronic dimension. Models are sometimes made diachronic on the basis of stages, for example, by invoking the passing from one configuration to another; however, overall an organizational model belongs to the long-term category. This may be said without any real sectorial conditions; for example, the Toyota model extends beyond the automotive sector, just as the Ford model did. This is true even if an old model is revived. However, a business model has a shorter term and sectorial contingency (for example, Google's business model). Also, a model sets out the organizational elements as a coherent whole, whereas a business model comes from 'arrangements' of the market.

Also worth stressing are the socioeconomic and/or sociopolitical conditions of an organizational model. Here are three examples with dates:

1. 15 August 1971: the end of the gold standard for the dollar (parity), the shift to a flexible rate of exchange and the arrival of the Japanese organizational model, which would emphasize flexibility.
2. 3 October 1989: the fall of the Berlin Wall and the development of globalization as well as general externalization (delocalization, off-site management).
3. 8 August 2007: the subprime crisis and the appearance of risk as a topic.

Actually, these are organizational layers that have accumulated. Crises in capitalism give rise to both institutional and organizational creativity in correlation with whatever triggered the crisis and, in that respect, a CSR organizational model may be characterized more by difference than by breakdown.

The time has come to stress the difference between an organizational topic (ten-year life cycle synonymous with 'concern' – like quality, which appeared during the 1980s; financial value, in the 1990s; and CSR, from 2000 to 2010) and the recurring issue of organization. To make matters more complicated, CSR exists as an issue, correlated to the development of mass production, and as a topic, correlated to organizational transformations linked to globalization. A fashion usually lasts about five years and creates reminiscence, or an echo. A management topic adds a symbolic and imaginary component to whatever the object of study, which continues to mark managerial representations after its 'golden age'. For example, quality left us its norm, which remains today the mother of managerial norms. Most likely the same will occur with CSR.

A model is both a norm and an attractor. An analysis of this so-called attractor normally includes the following aspects:

1. Epistemological contours related to creation of the discourse linked to the objects (of study).
2. Fundamentals of the organizational ideology associated with the model.
3. Evolution of the representations of the organization in terms of the analysis of change in discourse.

If discussing a CSR organizational model, we would have to assign specific alchemical potentials to these three aspects to calculate their contribution to organizational science in a given place (USA) and time (essentially 2000–10). However, even if a topic tends to influence a model, it remains a topic and does not automatically change into a model.

4.4   THE CSR ORGANIZATIONAL MODEL AMERICAN STYLE

If talking about an 'American' CSR model, we must reflect on whether

1. It is an organizational model. In this case CSR would be a structuring component in terms of the circumstances of companies, but it is also a sign that their management focus is shifting from tasks to people.
2. It may possibly be used at least within a culturalist interpretation, in which case, a comparative reference would be required, for example, a 'European' model.

The American CSR model tends to refer to cultural models of reference with preference given to a so-called American culture. Farnetti and Warde (1997) help shed light on this perspective herein. Basically, the transmission of an American model seems to have occurred through borrowings and blendings. After the Second World War, American management methods essentially dominated everywhere. However, they fed upon others, so that comparing an American and a European CSR model is more confusing than it might seem at first glance.

Indeed, anthropological research (Bastide, 1970) has shown how the transmission of models obeys two paradoxes. The first paradox relates to the effect of importing a model that cannot generate the same results as those observed in the country of origin. The second paradox involves the frequent case of a model that gets revamped and returned to the country of origin, which then benefits from it. Models thus cross-fertilize and have different effects according to where applied. All this helps explain why they are far more difficult to distinguish than it first seems.

The American model could thus be distinguished from that of the Rhine-Japanese by the predominance of finance in the economy and by short-term profit, since the model embodied by Germany and Japan is known for the predominance of industry in the economy and for the difficulty of generating short-term profits. This first foray reveals a lack of intellectual rigour caused perhaps by the hasty naming of the so-called American model of CSR and the implicit opposition thus introduced

Table 4.1   CSR: American view versus European view

US View of CSR	European View of CSR
1. Avoidance of damage to company's stock value and reputation	1. Integral part of managerial philosophy in terms of organization's culture and management based on certain values
2. External request leading to codes of ethics	2. Management cannot ignore democracy in the workplace
3. Allegiance to Republican tradition of civicism (especially the civic virtue of honesty)	3. 'Ethical' perspectives come from social partners
4. Importance given to formal training on values	4. Importance given to understanding values
5. Legal tradition of common law, allowing room for conflict and interpretation	5. Legal tradition of Napoleonic Codes and labour codes
6. Importance of anti-corruption legislation	6. Voluntary (non-binding) aspect
7. Codes of ethics are almost laws	7. Codes of ethics are non-obligatory guidelines
8. Federal Sentencing Guidelines	8. Partnership: employers-employees (including unions)
9. Courses on business ethics in management curricula	9. Courses on the economic implication of professional life from an ethical perspective

concerning a European model. Given the implicitly cosmopolitan character of the American model, does this imply the militant minoritarianism (read communitarianism) of a European model? Globalization seems to tip the scales towards an era of great change in organizational structures with the ideology of a unique form, that of the American model (including its version of CSR), and in terms of resistance, that of the European model, for example.

As seen above, geographical references create some ambiguity between the macro political perspective of sustainable development, which necessarily relates to a geopolitical and economic framework with reference to the states that show concern about sustainable development (each in its own way), and the micro political perspective of CSR, such as the strategies set out by corporate boards.

Only with a point-by-point comparison can we develop a culturalist overview that enables us to contrast the American and European understandings of CSR on the basis of patterns, which we hope are not prejudices.

Of course, once we speak of an American pattern of CSR, we have to find a comparable European version (Table 4.1).

In fact Segal (2003) approached this very issue by emphasizing, along with CSR, the contours of an intercultural situation rich in lessons from a concept flush with American references.

The following is from the *Green Paper* (2001), published by the Commission of the European Communities:

> Corporate social responsibility is essentially a concept whereby companies decide voluntarily to contribute to a better society and a cleaner environment. At a time when the European Union endeavors to identify its common values by adopting a Charter of Fundamental Rights, an increasing number of European companies recognize their social responsibility more and more clearly and consider it as part of their identity. This responsibility is expressed towards employees and more generally towards all the stakeholders affected by business and which in turn can influence its success . . . . Although the prime responsibility of a company is generating profits, companies can at the same time contribute to social and environmental objectives, through integrating corporate social responsibility as a strategic investment into their core business strategy, their management instruments and their operations.

This noticeably broad definition opens the door to several interpretations, but the inherent American culturalist influence must still be pointed out. As actually confirmed by the section 'Employment, Social Affairs, Citizenship' from the European Social and Economic Committee on the 'Instruments of Measurement and Information on Corporate Social Responsibility in a Globalized Economy', the following definition of CSR emerges:

> [T]he voluntary integration by corporations of social and environmental concerns into their commercial activities and relations with stakeholders [in the name of a European concept of sustainable development, and with reference to] a highly competitive social market economy which tends towards full employment and social progress.

The latter definition highlights the divergence from the previous culturalist view.

According to Ségal (2003), this definition introduces four key dimensions around which the intercultural debate would take shape:

- The voluntary nature of the endeavour, which means it is company management that takes on commitments in this area, going beyond its existing legal and contractual obligations. This voluntary commitment has the moral value of exemplarity and associates altruistic values with long-term consequences. In a way, this confers on the corporation the right to expect some form of recognition from stakeholders (shareholders, consumers, employees, citizens and so on).

- The sustainable nature of the endeavour, which affirms how serious and strategic the corresponding commitment is.
- The transparent nature of the process, which relies upon the gathering and publishing of information distributed internally and externally and enables others to verify the declared good practices and to measure any progress.
- The capacity to get new stakeholders involved.

The question of CSR profitability is thus raised without soul-searching, by showing what the owners of the corporation and/or their administrators have the right and duty to do in terms of the values of 'their' company. This they do knowing that developing the corporation's economic value is considered inseparable from its political correctness. Here we find ourselves within a liberal universe in which self-regulation is supposed to play a major role. In the end, European cultural heterogeneity raises the question of whether a European CSR model, thus a 'convergent' European CSR model, could ever exist.

Yet the circumstances surrounding CSR, as a waning or exhausted topic, mean that it will not become a model. It is the correlation of the five crises mentioned earlier that might be the trigger needed for any eventual model.

4.5 COMMENTS ON THE EXHAUSTION OF CSR AS A TOPIC

CSR was indeed a subject that could at least be placed in the category 'continuation-amplification' within the broader topic of business ethics, which was less dominant in references when CSR was developing during the 1990s. In this respect, CSR is an act of general business administration whose importance now puts it among the categories of organizational behaviour. In short, CSR serves as a sort of alternative project to communism as a mode of economic and social development because we are supposedly at the 'end of ideologies' (Fukuyama, 1992). It is thus also an ideological project. No doubt this last point is what gives CSR one component of model building, that normative side.

As already pointed out, CSR belongs to a long history of charity traced in the West since the Middle Ages. However, this was an ostentatious charity, hence the countless efforts to take it into account outside the traditional categories of financial communication. Examples of CSR come closer to protection (for example, animal species, plants and people, given the links forged among innumerable, disparate NGOs) than to charity or solidarity. Given the organized ostentation found in corporate communication on CSR, one could even speak of the company as a patron who certainly does good, but according to his or her interests while serving up an infantilizing discourse for the stakeholders.

Another noteworthy feature is anything involving secularization, be it economic, moral or political, within a postsecular society, to adopt the term used by Habermas (2003). Among the categories of a liberal moment in which the genetic conditions for the 'heterodetermination' of humans develop, the corporation – a privileged site for achievements in science and technology – becomes a place where a heteronymous order of autonomy will be dictated as a condition for the possibility of the corporation's moral and political legitimacy. In fact, the corporation becomes institutionalized, almost signifying the fulfillment of the criticism by Friedman (1962) of the return to self-designated private individuals who decide what is in society's interest.

It seems that the current correlation of CSR and risk, including risk management in its broadest sense, leads to the real and potential designation of individuals who are both inside and outside the borders of the corporation. In terms of correlation, during the liberal moment, we witnessed a 'conjunction-disjunction-contradiction' among the legal, economic and social perimeters of a corporation. The disjunction actually creates risks, which must be managed, of course. Hence the 'triple bottom line' (TBL: people, planet and profits) enters into the equation and lays the foundation for CSR in the sense that the consequences of the life of a company exceed the legal perimeters that traditionally limit a corporation's legal responsibilities.

Yet, for any business administrator, expecting results from a social responsibility policy means the following:

- bringing together social responsibility policies and the logic of cost-advantage analysis, hence the development of a whole set of tools;
- selecting from among social problems (in general gutting the theme of a handicap for it to subsist as needed only in discourse form with respect to the importance given it, for example, the fight against the spread of AIDS);
- legitimizing the inherent gerontocracy in pension funds (this goes along with the idea of so-called ethical investment funds);
- managerial 'confiscating-retrieving' of sustainable development combined with a recursive confusion about the planet's sustainable development with that of the corporation, hence an intrusion of the

corporation into the definition of the 'common good' in the relationship between Man and Nature;

- seeking legitimacy in terms of the slackening of legislation and through imitation, hence the reference to norms and models; for the latter, there is also the idea of taking advantage of their symbolic potential;
- acting, as in the behaviour found in the 'Anglo-American' CSR model, which involves American cultural supremacy in its vocation of suggesting norms for business operations.

This may explain why the very topic of CSR leads to stances like these:

- take advantage of the opportunity (for example, launch 'bio' products);
- be cautious, which means do everything to avoid catastrophes;
- show another type of caution, which means do everything to be 'forgotten';
- use PR to spin a vice into a virtue.

CSR has thus served as a pragmatic response (cf. best practices) and a proactive response to the pressures related to environmental and sociopolitical perspectives addressed to the corporation by society. Here we face a new agonistic[2] manifestation (Mouffe, 1994) of the managerial project; that is, the utopia of refusing to recognize that antagonism exists within the company. The development of CSR as a topic initially arose from the order to avoid and repair social damages. This stems from the American ethical tradition of the 'moral minimum' (Simon et al., 1972). In short, it reveals the necessity of providing a response when it is impossible to avoid a negative injunction, even if the notion of social damage is both imprecise and time-sensitive. It is undoubtedly this traditional foundation that led to the referencing of a CSR model as 'American'.

CSR implies that the relationship between a company and society is understood to be contractual (Dahl, 1972). Today this ideology lends legitimacy to the continuum 'law-contract-responsibility'. Moreover, the whole structure of commercial exchange relies upon extra- or para-economic basics like confidence, which is in itself based on moral principles. It was really a case of basing this 'contractualism' on ethical views. In fact, the result is a repackaging of economic liberalism, which makes the wealth of corporations that of nations; that is, the contractualism of the corporation creates, by mere association, the social contract.

Obviously many political and ideological ingredients have been used to legitimize reference to an organizational model of CSR, independently of any culturalist interpretations.

4.6 CONCLUSION: THE END OF CSR AS A MANAGEMENT TOPIC

Let us recall some of the previously mentioned elements used to determine the existence of an organizational model in order to define a management topic and how CSR may be considered as such.

- First, a management topic stands out from a fashion by its duration (approximately one decade). CSR appeared early in the decade begun in 2000 and is fading now, so CSR was more than a fashion.
- CSR offered a unifying managerial vision. Also, CSR brought together disparate practices by giving them a formal coherence (fair trade, ethical business, ethical marketing, ethical investment funds, socially responsible investments, stakeholders' reports, ethics audits and so on).
- Management methods existing outside CSR were reinterpreted as reporting, which would go beyond financial to become both societal and environmental. Management 'tools' existing before the arrival of CSR would take on a new dimension (for example, charters of ethics). New methods also appeared, as happens with everything involving social monitoring or accounting.
- As a management topic, CSR had certain inherent dimensions that led to the reinterpretation of the development of performance, reference to a social 'game', procedures and values and so on, as in the 'triple bottom line'. However, a closer look reveals that more often than not we were staring at a 'reinterpretation-accentuation' of some pre-existing concept or method that borrowed from measurements of financial performance or quality management. Existing managerial methods were thus rediscovered and reinterpreted in CSR.
- CSR interacted with managerial logic, such as corporate governance, then shifted to global governance through the very reference to CSR.
- CSR drew upon the available concepts to found the notion of 'stakeholders'.
- Tangible symbolic achievements, such as the 'Danone Way', remain.[3]
- Lastly, given the tremendous development of management practices that CSR has generated, it will surely leave something after it exhausts itself.

Like any organizational model, a management topic shares the following discursive features (Austin, 1970):

- Locutionary (what is expressed at the first level): the CSR discourse relied on several declarative perspectives. This may be readily said of charters of values, for example.
- Illocutionary (what is prevented from being expressed): the fact that this management topic takes over from that of financial value is not neutral. Here the bourgeoisie has been able to continue evolving in camouflaged fashion.
- Perlocutionary (the concrete acts resulting from the topic).

However, a management topic, because it is a topic and not a model, tends to have more clearly ideological contents:

- Simplification and incantation (that is, blinding through the down-grading of political categories, for example, political life of the city with its political events and politicians). Citizens may ask what, exactly, the state is doing to protect species on the verge of extinction while the World Wide Fund for Nature with millions donated by Lafarge is handling the issue so well!
- Distinction between 'friend' and 'foe' factors (that is, the construction of a partiality, and CSR is certainly partial).
- Phagocytosis of sustainable development, understood in its macro political sense.

No management topic falls from the sky, as demonstrated in the case of CSR by

- concrete examples of business ethics with its favourite tool, the code of ethics, or proclamations formulated by administrators of some of the largest firms – all of these existed before, yet now there is an accumulated experience of the problem of everyday compliance;
- the catalytic force of such aspects as the 'charity business', which served as an opportunity for learning;
- the fact that interactions with society legitimize it (for example, grassroots reactions like alterglobalization, geographic disparities, ecological problems like global warming, 'ethicalization' of representations of the political fact with the increased legitimacy of appealing to civic virtues, to name a few examples).

CSR created the ambiguities needed to develop a 'meaning' because it

- provided a means to reinterpret the managerial dialectic, which was important as underscored by Simon (1993), who showed all the managerial problems involved in the shift from values based on principles coming from a universalizing perspective to facts coming from the consequentialist view. Here we see the importance of logic in the dilemmas that mark business ethics;

- established incomplete and partial discourses, thus heralding the triumph of a communicational activity, given some concrete elements (for example, the 'Danone Way', which really takes into account the categories of human rights in different forms of managerial logic, but yogurt containers fill our dumps and yogurt fulfils our basic desires through commercial communication based on stimulating our taste buds);
- led to the seizing of a political field by businesses whose legitimacy in CSR remains to be seen. This in turn has yielded the development of a political element that took over the notion of sustainable development and appears to be the only one ready to face crises like those mentioned in the Introduction.

CSR as a management topic has thus lost its steam. One of the main benefits of CSR policies was the questioning of corrupt practices. However, concrete CSR actions have made the procedural side of business operations considerably heavier. This increased bureaucracy has met with other procedural tensions, such as the QSE formula (Quality, Safety, Environment). The more cumbersome procedural side has also created tension over efficiency. Yet it is this same tension that reveals how CSR is waning as a management topic, at least internally. Exhaustion of this topic turns the spotlight onto another management topic – possibly risk – as an alternative. Yet it is the flaw of institutionalization of the corporation that confirms the exhaustion of CSR as a management topic. In fact, this institutionalization may be defined as working on (a) mentalities, such as through representations of the role of a corporation and its relationship with society, (b) discourses, such as the way in which CSR is treated; (c) practices specific to CSR; (d) institutions, such as those which take part in training managers and those which either generate or legitimate CSR norms; and lastly, (e) knowledge, such as the understanding of what CSR is.

With the corporation inserted into the definition of the common good, managerial voluntarism seemingly outdid itself in trying to make the rules established by business administrators omniscient rather than those of public authorities. Companies achieved this with no proof of representation, using the two-pronged argument of functionality and efficiency. The size and power of multinationals, as well as their combined clout as a bloc, has impacted the very definition of rules for living in society through CSR policies. On the other hand, the same companies have become involved because they can no longer do otherwise. By 'substituting' for public authorities (which are sometimes deficient, as in developing countries, for example), corporations have more or less enshrined the conditions for the constitution of a state, which is sorely lacking. From a 'micro' political perspective (including CSR), we have moved without realizing it to a 'macro' political definition of the common good. Sustainable development (the macro political) has replaced CSR (from the micro political). However, the arrival of the crises listed earlier has not led to any effort at resolution except through massive state interventions, thus bringing CSR back to issue status, as before.

NOTES

1. This term comes from Pesqueux (2007).
2. The term 'agonism' derives from antagonism but indicates a lesser degree of opposition. Enemies (of antagonism) find their match in adversaries (of agonism). Agonism shades the contours of a society (organization in this case) in which seeking consensus takes the place of recognizing conflicts.
3. http://www.danone.com (accessed December 2007).

REFERENCES

Allouche, J., I. Huault and G. Schmidt (2005), 'La responsabilité sociale de l'entreprise (RSE): discours lénifiant et intériorisation libérale, une nouvelle pression institutionnelle', in F. Le Roy and M. Marchesnay (eds), *La responsabilité sociale de l'entreprise*, Paris: Editions ems, pp. 177–88.
Austin, J.L. (1970), *Quand dire c'est faire*, Paris: Seuil.
Bastide, R. (1970), *Le prochain et le lointain*, Paris: Cujas.
Castel, R. (1995), *Les métamorphoses de la question sociale*, Paris: Fayard.
Commission of the European Communities (2001), *Livre Vert, Promouvoir un cadre européen pour la responsabilité sociale des entreprises*, 18 July.
Dahl, R. (1972), 'A prelude to corporate reform', *Business and Society Review*, **1** (Spring), 17–23.
Farnetti, R. and I. Warde (1997), *Le modèle anglo-saxon en question*, Paris: Economica.
Friedman, M. (1962), *Capitalism and Freedom*, Chicago, IL: University of Chicago Press.
Fukuyama, F. (1992), *La fin de l'histoire et le dernier homme*, Paris: Flammarion.
Habermas, J. (2003), *L'avenir de la nature humaine – Vers un eugénisme libéral*, Paris: Gallimard, collection 'nrf essais'.
Hatchuel, A. (2000), 'Y a-t-il un modèle français? Un point de vue historique', *Revue Française de Gestion Industrielle*, **17** (3), 9–14.
Martinet, A.-C. (1984), *Management stratégique, organisation et politique*, Paris: McGraw Hill.

Mouffe, C. (1994), *Le politique et ses enjeux – Pour une démocratie plurielle*, Paris: La Découverte/MAUSS.

Noël, C. (2004), 'La notion de responsabilité sociale de l'entreprise: nouveau paradigme du management ou mirage conceptuel', *Gestion 2000*, **3** (September–October), 15–33.

Pasquero, J. (2005), 'La responsabilité sociale de l'entreprise comme objet des sciences de gestion: un regard historique', in M.-F. Bouthillier-Turcotte and A. Salmon (eds), *Responsabilité sociale et environnemental de l'entreprise*, Montréal, QC: Presses universitaires du Québec.

Pesqueux, Y. (2007), *Gouvernance et privatisation*, collection 'La politique éclatée', Paris: PUF.

Ségal, J.-P. (2003), 'Pluralité des lectures politiques de la responsabilité sociale de l'entreprise en Europe', *Colloque interdisciplinaire*, Audencia Nantes, Ecole de Management, 16–17 October.

Sfez, L. (2002), *Technique et idéologie – Un enjeu de pouvoir*, collection 'la couleur des idées', Paris: Seuil.

Simon, H.A. (1993), *Administration et processus de décision*, Paris: Economica.

Simon, J.S., C.W. Powers and J.P. Gunnemann (1972), *The Ethical Investors: Universities and Corporate Responsibilities*, New Haven, CT: Yale University Press.

PART 2

Ethics in the market

5. Moral virtue, philanthropy and the market

Kevin T. Jackson

It is extraordinary to me that you can find $700 billion to save Wall Street and the entire G8 can't find $25 billion to save 25,000 children who die every day of preventable treatable disease and hunger.

Bono

5.1 INTRODUCTION

Reflection on philanthropy prompts puzzling questions: how virtuous are high-profile givers, really? Is money donated with trumpet blasts accomplishing more good than simply running a business? How are generosity and philanthropy connected, and why is generosity deemed a moral virtue? How is the rationale for charitable giving distinct from that of investing in a business? With emerging models like venture philanthropy, is the distinction tenable?

Before year 2000, Bill Gates was not, as now, immersed in philanthropy. Cynics linked the birth of the Bill and Melinda Gates Foundation to bad press from Microsoft's anti-trust case. Addressing the World Economic Forum on AIDS in Africa in 2002, Gates began earning a reputation for posing disquieting queries such as: 'Do people have a clear idea what it is like to live on $1 a day?' Conceding an earlier naivety in fancying that computers could solve the world's problems, Gates declared:

That's why my wife, Melinda, and I decided to make polio eradication one of the primary goals of [our] Foundation. And once polio has been wiped out, just as smallpox was eradicated in 1977, we want to reduce or eliminate other diseases.

In 2007 his foundation donated $100 million to combat a resurgence of the polio virus in India. In 2009 another $255 million was pledged, followed by a commitment to eradicate malaria, a goal deemed even more difficult than ending polio (Brown, 2009). Recently, the Foundation pledged $10 billion over the next decade for researching vaccines and making them available to impoverished countries (Higgins, 2010).

Peter Singer questions whether Gates is generous enough. Invoking the classic supererogatory duty debate, Singer avers that 'even though we did nothing to cause the child to fall into the pond, almost everyone agrees that if we can save the child at minimal inconvenience or trouble to ourselves, we ought to do so.' Singer argues, by extension, that as much as Gates has done for the poor already, there is still more he could do – and not doing so is the same as leaving the child, or lots of children, in the pond to drown. Gates' '66,000 square-foot high-tech lakeside estate near Seattle is reportedly worth more than $100 million', Singer observes. 'Among his possessions is the Leicester Codex, the only handwritten book by Leonardo da Vinci still in private hands, for which he paid $30.8 million in 1994. . . . Are there no more lives that could be saved by living more modestly and adding the money thus saved to the amount he has already given?' (Singer, 2006). Singer's formula for charitable giving prescribes that the richest 0.01 per cent of Americans should give away one-third of their income; the top 0.1 per cent earners should give away 25 per cent of their income; the top 1 per cent should give 15 per cent and so on. On the other hand, those who feel that Singer is too hard on Gates, might find support from Harvard economist Robert Barro's observation that by creating Microsoft, Gates has already benefited humanity to the tune of about 1 trillion dollars. As Barro puts it: 'Microsoft has been a boon for society and the value of its software greatly exceeds the likely value of Gates' philanthropic efforts' (Bishop and Green, 2008, p. 267).

5.2   GENEROSITY AS A MORAL VIRTUE

Generosity is considered an important virtue across moral traditions. As well, virtually every religion from Christianity to Buddhism encourages it. Confucius identified charitable conduct within *ren* (benevolence, charity, humanity) a cardinal virtue.

To sceptics, however, 'generosity' can mean making sizeable contributions while being clueless about consequences. We feel good handing money to street people, yet for all we know we're subsidizing hookers, drugs, booze or gambling. And while some advocate eliminating the debts of poor countries, such a move might help corrupt dictators build up their armies, and provide financial backing to eradicate inconvenient political opponents.

Ancient thinkers would deem much of what passes today as altruism to be self-indulgence, partaking more of vice than the virtue of generosity. What they would find missing is discernment.

Listen to Aristotle's words from *Nicomachean Ethics* (Williams, 1869, p. 56):

> To give away money is an easy matter and in any man's power. But to decide virtuously who to give it to, the amount to give, when, how, and for what purpose, is neither in every man's power, nor an easy matter.

Aristotle identifies generosity (or 'liberality') as the chief virtue connected with wealth. This virtue governs one's inclinations for affluence. At one extreme sits the spendthrift, inclined to either give away or spend more than he makes. The spendthrift's hang-up is this: sooner or later he depletes his assets, making him ill-equipped to carry out any virtuous acts. Apart from this impediment, Aristotle deems profligate people to at least share a commendable attribute with generous people: an inclination to be on the giving rather than the receiving end of things. It's just that the profligate person, or 'prodigal', is not careful about tracking expenditures relative to income and keeping them in correct proportion.

> The characteristics of prodigality are not often combined; for it is not easy to give to all if you take from none; private persons soon exhaust their substance with giving, and it is to these that the name of prodigals is applied – though a man of this sort would seem to be in no small degree better than a mean man. For he is easily cured both by age and by poverty, and thus he may move towards the middle state. For he has the characteristics of the liberal man, since he both gives and refrains from taking, though he does neither of these in the right manner or well. (Aristotle, *Nicomachean Ethics*, Bk. IV, Ch. 1, 1121a 16-24 at 987)

What is less worthy is the extreme coming from the other direction: being tight-fisted and profiting from disgraceful and seedy undertakings. Aristotle points to those running two-bit gambling rings, pimps and loan sharks.

> Others . . . exceed in respect of taking by taking anything and from any source, e.g., those who ply sordid trades, pimps and all such people, and those who lend small sums and at high rates. For all of these take more than they ought and from wrong sources. What is common to them is evidently sordid love of gain; they all put up with a bad name for the sake of gain, and little gain at that. For those who make great gains but from wrong sources, and not the right gains, e.g. despots when they sack cities and spoil temples, we do not call mean but

rather wicked, impious, and unjust. (Aristotle, *Nicomachean Ethics*, Bk. IV, Ch. 1, 1121b 30-1122a 6 at 988)

Such activities display a penchant for taking advantage of people in vulnerable and desperate situations together with a willingness to surrender one's reputation in exchange for paltry payoffs (Rivlin, 2010). Contemporary manifestations of this inclination would include instant tax refunds, payday loans and other mercenary devices. Aristotle admits that our level of savings and investments declines insofar as we practise generosity. Plus, generous people tend to get the short end of the stick in business deals (Aristotle, *Nicomachean Ethics*, Bk. IV, Ch. 1, 1121a 5-8 at 986):

> . . . the liberal man is easy to deal with in money matters; for he can be got the better of, since he sets no store by money, and is more annoyed if he has not spent something that he ought than pained if he has spent something that he ought not . . . .

Aristotle observes that the ethical person mulls over questions like these: is the recipient worthy of assistance? Is this the best among many worthy causes? How much is required? Will the money actually improve the recipient's lot? Might the recipient require something more than just money? For Aristotle, underlying motivation counts: am I giving this money away for my good, or for the good of others? And yet, in addition to being a 'good Samaritan' – having a sincere motivation to help others – in business there are many reasons to donate: maintaining social status and a reputation for generosity, practising conspicuous consumption, seeking immortality, making atonement and expressing contrition, deflecting attention away from wrongdoing and realizing tax benefits.

5.3   THE VIRTUE OF MAGNIFICENCE

According to Aristotle, what makes you a magnificent person is having the good taste to divert big money appropriately and to advance a laudable end. In contrast to a vulgar cuss, you are not gaudy, showing off your affluence by spending more than circumstances warrant.

> . . . the man who goes to excess and is vulgar exceeds . . . by spending beyond what is right. For on small objects of expenditure he spends much and displays a tasteless showiness; e.g. he gives a club dinner on the scale of a wedding banquet . . . . And all such things he will do not for honour's sake but to show off his wealth, and because he thinks he is admired for these things, and where he ought to spend much he spends little and where little, much. (Aristotle, *Nicomachean Ethics*, Bk. IV, Ch. 2, 1123a 18-27 at 990-91)

We can perhaps find no better portrait of Aristotle's notion of vulgarity through tasteless excess than the image of Dennis Kozlowski, the Tyco International CEO who fell from grace due to a string of malfeasances associated with his receipt of unauthorized bonuses and his misappropriation of corporate assets. His criminal trial divulged details of the $2 million, week-long birthday bash (the 'Tyco Roman Orgy') for his second wife on the island of Sardinia, complete with dancing nymphs, models dressed as gladiators and Roman servants, a performance by Jimmy Buffett and his group (flown in to the tune of $250,000), a birthday cake shaped as a woman's body with sparklers protruding from her breasts, and an ice sculpture of Michelangelo's statue of David urinating Stolichnaya Vodka. Kozlowski was noted for leading an extravagant lifestyle supported by the booming stock market of the latter 1990s and early 2000s. Purportedly, he arranged to have Tyco shoulder the cost of his $30 million Manhattan apartment on Fifth Avenue, which included a $6,000 shower curtain in the maid's room, a $15,000 umbrella stand and a $17,000 travelling toilette box.

At the other end of the spectrum is the petty person fussing over the smallest details of every financial layout. Hear what Aristotle has to say about that (Aristotle, *Nicomachean Ethics*, Bk. IV, Ch. 2, 1123a 27-32 at 991):

> The niggardly man . . . will fall short in everything, and after spending the greatest sums will spoil the beauty of the result for a trifle, and whatever he is doing he will hesitate and consider how he may spend least, and lament even that, and think he is doing everything on a bigger scale than he ought.

Steering clear of the excesses of vulgarity and pettiness, you could be magnificent by allocating some wealth to the development of public goods, for instance, by building a library, being a patron of the arts or adding a new wing to a hospital. Turning back to Bill Gates, recall that his foundation contributed $4.2 billion for ameliorating health throughout the developing world.

Given the choice between, say, stretching beyond financial means to outfit one's residence with fancy, new-fangled gizmos and keeping to a budget with understated, more durable alternatives, a magnificent person goes for the second of these.

> A magnificent man will . . . furnish his house suitably to his wealth . . . and will spend by preference on those works that are lasting (for these are the most beautiful), and on every class of things he will spend what is becoming. (Aristotle, *Nicomachean Ethics*, Bk. IV, Ch. 2, 1123a 6-9 at 990)

For a suitable modern contrast consider, on the one hand, Nicolas Cage (whose gaudy foreclosed Bel-Air mansion was described by a real estate agent as a 'frat house bordello' (Beale, 2010) and Warren Buffet (among the world's richest, who still lives in the modest home he bought for $31,500 in 1958, yet gives $30 billion to charity), on the other. Given his opposition to the hedonistic life, for Aristotle, the bottom line is that your consumption should be balanced, under the guidance of what self-perfection requires.

5.4   OVEREMPHASIZING THE VIRTUE OF GENEROSITY

M.C. Escher's well-known painting of staircases extending in multiple spatial directions is, I think, an apt metaphor for a predicament: We might think we're doing good in being generous and charitable (moving up the stairs), yet from another perspective, we're doing harm (moving down the stairs).

For instance, a business might appear to satisfy all of the conditions of generosity while at the same time giving money to people and organizations that waste and misuse it. Aristotle claims the generous person 'will give the right amount, to the right people, at the right time, and with all other qualifications that accompany right giving'. But he does not explain the 'right' conditions. Normally, people do not scrutinize generosity before praising someone for it. They worry about motivation, amount given, and maybe the level of sacrifice, but rarely ask for more. One might argue that we should not worry about a little waste as long as the funds are doing at least some good. Yet given the urgency of today's social and environmental problems, and the scarcity of resources to address them, wasting funds that could be put to better use is a serious moral issue that can be missed with an exclusive focus on generosity.

In other words, philanthropic activity imposes opportunity costs in the contemporary world. The reason is that wealth carries socially beneficial alternative uses that were non-existent in Aristotle's age. When ancient norms favouring generosity and charity emerged, excess wealth was by and large stored for future use or no use at all. It was not being used productively for society. Now, most wealth is saved with financial institutions or invested in financial instruments. It is part of the capital stock that drives productive capacity. Savings are used to make loans that help businesses grow. Investments allow firms to build for the future and governments to complete capital projects for which current tax revenues are insufficient. Modern societies cannot thrive without sufficient capital to support economic activities. Economic activities create jobs, and many would claim that job creation is the best antidote to poverty.

Having a job is certainly superior (for individuals and society alike) to being dependent on charity.

Giving wealth away means not investing or saving. This has opportunity costs, not just the forgone financial returns to the wealthy individual, but also the loss of capital in the financial system (and resulting increased cost of capital) for business and government. Nowadays, the wealthy have options to invest in businesses that directly address social and environmental problems, instead of simply giving their wealth away. Funds devoted to developing capital markets for local entrepreneurs in developing countries may have greater positive impact than direct philanthropy to those same countries. Philanthropy need not be understood just as a 'gift'; it can also function as an alternative 'investment', a way to use wealth productively for social benefit.

Moreover, an overemphasis on the generosity behind charity can lead to smugness, when people feel good about being generous, and become self-satisfied about their moral worth. As normally understood, the virtue of generosity does not require that one follow up to see what impact one's generosity has had. The donor has given generously and that is noble. Why spoil it by questioning the effects? Without taking a critical perspective, generous people do not learn; they simply feel good, though they may, at the end of the day, be doing little good. This has a secondary effect on the organizations that benefit from the generosity. They have little incentive to assess their own performance if their donors are not asking for such an assessment.

Focusing exclusively on generosity provides no incentive for deliberation, due diligence and learning on the part of philanthropists, and overlooks the need for rigorous performance measurements by the organizations they support. Misguided philanthropy is akin to what M. Scott Peck calls 'injudicious giving'. 'Judicious', he says, 'means requiring judgment and judgment requires more than instinct; it requires thoughtful and often painful decision-making' (Peck, 1978, p. 111). Self-congratulatory givers may never realize that they are perpetuating problems they intend to mitigate and harming people they intend to help.

Another way generosity and charity can go awry is expressed by Muhammad Yunus, the 2006 Nobel Peace Prize winner and founder of Grameen Bank (Yunus, 1999, p. 237):

> When we want to help the poor, we usually offer them charity. Most often we use charity to avoid recognizing the problem and finding a solution for it. Charity becomes a way to shrug off our responsibility. Charity is no solution to poverty. Charity only perpetuates poverty by taking the initiative away from

the poor. Charity allows us to go ahead with our own lives without worrying about those of the poor. It appeases our consciences.

Finally, efforts at generosity, particularly in the form of charity, can harm those it is intended to help, and can also harm the one who gives. Michael Walzer (1983, p. 92) comments that: 'Private charity breeds personal dependence, and then it breeds the familiar vices of dependence: deference, passivity, and humility on the one hand [among recipients]; arrogance on the other [givers].' Many have noted that when generosity is not part of some mutual system of support, when it flows one way, it establishes one party as inferior and the other as superior. Few people wish to be objects of charity. Consider what happens when one offers to help a friend or relative by giving them money. The recipient will insist on calling it a 'loan' rather than an outright gift (even when repayment seems unlikely). Making a loan is not as 'generous' as making a gift. It involves less sacrifice for the giver, but it better preserves the recipient's dignity. This is one reason Yunus favours microcredit over charitable assistance, and one reason Habitat for Humanity requires beneficiaries to work on their own houses and pay a small mortgage for them.

5.5   MAINTAINING HUMAN DIGNITY

The concern for preserving dignity is embodied in the 'ladder of charity' of twelfth-century Rabbi Moses Maimonides (Table 5.1, see also Salamon, 2003, pp. 166–8):

The morally highest level involves assisting someone in finding employment, establishing a business partnership with them or providing a gift or loan enabling the person to become self-sufficient. A loan or a partnership might not seem as 'generous' as an outright gift, but according to Maimonides they are superior because they protect a recipient's sense of dignity and lead to better outcomes for all concerned. Maimonides' second highest level involves complete anonymity, with neither donor nor recipient having awareness of the other party's identity, reducing the likelihood of indignity.

Protecting dignity is complicated by the fact that the intended beneficiaries of generosity rarely complain. Since generosity takes the form of a gift, complaint is inappropriate, even rude, as evidenced by the time-worn adage 'never look a gift horse in the mouth'. Also, one may so desperately need the money one takes the hit of indignation. So givers often go away confirmed in the goodness of their generosity.

Table 5.1   Maimonides' ladder of charity

Helping someone get a job, forming a business partnership with them, or giving
  a gift or loan that enables recipient to become self-sufficient, no longer
  dependent on charity.
Giving with total anonymity. Neither donor nor recipient knows identity of the
  other. Minimizes potential indignity.
Giving when you know who is benefiting, but recipient does not know your
  identity.
Giving when you do not know who is benefiting, but recipient knows your
  identity.
Giving before being asked.
Giving cheerfully and adequately, but only after being asked.
Giving cheerfully, yet not enough.
Giving begrudgingly, making recipient disgraced or embarrassed.

The central point here is not that charity as such is morally wrong.
Rather, it is that generosity can be exercised not only poorly (wastefully,
ineffectively) but also badly (creating moral harm, perpetuating problems).
Hence, focusing on generosity alone (or even primarily) can obscure the
challenges of effective and morally sound philanthropy.

5.6   COMPARING RATIONALES FOR GIVING VERSUS INVESTING

Oracle CEO Larry Ellison said he could do more good investing in for-
profit start-ups than through philanthropy. He asked: 'Which did more
good for the world, the Ford Motor Company or the Ford Foundation?'
But one may wonder whether that is a fair way to frame things. Granted
that both Ford organizations have done great good, their respective purposes and methods rest on different footings. At least from the standpoint
of received economic thinking, the act and consequences of business
investing are distinct from the act and consequences of charitable giving.
In the case of the former the subtext reads: 'I embark on this business
venture for myself, intending to attract a profit, understanding that you,
also, may benefit as an unintended result of my rational self-interested
conduct.' In the case of the latter, however, the undertone is: 'I make this
charitable contribution for you, for your benefit, at my expense, and with
no expectation of reward or thanks.' The good done by the Ford Motor
Company, in terms of job and wealth creation and contributions to community tax rolls, is a consequence of its business activity, not its purpose.

5.7   A CULTURE OF PROFIT MAXIMIZATION

Colin Powell admonished business leaders to give because '[i]f you want to keep making a profit, then you've got to keep growing the society, so that you have people out there who are workers and consumers'. Powell's comment harkens back to Henry Ford's 1907 justification for paying his workers the obscene sum of $10 a day: so they could afford to buy a Ford for themselves.

Henry Ford's standpoint is worth examining. In 1919, the Dodge brothers, original shareholders in the Ford Motor Company, and later competitors, initiated a lawsuit alleging that Ford's strategy to hold back a special dividend should be enjoined as contrary to the best interests of the firm and its stockholders (*Dodge v. Ford Motor Company*, 1919, p. 668). Take note of the mindset reflected in Ford's personal account: 'My ambition is to employ still more men, to spread the benefits of this industrial system to the greatest possible number, to help them build up their lives and their homes. To do this we are putting the greatest share of our profits back in the business.' As the Supreme Court of Michigan put it, Ford believed his company had amassed 'too much money, has had too large profits, and that, although large profits might be still earned, a sharing of them with the public, by reducing the price of the output of the company, ought to be undertaken' (*Dodge v. Ford Motor Company*, 1919, pp. 683–4).

However, the Court's retort was not exactly philanthropy-friendly (*Dodge v. Ford Motor Company*, 1919, p. 684):

> A business corporation is organized and carried on primarily for the profit of the stockholders. The powers of the directors are to be employed for that end. The discretion of directors is to be exercised in the choice of means to attain that end, and does not extend to a change in the end itself, to the reduction of profits, or to the non-distribution of profits among stockholders in order to devote them to other purposes.

According to the *Dodge v. Ford* ruling 'it is not within the lawful powers of a board of directors to shape and conduct the affairs of a corporation for the merely incidental benefit of shareholders and for the primary purpose of benefiting others' (*Dodge v. Ford Motor Company*, 1919, p. 684). The words echo those of Milton Friedman's well-known article: 'The social responsibility of business is to increase its profits' (Friedman, 1970).

Yet even conceding the priority of the objective of profit maximization, surely only the most narrow-minded accounts would deny that maintaining a corporation's long-term profitability demands vigilant sensitivity as to the way the firm's decisions and conduct affect stakeholders inside and outside the firm.

So what are we to make about newfangled alternative business models according to which a substantial proportion of a firm's profits gets channelled to wider community development, say, as direct aid to the indigent, or to underwrite educational initiatives that seek to foster a culture of generosity, dignity and the common good? One response would be that such businesses could not be designed to be publicly traded; so any such organization lies at the margins of the prototypical for-profit enterprise. Such a business seems to run afoul of the core of established corporate jurisprudence and received corporate philosophy.

Legal norms of accountability and transparency that constitute the basis of corporate laws enable public participation in the market. Such norms are based on the premise that market relationships are anonymous, devoid of potentially partial commitments or interests. Should individual investors happen to desire to divert their personal assets to the amelioration of poverty, that's their choice. However, the present constitution of large publicly held companies does not render them capable of accommodating complex social commitments.

And yet, there are business models around the world today – not to mention family businesses – built around networks of close interpersonal relationships. Such firms represent the direct opposite of the sort of anonymity which typifies publicly traded firms.

Accordingly, even granting that some of the more philanthropically oriented business models may not conform to legal constraints of large publicly traded firms, they nevertheless provide a heuristic reference point for reflection on critical economic, moral and cultural facets of business life. Indeed, by thinking outside the box to study linkages between humanitarian values and corporate decision making, a more fertile line of investigation would appear to be one aimed at smaller, tightly held firms which permit greater leeway in assimilating alternative value systems.

For instance, it is worth investigating the extent to which applying humanitarian values and norms via venture philanthropy enterprises creates relational goods and social capital. This kind of approach would pave new avenues towards grasping the importance and potential of strategies for long-term profitability. Likewise, research into the extent to which venture philanthropy enterprises that model horizontal conceptions of management and governance relationships enhance profitability would defy traditional suppositions that top-to-bottom management and governance models are sacrosanct. Lastly, venture philanthropy's stance towards poverty and development, particularly to the extent it stresses equal human dignity in sharing needs and allocating resources, can contribute to thinking about sustainability and corporate social responsibility in the global economy.

5.8   VENTURE PHILANTHROPY

Time magazine's special section devoted to 'The New Philanthropy' observes:

> This new breed of philanthropist scrutinizes each charitable cause like a potential business investment, seeking maximum return in terms of social impact – for example by counting the number of children taught to read or the number inoculated against malaria. (Greenfeld, 2000, pp. 48, 51)

Aristotle says it is both prudent and virtuous to make sure money one gives is used wisely and for the intended purpose. So venture philanthropy's measures of efficiency and effectiveness appear to be relevant in moral deliberations about alternative uses of charitable funds. But will bringing concepts from marketing and finance into the picture drive out moral principles? Venture capitalist John Doerr makes philanthropic decisions the same way he makes investment decisions in start-ups, stressing issues like 'pricing, revenue assumptions, and sustainability'. While importing efficiency into the non-profit world is a plus, as was discussed earlier, from an Aristotelian perspective the rationale for charitable giving is different from investing in a business. If the two were identical, solutions to all social problems could be turned into self-sustaining businesses, and there would be no need for charities.

Moreover, thinking about philanthropy as a creature of venture capitalism obscures the fact that the neediest causes almost always are the least efficient in market terms. Clearly, there is no virtue in throwing money away, but should charity be based on measures of cost-effectiveness? Investments in medical research are particularly difficult to justify using conventional metrics: billions have been spent, so far without great results, on finding cures for cancer. While these investments have not been particularly effective, few would argue they were wasted, or shouldn't continue to be made. It is also difficult to demonstrate justifiable returns on investments in education.

Thus, what we saw earlier in Maimonides' regard for preserving the dignity of the recipient must in turn be balanced against the reality that charity is not likely to be completely replaced by impact-and-efficiency-driven venture philanthropy.

Viewing things from another perspective, note that practical activities like philanthropy rank below engaging in the life of the mind on Aristotle's hierarchy of virtues. For Aristotle first things come first. One must have a clear understanding of a problem, and a clear sense of what one should do to solve it, before acting. From such a standpoint, the first order for philanthropists is to understand that the purpose of their actions is to create conditions under which others can realize their own potential. Aristotle argued we cannot realize the potential of others for them; the best we can do is remove the obstacles preventing them from doing virtuous things for themselves. So the question a philanthropist must ponder is the same one a virtuous politician or business leader must ask: 'What can I do to provide conditions in which others can pursue happiness?' The philanthropist begins by asking what others need; indeed, by first asking them what they need.

Sociologist Jane Addams advocated, in the late nineteenth century, that philanthropists engage recipients in identifying their needs. American writer Louis Menand portrays how Addams developed her philosophy while co-founding (with Ellen Gates Starr) Hull-House, the Chicago neighbourhood centre in 1889 (Menand, 2001, p. 311):

> She found that the people she was trying to help had better ideas about how their lives might be improved than she and her colleagues did. She came to believe that any method of philanthropy or reform premised on top-down assumptions – the assumption, for instance, that the reformer's tastes or values are superior to the reformee's, or, more simply, that philanthropy is a unilateral act of giving by the person who has to the person who has not – is ineffectual and inherently false.

5.9   RELATIONSHIP TO ECONOMIC THEORY

It bears mentioning that throughout the history of Western civilization, one repeatedly finds business ventures embodying humanitarian endeavours. Monasteries in the Middle Ages were, in effect, incipient institutions of economic activity. Likewise, as far back as the fifteenth century, the Franciscans provided philanthropic impetus in the form of the *Monte di Pietà*, a precursor of the modern bank, which grew up not seeking profit, but instead trying to bring reform to usurious lending practices and providing charity to the impoverished in the wake of economic hardship (Menning, 1993). As well, the nineteenth century provided for a merging of economic and humanitarian objectives as the bulk of European welfare establishments and hospitals emerged out of spiritual associations.

What is not ordinarily acknowledged is that classical economic theorists espoused principles which are much in line with a robust spirit of philanthropy. Barely one hundred years have passed since economic theory changed tracks to favour an individualistic mindset grounded in the notion of scarcity and the view that people participate in the market purely as self-regarding profit maximizers.

Notwithstanding this relatively recent transition in economic thought, an idea upon which philanthropy and classical economic theory comes together is the concept of public happiness or the common good. The term 'public' underscores the reciprocal character of happiness, as opposed to affluence. One can be affluent alone, but to be happy requires others. Public happiness is diagnosed in a stream of economics literature stressing the concept that commodities and profits engender prosperity only when situated within a broader context of meaningful interpersonal relationships.

Moreover, in the eyes of many classical economists, instead of contravening civil society, the market was in fact the very embodiment of it. Proper functioning of the market depended on contracts, cooperation, institutions and trust. And these in turn served to promote reciprocity. Throughout the classical Latin tradition, economic activity was viewed as providing a setting wherein humans manifest their social being and reveal their thirst for camaraderie in relationships of equality and dignity.

Given contemporary understandings about the market, such characterizations no doubt appear strange, perhaps incomprehensible. Nevertheless, the crucial insight is this: the market reveals itself as a manifestation of social life the moment we discern beneath it a shared sense of the common good, and this is something logically prior to bargaining. By building good and just institutions, by forming agreements grounded in authentic trust rather than on the basis of deceptive and disingenuous corporate images, market interactions will take on a wider and more virtuous role. From this vantage point, a strong philanthropic business orientation acquires nourishment from a tradition of thought common in ancient economies.

An idea of more recent vintage that a philanthropically oriented business mindset may wish to revisit is the nature of the entrepreneur. Writing at the advent of the twentieth century, Thorstein Veblen offered a nuanced distinction between entrepreneurs and speculators. Veblen characterized the entrepreneur as a businessperson with a project, who calculates the success of his business according to its realization of that project. To the entrepreneur, however, profit represents a gauge of the goodness of the activity, not the end-all-and-be-all. A speculator, on the other hand, pursues projects with the objective of making money. The material object of the activity is purely inconsequential. Indeed, a speculator will switch ventures or change to a different economic sector the moment he finds a more profitable pathway to generate money (Veblen, 1904). Applying this idea to the context of venture philanthropy, one may hope to find, in opposition to the dynamic of plain speculation, the presence of entrepreneurs having a venture, or better, a vision, to bringing about from their economic activity a more just world, to realizing the common good.

5.10 SQUARING ECONOMIC RATIONALITY WITH GENEROSITY

Scholarship in economics has investigated the inadequacy of instrumental rationality to attain loftier human ends like reciprocity or happiness. Here we find an irony: reciprocity is necessary, yet does not show up when pursued directly. Authentic happiness emerges from disinterested, gratuitous conduct undertaken in a spirit of openness towards another. So although one requires reciprocity to be happy, one cannot just force it into existence.

Can such apparently contradictory features be reconciled: at one end, gratuitous generosity, and at the other end, rational egoism? It is instructive to notice recent trends. Capitalistic enterprises focused on the profit motive are turning more and more socially conscious, while non-profit volunteer ventures are coming to resemble businesses. The question arises: will venture philanthropy enterprises be contributing anything new in a world in which most businesses have turned socially aware? Conversely, will the stark demands of the market spell doom for attempts to cultivate a culture of generosity at the heart of business enterprises?

We would do well to keep in mind that the virtue of generosity, along with all of the virtues vital to the functioning of economic life, are not completely captured or translated into contract, even in its more elaborate guises. In this regard, venture philanthropists are advised to adopt a few precautions. First, by valuing their relationship with people lacking material resources. To such a way of thinking, the destitute are not deemed a burden, that is, as making lousy contractual partners, but instead an opportunity to create reciprocity, and a means by which a business community may embrace the primordial significance of brotherhood. Second, by aiming to build a business culture which cultivates the virtue of generosity at the core of the business, rather than being relegated to the margins. Third, a culture of generosity must be translated into the procedures and practices of an organization's day-to-day operations.

5.11 THE MARKET AS A SPACE FOR COMPASSION

Economic history reminds us that mutual assistance in business was the norm. Cooperation in the context of particular businesses was an elemental form of a more generalized style of cooperation forming the heart of the division of labour, and hence, of the market. As Mill states, 'The peculiar characteristic, in short, of civilized beings, is the capacity of cooperation; and this, like other faculties, tends to improve by practice, and becomes capable of assuming a constantly wider sphere of action' (Mill, 1872, p. 423). Unlike Marxist accounts, Mill interpreted collaboration, not class conflict, as essential to the market. Viewed from the standpoint of today's highly competitive global economy, Mill's observation assumes special significance: 'there is no more certain incident of the progressive change taking place in society, than the continual growth of principle and practice of cooperation' (Mill, 1872, p. 423).

The reality that philanthropy-centred enterprises worldwide are not simply surviving but flourishing challenges narrow postulations of economists, executives, corporate legal scholars and others. By placing the notions of generosity, dignity and the common good squarely into the market, perhaps the emerging philanthropy paradigm will show that the market is more multifaceted than normally thought. The market can then become a space typified not just by efficiency, but also by an ethos of generosity and compassion.

REFERENCES

Beale, L. (2010), 'Foreclosure auction of Nicolas Cage's mansion is a flop', *Los Angeles Times*, 8 April, B1.

Bishop, M. and M. Green (2008), *Philanthrocapitalism: How the Rich Can Save the World*, New York: Bloomsbury Press.

Brown, D. (2009), '635 million is donated to fight polio', *Washington Post*, 22 January, A10.

Dodge v. Ford Motor Company (1919), 170 N.W., Michigan.

Friedman, M. (1970), 'The social responsibility of business is to increase its profits', *New York Times Magazine*, 13 September.

Greenfeld, K.T. (2000), 'A new way of giving', *Time*, 24 July.

Higgins, A.G. (2010), 'Gates Foundation pledges $10 billion to vaccine research', *Washington. Post*, 30 January, A2.

McKeon, R. (1941), *The Basic Works of Aristotle*, New York: Random House.

Menand, L. (2001), *The Metaphysical Club: A Story of Ideas in America*, New York: Farrar, Straus and Giroux.

Menning, C.B. (1993), *Charity and State in Late Renaissance Italy: The Monte di Pietà of Florence*, Ithaca, NY: Cornell University Press.

Mill, J.S. (1872), *Principles of Political Economy*, New York: Lee, Shepard, and Dillinghan.

Peck, M.S. (1978), *The Road Less Traveled: A New Psychology of Love, Traditional Values and Spiritual Growth*, New York: Touchstone Edition.

Rivlin, G. (2010), *Broke, USA: From Pawnshops to Poverty, Inc. – How the Working Poor Became Big Business*, New York: HarperBusiness.

Salamon, J. (2003), *Rambam's Ladder: A Meditation on Generosity and Why It Is Necessary to Give*, New York: Workman Publishing.

Singer, P. (2006), 'What should a billionaire give – and what should you?', *New York Times Magazine,* 17 December.

Veblen, T. (1904), *The Theory of the Business Enterprise*, New York: Charles Scribner's Sons.

Walzer, M. (1983), *Sphere of Justice: A Defense of Pluralism and Equality*, New York: Basic Books.

Williams, R. (1869), *The Nicomachean Ethics of Aristotle*, London: Longmans, Green, and Co.

Yunus, M. (1999), *Banker to the Poor: Micro-lending and the Battle Against World Poverty*, New York: PublicAffairs.

6. The ethics of PE buyout deals: the impact on stakeholders and society

Eleanor O'Higgins

6.1 INTRODUCTION

Since the late 1990s there was a worldwide surge in private equity (PE) buyouts, accelerating from 2004 until the credit crunch of 2007/8. The boom in PE buyouts of household name companies, such as Boots the Chemists in the UK, brought the PE industry into the spotlight, as observers and stakeholders debated the pros and cons of this form of capitalism. Proponents of PE buyouts suggest that these deals benefit everyone, taking bloated poorly managed companies and turning them into strong firms. Meanwhile, partners generate handsome profits, managers are rewarded with exceptionally high compensation (and low taxes), and investment banks, lawyers and accountants earn good fees (Maxwell, 2007).

However, do these deals really benefit the public interest? Can society as a whole benefit if there is an inherent inequality in the spoils of PE deals? Questions remain about the treatment and effects on various stakeholders.

6.1.1 Defining PE and its Parameters

PE refers to investments in unlisted, as opposed to publicly listed companies. Investors, known as 'limited partners' (LPs) are typically institutional investors and high net worth individuals, with limited liability and control. They invest significant amounts in designated PE funds for a fixed period of time, usually up to ten years during which they cannot access their money. 'General partners' (GPs), who manage the invested funds belong to the PE firms themselves. Companies purchased by PE funds are 'portfolio companies'. Buyouts of private firms and divestments of divisions account for the largest share of deals. However, high-profile public-to-private (PTP) deals in the form of 'leveraged buyouts' (LBOs) were increasing in numbers and size, up to 2008.

PE buyouts are usually funded by debt, which comprises 70–80 per cent of the investment, leading either the acquirer or the acquired businesses (or both) to become highly leveraged (hence the notion of LBOs or leveraged buyouts) with the portfolio company as collateral. The first few years of private ownership is concentrated on generating sufficient cash flow to service the debt, whilst capital repayment is deferred.

The most noticeable PE activity from the point of view of investors is the takeover of listed companies. PE investors are deemed to have a significant influence over management and much better access to financial information. The idea is that the PE buyer will be in a better position to transform the business than existed under dispersed shareholders. Having transformed the business, the PE firm will seek an exit via an initial public offering (IPO) on the stock market, or sale to a trade buyer, or via a secondary sale to a PE firm. Large deals may be beyond any one PE firm and 'club deals' involving two or more PE houses are often put together. An example is the 2006 $21 billion buyout of Hospital Corporation of America (HCA) by Bain, KKR and Merrill Lynch. At exit, if everything has gone to plan, any return on the total firm is magnified in relation to the small initial cash outlay, thanks to tax breaks. PE firms and their partners share in the returns, in addition to the money they collect in fees.

Leveraged buyouts led by investors without the collaboration of incumbent management usually result in replacement of existing top management (management buy-ins or MBIs). However, often, incumbent management of a target firm collaborates with a PE firm or consortium of firms to bring about a buyout (management buyouts or MBOs), so they can lead the acquired company.

6.2   PE AND STAKEHOLDERS

The ethics of PE buyouts are explored with respect to the deal process itself and effects on various stakeholders. This involves the effects of PE LBOs on these stakeholders, concentrating on PTP deals. The stakeholders include pre-buyout shareholders, PE LPs, GPs, pre- and post- buyout management of the portfolio company, debt holders, employees and retirees, the portfolio company itself and society. The parameters that affect the impact on these stakeholders include the deal's structure, the extent of debt financing, the approach of the GPs with respect to operational and strategic change, exit options and timing of exit.

6.2.1   General Partners (GPs) of PE Firms

GPs are the main protagonists in devising buyouts and charged with creating value. Net value is measured by the size of the premium realized on exit, irrespective of what has happened along the way. Value creation comes from active management with 'a ruthless focus on performance' and a single-minded 'focus on cash . . . stripped down capitalism' (Czerniawska, 2007, p. 5). GPs share in all the benefits of buyouts: the typical 20 per cent 'carry' from profits on exit, 2 per cent management and transaction fees, and proceeds from refinancing. GPs may themselves have invested in their funds, so they also reap the same benefits as LPs. GPs associated with a deal usually sit on the board of directors of the portfolio company, keeping a close eye on it. PE advocates argue that this close scrutiny and control of portfolio companies, along with the rich rewards from successful deals, means that the interests of limited investors are better aligned with those of the board of directors than is the case in quoted companies, especially where GPs have made personal investments.

However, it can be argued that, whatever happens, the downside risk for GPs is far less than it is for other stakeholders. It is the portfolio company, not the PE firm, that is liable for the debt incurred. Even if a portfolio company goes bankrupt, the PE firm will still have collected its fees, at the very least. Continuing management fees are an incentive to keep 'zombie' companies going (Tett, 2009). (Zombies are judged to be worth less than they owe to creditors, that is, the walking dead.)

The favourable tax treatment given to the 'carry' means that GPs pay relatively low taxes. In the UK, the tax benefits enjoyed by PE firms have been under scrutiny, with many claiming they create an unfair advantage. PE executives paid just 10 per cent capital gains tax on carried interest, rather than the 40 per cent income tax that critics say they should have to pay. Nicholas Ferguson, a leading figure in the UK PE industry, has criticized these rules as leaving buyout executives 'paying less tax than a cleaning-lady' (Arnold, 2007). Warren Buffett has criticized the US tax system as allowing him to pay a lower rate than his secretary and his cleaner (Bawden, 2007).

Generally, PE firms have come in for condemnation, on account of the lack of transparency in their reporting as to how they make their money, and a perceived unfair distribution of the gains of PE deals, skewed in their favour. The former relates to alleged asset stripping and the latter to taking advantage of tax regimes. Also, in the USA, some of the nation's largest buyout firms have captured the attention of the Department of Justice on account of possible collusion when rival firms agree not to bid for a particular deal during an auction process as a way of restricting competition to keep prices down. Then, after the deal is agreed, non-bidding firms will be offered a stake in the deal (Cumming et al., 2007).

In the UK, the PE industry has fought back against recriminations in various ways. The industry has published new rules on transparency and declared its own contributions to society (discussed below). A survey conducted by Grant Thornton with 100 PE executives involved in deals worth at least £5 million revealed that they felt unjustly criticized and confident in the correctness of their own behaviour. Fewer than a quarter of the firms represented had a formal code of ethics, but two-thirds claimed to have an informal code.

6.2.2 Limited Partners (LPs)/Investors in PE

Barber (2007) declares that, in contrast to publicly quoted companies where investors hire managers to manage their assets, with PE, the balance of power is inverted – managers go out to hire investors' money. However, by 2009, PE was suffering with a collapse in the value of investments and crippling debt, with no way out via exits. LPs were offloading their investments for up to 80 per cent discounts and one in ten was likely to default on their investment commitments. The balance of power had shifted with the mean management fee dropping from 2 to 1.8 per cent, and changes in non-economic terms, such as no-fault divorce clauses which allow LPs to remove GPs or dissolve funds without cause (Preqin, 2009).

Much research attempting to prove the positive results from PE shows that LPs have gained better returns from PE investments than they might have expected from other vehicles (BCVA PricewaterhouseCoopers, 2008; Cumming et al., 2007; Ernst & Young, 2008; World Economic Forum, 2008; Wright et al., 2009). The British PE and Venture Capital Association (BCVA), in conjunction with PricewaterhouseCoopers (PwC), reported in 2008 UK PE industry ten-year returns of 20.1 per cent compared with 6.2 per cent for the FTSE All Share Index. On a global basis, the news was also good – Ernst & Young reported that enterprise value of the 2007 100 top global PE exits grew enterprise value at 24 per cent, double that of public company benchmarks. However, the best returns were seen among private company acquisitions at 32 per cent, rather than PTPs at 17 per cent, and already exited LBOs are bound to show a more positive picture than LBOs in general.

Many of the glowing results are reported by PE firms themselves or advisors sympathetic to them. More objective reports suggest that, in the USA, ten-year rates of return on buyout investments have been similar to those from the stock market (Barber, 2007). Cumming and colleagues (2007) take a more nuanced view, examining a large number of studies in an international context. They conclude that overall, buyout performance demonstrates superior risk-adjusted performance compared to same industry benchmarks, but more especially insider-driven deals. Sources of investor gains have been identified as undervaluation of the pre-transaction target firm, tax shields, add-on acquisitions and incentive realignment and/or replacement of managers (Cumming et al., 2007; Renneboog et al., 2007). Basically, studies show how difficult it is to compare like-with-like, particularly on the basis of potentially manipulated accounting measures, the problematic nature of event study methodology, the form of the acquisition and metric used, the type of exit and the time period under scrutiny (Wright et al., 2009).

While generally upbeat on the relatively higher positive returns to PE, backed by superior strategy, the studies show a lack of clarity due to difficulty of measuring and comparing. These optimistic conclusions are mitigated further by studies which provide evidence that PE investors actually do worse than if they invested in the stock market when a number of factors are taken into account – fee payments, adjustment of values of firms which have not yet been exited resulting in inflated accounting valuation, biased selection of firms in the database and higher risk (Hall, 2007a). When adjusting for these distortionary factors, Phalippou and Gottschalg (2009) found an average net-of-fees fund performance of 3 per cent per year below that of the S&P 500. Fees are estimated at 6 per cent per year. Adjusting for risk brings the underperformance to 6 per cent per year.

Barber (2007) points out the illiquidity of PE investment, and the lack of opportunity to diversify risk compared to public markets. Since the credit crunch, some funds have offered negative returns, prompting observers to claim that what looked like previous high returns due to a superior business model are exposed as financial engineering, overdependent on leveraging. 'As Warren Buffett notes, when the tide is going out, we find out who has been swimming without their shorts' (Gordon, 2008).

Cumming et al. (2007), the OECD (2007), Ernst & Young (2008) and the World Economic Forum (2008) are also positive about the non-financial aspects of firm performance and strategy after buyouts. Cumming et al. (2007) and the OECD (2007) show dramatic gains in productivity in MBO establishments, albeit that these establishments were less productive than comparable plants before transfer of ownership. Ernst & Young (2008) discovered that 2007 exits had 33 per cent higher productivity than public company benchmarks. It is suggested that the productivity is due to reduced labour intensity and outsourcing. The evidence on capital investment and R&D is less clear. R&D may be reduced, but where it continues it may be more effectively focused on economic objectives (Cumming et al., 2007; World Economic Forum, 2008). A study conducted by the BVCA purports to have found that PE-backed IPOs outperform other IPOs and that 'the figures on spending on R&D and capital investment underline the big contribution that PE make to creating both business and an economy that are more innovative' (Van der Luijt, 2008). However, it is suggested that lower debt levels may be needed to allow investment to exploit opportunities for innovation.

The theme of non-value creation by PE is carried forward by others who accuse the industry of short-termism, engaging in 'quick flips', relisting their PTPs after a couple of years with more leverage, but no real improvements (Rigby, 2007; SEIU, 2007). Indeed, the World Economic Forum (2008) found that 12 per cent of buyouts exited within two years, whereas 58 per cent exited after more than five years, and the remaining 30 per cent exited between two to five years after the deal. The OECD (2007) found that the average time for exit was four to five years.

6.2.3 Creditors

Financial institutions providing debt finance for PE deals are key stakeholders. LBOs occurred during a period of relatively low interest rates and steady economic growth. Borrowings for PE deals were repackaged and sold on, resulting in chains of senior and junior debt. During the lending boom, there was limited due diligence on the part of either original or new lenders, and loans were granted on 'covenant light' or even 'covenant free' terms, as financial institutions vied with each other for PE business. Even when companies have been offloaded by PE firms back into public ownership, they are still saddled with debt, which increases risk for their creditors. Research shows that in the UK, during the 1985–2005 period, 12 per cent of buyouts had entered protection from creditors, who recovered 62 per cent of their loans, on average (Cumming et al., 2007). Also, financial institutions, distressed during the credit crunch, have been provoked into selling back the original debt to PE firms at a huge discount, even providing a second tranche of leverage. It must be concluded that lenders to PE have borne considerable risk, although voluntarily. This readiness to lend at such high risk is, of course, partially explained by conflicts of interest when lending institutions offer various services to their debtors. In fact, various financial institutions who advise the target company have switched sides to advise the buyout group during the course of a bid. Examples are Goldman Sachs and Merrill Lynch.

6.2.4 Management

PE is supposed to work because delisting means that the agency problem is solved, as management interests are more closely aligned to those of the owners. Instead of dispersed shareholders represented by a passive board of directors, easily controlled by management, we have a small active board comprised of GPs who are closely involved with the oversight of the portfolio company (Jensen et al., 2006). The senior management is also likely to have a significant stake in the company, and a majority of its remuneration is performance related on favourable tax terms. Moreover, unlike quoted companies which have to report on remuneration of senior managers, unquoted companies do not have the same reporting require-ments. Thus, when senior managers make huge sums of money, boards which have sanctioned these rewards are not accountable. Management in PE-owned firms is also supposedly motivated by the discipline of produc-ing cash flow to service the huge indebtedness (Wright et al., 2009).

It is claimed that PE has given rise to an entirely new way of managing (Colvin and Charan, 2006). Managers are conditioned by the fact that the goal from day one is to sell the company at a profit, fostering a sense of urgency. With their own money on the line, they simply try harder. PE can headhunt the best executives, and pay them whatever it takes, since they do not have to disclose this information publicly, or answer to sharehold-ers, as in public companies. Managers are generally freed from spending time dealing with shareholders. Czerniawska (2007) summarizes the merits of PE strategic management as due to:

- active owner participation;
- ruthless focus on performance;
- a focus on cash and value creation;
- an objective view;
- the need for speed.

Generally, managers can share huge gains from PE when things go well. In the case of MBOs, managers have usually contrived to bring about the buyout of their own company from previous shareholders. They may have done this for asset-stripping purposes, or to avail entrepreneurial opportu-nities which they had identified, but prevented from exploiting by bureau-cratic structures (Cumming et al., 2007; Wright et al., 2009). Thus, under PE ownership, they could be liberated. There is little hard evidence that liberation from constraints is really the reason for incumbent managers to bring about an MBO. Colvin and Charan (2006) suggest that managers of PE-backed firms simply try harder, suggesting that they were not inclined to do their best as heads of public companies. Also, when they team up with a PE firm to buy out their own company, they get into a position whereby they are bargaining down the price.

Managers who are the subjects of MBIs do not do as well. In many instances, these managers resist the PE buyout, because it could sacrifice long-term developmental plans for the enterprise in favour of a quick flip. On the other hand, incumbent managers may resist the buy-in because they are likely to lose their jobs, to be replaced by more aggressive types who have a stake in the PE firm's plans to prepare the business for a resale. Quoted businesses targeted by PE may not have been run for maximum value added, and are in need of management change to develop their potential, for the sake of shareholders and other stakeholders alike. This could be an example of the agency problems so decried by PE enthusiasts. However, is PE ownership the only way to overcome the agency problem?

6.2.5   Workers and Pensioners

One of the biggest points of dispute about PE centres around its influence on employment, in terms of job creation/destruction, wages and work conditions, as well as the rights of pensioners.

Various studies have shown that buyouts may add employment (Cumming et al., 2007, OECD, 2007; Taylor, 2007). However, Cumming et al. and the OECD offer a shifting picture, whereby 60 per cent of MBOs increase employment after the fourth year, following an initial dip. However, in MBIs, an initial greater dip in employment is never reversed. It is not clear what the employment levels would have been like had the buyout never occurred so comparisons are incomplete in these studies.

Hall (2007b, 2008) has reworked data and interpretations from a number of previous studies carried out by PE firms themselves. He explains how a number of methodological and interpretational issues in previous studies skew results in favour of showing employment increases. The data may also be distorted since it is provided by respondents in PE companies themselves. Hall (2008) regards as authoritative and objective a study carried out by a team from the World Economic Forum and Harvard University, to which he contributes further insights. This study found that:

- workplaces of companies taken over by PE firms have 3.6 to 4.5 per cent fewer employees two years, and 10 per cent fewer employees five years after the takeover than if they had developed like similar workplaces not bought by PE; this takes into account greenfield entry rates and expansions, closure rates, acquisition and divestiture rates;
- companies taken over by PE have higher rates of closure, opening, acquisition and disposal of workplaces in the two years following a takeover than comparable firms.

Hall (2008) makes some additional points about worker insecurities wrought by a rate twice as high in PE-backed firms for acquisitions, divestitures, new plants and closures, so that 24 per cent of employees in PE-owned companies will have experienced closure, sale or employment reductions during a two-year period.

When it comes to wages and employee empowerment, some studies have found that MBOs were associated with higher levels in both the UK and the Netherlands, but stronger in the UK (Cumming et al., 2007). Another study found PE-backed buyouts were found to have either neutral or positive effects on employee relations with a net increase in employee commitment for financial incentives and engagement. The effects were greater in less socially regulated countries (EVCA/CMBOR, 2008). This demonstrates the importance of institutional contexts. Also, these studies may be subject to some of the same distortionary effects as employment level studies, such as self-report and inappropriate comparators. What emerges from all these studies is that it is difficult to draw definitive conclusions about effects on employment with respect to job losses, wages or working conditions, since it depends on context.

PE ownership does not necessarily have to imply a loss of workers' rights and an unfair distribution of its benefits. Examples of PE owners interacting with workers to jointly resolve efficiency, development and marketing issues can result in a win-win conclusion. When Onex, a Canadian PE firm, took over three Boeing plants, two in Oklahoma and one in Kansas in 2005, it engaged in negotiations with the unionized workforce. In return for immediate pay reductions and some job cuts, Onex offered better medical insurance rights and stock in the company. The company did very well subsequently, creating more jobs. When the company was floated in 2006, the workers shared in the capital gain realized and retained stock in the floated company. With respect to this example, it must be borne in mind that PE purchases of selected plants differ to LBOs of entire quoted companies.

Following on from the issue of diminished rights for workers in some PE deals is the question of observing the pension rights of workers, especially those on defined benefits schemes, a big bone of contention. First, there is the question of PE firms arranging to continue contributing to company schemes after a buyout. Shortfalls in many company pension schemes, due to falls in the values of equities, make such contributions all the more urgent. Given the risk of failure in highly leveraged companies typical of PE ownership, pension schemes could be jeopardized.

6.2.6   The Portfolio Company

How does the original subject of the buyout, that is, the bought-out company, fare, short, medium and long term?

The deal starts with the original owners of the company, who are willing to sell, implying they are realizing more from selling than from keeping the company. On average, pre-transaction shareholders reap a benefit of approximately 40 per cent (OECD, 2007; Renneboog et al., 2007). Of course, in instances of club deals or collusion among PE firms not to bid against each other, original owners might have done even better. Or, they might do better where incumbent management does not join up with PE to buy out its own firm.

Research found that UK buyout IPOs outperformed other IPOs by 9 per cent in their first year of trading, outstripping the FTSE All Share Index by 20 per cent. However, since PE-backed IPOs floated at lower average earnings multiples than other IPOs their outperformance may be due to more conservative pricing at the outset. The espoused improvements in PE-backed companies are purportedly derived from 'market nimbleness, adaptability to changing conditions, broad experience with varied investment rationales, effective governance and increasing prowess at operational improvements to accelerate business growth' (Ernst & Young, 2008, p. 3). One of the questions arising about reported improvements in productivity and enhanced performance in companies bought out by PE is whether these improvements could have been effected in public ownership through greater monitoring by shareholders and better corporate governance to encourage improved management (Tomorrow's Company, 2008). Evidence on this point is unclear (Cumming et al., 2007). Moreover, the nature of the exit and sustainability of the gains after further changes of ownership are difficult to attribute.

If the original PE owners have optimized the potentional of the bought-out company, what further value can be squeezed from the company after exit? Increasingly, exits are taking the form of secondary buyouts by other PE firms, as difficulties in equity markets make IPOs less favourable. In fact, as buyout markets mature, even tertiary and fourth-time-around deals are not uncommon. What then, are the motives of the buyers and sellers in these circumstances?

In terms of exits, the PE seller may retain a stake in the IPO. However, there is a growing belief among PE executives that selling companies outright is a safer way to lock in the gains of a deal. In IPOs, there may be restrictions in selling out a stake and exit is longer and less certain.

Even in IPOs, why should new shareholders pay such a huge premium over the original buyout price. This is only reasonable if the PE owners have positioned the company for long-term growth. This may well be the case when PE owners have overseen innovations that will sustain future growth. The OECD (2007) reports that 69.6 per cent of PE buyouts increased their product range, 62.5 per cent expanded into new markets,

53.7 per cent invested in new sites and 52 per cent developed existing sites. However, these are self-reports from PE firms, and what constitutes new products and new markets is debatable. Also, given the active opening/ closing dealings of buyout owners, new sites may be substitutes for old sites which have been closed. Further, the OECD reports that the most common ways of attempting to create value are through add-on acquisitions (53 per cent) and replacing top management (43 per cent). A fifth of cases involved strategic realignment, including cost-cutting and restructuring.

It is difficult to interpret the OECD figures from the point of view of how significant is the proportion of deals which do not take any developmental initiatives. We do know that most buyouts occur in low-tech industries that concentrate on continuing efficiency gains, rather than sustainable advantage. For example, one study found that improvement in economic performance of MBOs occurs through the reduction of labour intensity through outsourcing (OECD, 2007).

One of the biggest issues is the heavy level of indebtedness that encumbers the company subject to an LBO. The PE industry itself was predicting casualties in some PE firms' portfolios, as inflated prices had been paid for some companies acquired in 2006 and early 2007 (Preqin, 2008). LBO companies already had a level of bankruptcy twice the average in 2007 (Hall, 2008). In the UK, the combination of economic recession and the credit crunch saw nearly 75 per cent of private equity exits end in receivership in the first half of 2009 (Arnold, 2009). Increasingly, companies saddled with debt after PE buyouts were becoming zombies. The phenomenon of overdebted companies has been exacerbated by 'refinancing' by PE firms to pay themselves special dividends, or to buy back their debt, by incurring even more debt for the portfolio company.

Some PE firms do opt to keep their acquisitions and manage them for longer-term growth, developing conglomerate style stables of companies, rather than returning them to the listed market. Warren Buffett's Berkshire Hathaway is such an example, but this diverges from the leveraged buyout, for-exit model.

6.2.7   Society

Is PE good for society? This question is certainly hard to answer definitively, since how do you define society? Former UK Prime Minister Margaret Thatcher declared there was no such thing as society. Also what are the criteria for goods and harms? We can consider only certain issues.

The corporation may see itself as part of society, or as a private body. PE would likely see itself in the latter camp, whereby companies are separate to society, defined as a nexus of contracts and a set of relation-ships between principals and agents (Kay and Silberston, 1995). In this view, the duty of the corporation to look after the interests of the princi-pals excludes notions of responsibilities to society over and above those pertaining to fulfilling explicit contracts, or, at most, regarding society and its constituents as instrumental stakeholders (Donaldson and Preston, 1995).

The philosophy of PE is redolent of Tennyson's phrase about 'Nature, red in tooth and claw'. It can be argued that PE suggests a 'survival of the fittest' type of view. Society benefits when companies become more competitive and customer aware, so customers are benefited by suppliers who are more answerable to their needs. On the other hand, continuous concentration on cost savings and efficiencies to maximize cash flow may result in lesser customer service. An example is the AA, the UK motorists' organization taken over by two PE firms, CVC and Permira. After the takeover, the AA reduced its frontline services, and the company, once rated the best motoring organization in the UK, has fallen to third place out of three (Maloney, 2007).

Nielsen (2008) makes the point that some PE investors, such as endow-ment funds, pension funds and sovereign wealth funds, apply their gains to social purposes, so they find their way into the betterment of society. PE firms themselves have also become involved in various philanthropic causes. A UK example is the PE Foundation, established in 2006 by PE firms and their advisors to support charities that help young people, investing both money and expertise into the designated charities. In its first year, it raised £4.5 million, while its sister US organization, the PE Foundation raised $1.7 million. How do these sums compare to the annual earnings of a typical PE general partner?

This kind of philanthropy should be weighed up against externalities PE may impose on the economy and society. Most obvious are the tax advan-tages. PE also imposes costs on society when it lays off workers to cut costs. These workers may have to resort to state resources to survive. The debt burdens on companies taken over also make bankruptcy more likely, so various stakeholders lose out, mainly suppliers, creditors and workers. This adds up to losses to the economy. Of course, PE also reduces choice for the average retail investor who cannot access PE. It also may reduce choice for buyers when companies go out of business.

While it is not possible to measure definitively the costs and benefits of PE in monetary terms to arrive at a pro or con consequentialist justi-fication, this is not the only way of assessing the effect of PE on society anyway (although it is one that PE enthusiasts would probably use). We have to look at the fabric of society as well, a more qualitative judgement.

6.3 CONCLUSIONS

When we analyse the pros and cons of PE LBOs from the point of view of the various stakeholders, it is impossible to say definitively that PE is 'good' or 'bad'. Under different conditions, some stakeholders may do well or badly. It depends on the structure of financing the deal, especially the extent of debt financing, the approach of the GPs with respect to operational and strategic change, exit options and timing of exit.

The foregoing inspection of the effects of PE LBOs on various stakeholders suggests that GPs comprise a group of stakeholders whose interests appear to be safeguarded, no matter what scenario materializes. Even if the deal is a failure in terms of turning an exit profit, the GPs will still get a cut, in terms of fees, dividends from refinancing and so on. If the deal turns out well on the investment front, this does not guarantee that it will turn out well for other stakeholders. For example, exiting at a profit may be due to short-term cosmetic operational changes – that is, putting lipstick on a pig – that cost jobs, services to customers, long-term development of the company and so on.

The issue is not necessarily private over public equity. Each has its place, and, in the first instance, it has to be considered whether PE ownership is, indeed, what a company needs to realize its potential. Has it been the case that to someone with a hammer, everything is a nail? There are advantages to PE ownership when appropriate. These have to do with an involved board with ownership stakes who run a company to create value. While PE ownership can have the effect of solving the public company agency problem with managers who have expropriated company resources for themselves, it has replaced it with an agency problem between GPs' pursuit of their own interests versus acting on behalf of limited investors, not to speak of other stakeholders. Can companies owned by PE investors be run to create long-term value for all stakeholders?

It would seem that if PE were to start with a different premise of adding value for all, not just a privileged few, this could extract the good from the concept. Those who control the company would act in a trusteeship capacity for the benefit of all stakeholders. This would imply structuring financing for developmental needs, not the other way around. Thus, debt could be used for the long-term development of the firm, and borrowings would be only as much as could be borne to repay principal and interest over a realistic time period. While cutting out some activities or selling off some divisions may make strategic sense, it should be not be done for its own sake, and then, with consideration for the fate of those affected. In the wake of turmoil in credit markets, the PE industry predicts that lower exit multiples will be realized, and even these would be more dependent on operating management in portfolio companies than previously. Also, deals were predicted to be done with much lower levels of debt and more equity (Preqin, 2008).

At least in the UK, the industry itself has attempted to tackle the issue of public accountability, by publishing a code with guidelines on transparency in reporting, after wide consultation within the industry (Walker Working Group, 2007). The code is voluntary, but company compliance with it will be monitored by an industry-appointed committee, consisting of five members, two from the PE industry, two independent outsiders and an independent chairman.

The main pillars of the code are:

- yearly publication of accounts;
- improved governance with outsiders on company boards;
- better collection and analysis of data about fundraising, fee payments and sources of returns;
- more detail of leverage, covenants and debt repayment schedules;
- greater communication to wider stakeholders and staff in a timely manner.

However, one key ingredient is that disclosure of pay and fees to GPs and portfolio company executives is not required, on the given rationale that investors are content with the arrangements. What is there to hide? There is also no provision for disclosure on relationships with stakeholders such as employees, pensioners and environmental sustainability. The industry reaction to this new disclosure regime has ranged from those PE firms which have produced bland but informative reviews, to those which have reacted very angrily and defensively (Arnold, 2008).

Meanwhile the PSE Group in the European Parliament has also put forward proposals for a more ethical PE industry. These include greater transparency, a fairer tax policy and upholding the social rights of various stakeholders (PSE Group in the European Parliament, 2007).

While setting a transparency code is a step in the right direction, another essential step is to enact a broader code of conduct, instilling moral sensitivities into PE agents, concentrating on ethical principles of conduct.

REFERENCES

Arnold, M. (2007), 'Buy-out tax rate is lower than a cleaner's', *Financial Times*, 4 April, 1.
Arnold, M. (2008), 'PE takes a less than clear view of transparency guidelines', *Financial Times*, 12 April, 16.

Arnold, M. (2009), 'Nearly 75% of private equity exits end with receiver', *Financial Times*, 2 July, 16.

Barber, F. (2007), 'Debate PE: changing Europe for the better?', *European Business Forum*, **28** (Spring), 25.

Bawden, T. (2007), 'Buffett blasts system that lets him pay less tax than secretary', *Times Online*, 28 June, accessed 19 December 2010 at www.timesonline.co.uk/tol/money/tax/article1996735.ece.

BVCA/PricewaterhouseCoopers (2008), *BVCA PE and Venture Capital Performance Measurement Survey 2007*, London: BVCA/PricewaterhouseCoopers.

Colvin, G. and R. Charan (2006), 'Private lives', *Fortune*, 27 November, 80–8.

Cumming, D., D. Siegel and M. Wright (2007), 'PE, leveraged buy-outs and governance', *Journal of Corporate Finance*, **13**, 439–60.

Czerniawska, F. (2007), 'Executing strategy: lessons from PE', *Strategy*, **12**, 3–7.

Donaldson, T. and L.E. Preston (1995), 'The stakeholder theory of the corporation: concepts, evidence and implications', *Academy of Management Review*, **20**, 65–91.

Ernst & Young (2008), *How do PE investors Create Value? A Global Study of 2007 Exits*, London: Ernst & Young.

EVCA/CMBOR (2008), *The Impact of Private Equity Backed Buyouts on Employee Relations*, European Private Equity & Venture Capital Association/Centre for Management Buyout Research.

Gordon, M. (2008), 'The PE boom was a clumsy trick', *Financial Times*, 1 April, 13.

Hall, D. (2007a), *Unhappy Returns to Investors in PE*, London: Public Services International Research Unit (PSIRU), Department of International Business and Economics, Business School, University of Greenwich.

Hall, D. (2007b), *Methodological Issues in Estimating the Impact of PE Buyouts on Employment*, London: Public Services International Research Unit (PSIRU), Department of International Business and Economics, Business School, University of Greenwich.

Hall, D. (2008), *PE and Employment – the Davos/WEF/Harvard Study*, London: Public Services International Research Unit (PSIRU), Department of International Business and Economics, Business School, University of Greenwich.

Jensen, M.C., S. Kaplan, C. Ferenbach et al. (2006), 'Morgan Stanley round-table on PE and its import for public companies', *Journal of Applied Corporate Finance*, **18** (3), 8–37.

Kay, J. and A. Silberston (1995), 'Corporate governance', *National Institute Economic Review*, **153** (August), 84–97.

Maloney, P. (2007), 'Debate PE: changing Europe for the better?', *European Business Forum*, **28** (Spring), 19–20.

Maxwell (2007), 'Debate PE: changing Europe for the better?', *European Business Forum*, **28** (Spring), 18–19.

Nielsen, R.P. (2008), 'The PE-leveraged buyout form of finance capitalism: ethical and social issues and potential reforms', *Business Ethics Quarterly*, **18** (3), 379–404.

OECD (Organisation for Economic Co-operation and Development) (2007), *The Implications of Alternative Investment Vehicles for Corporate Governance: A Survey of Empirical Research*, Paris: OECD.

Phalippou, L. and O. Gottschalg (2009), 'The performance of PE funds', *The Review of Financial Studies*, **22** (4), 1747–76.

Preqin (2008), 'Credit crunch special issue', *Preqin*, **4** (10), 2.

Preqin (2009), 'Terms and conditions: after the scandal', *Preqin* (special report), 1 July.

PSE Group in the European Parliament (2007), *Hedge Funds and Private Equity; A Critical Analysis*, Brussels: PSE-Socialist Group in the European Parliament.

Renneboog, L., T. Simons and M. Wright (2007), 'Why do public firms go private in the UK? The impact of PE investors, incentive realignment and undervaluation', *Journal of Corporate Finance*, **13**, 591–628.

Rigby, E. (2007), 'Flip or flop? The inside story of a PE deal', *Financial Times*, 6 August, 9.

SEIU (Service Employees International Union) (2007), *Behind the Buy-outs: Inside the World of PE*, April, Washington, DC: SEIU.

Taylor, A. (2007), 'PE deals that cement business growth', *Financial Times*, 2 April, 3.

Tett, G. (2009), 'Curse of the zombies rises in Europe amid an eerie calm', *Financial Times*, 3 April, 34.

Tomorrow's Company (2008), *Tomorrow's Owners: Stewardship of Tomorrow's Company*, October, London: Tomorrow's Company.

Van der Luijt, A. (2008), 'Private equity IPOs outperform market', *Director of Finance Online*, 29 April, accessed 19 December 2010 at www.dofonline.co.uk/content/view/1719/116/.

Walker Working Group (2007), *Guidelines for Disclosure and Transparency in PE*, London, UK.

World Economic Forum (2008), 'The global economic impact of PE report 2008', *Globalization of Alternative Investments working papers Volume 1*.

Wright, M., K. Amess, C. Weir and S. Girma (2009), 'Private equity and corporate governance: retrospect and prospect', *Corporate Governance*, **17** (3), 353–75.

7. Sovereign wealth funds – a significant and growing global force

Jane Collier

'High finance can no longer be separated from high politics'
Benjamin J. Cohen (1996)

7.1 INTRODUCTION

Management of official holdings of foreign assets, in particular in the form of sovereign wealth funds, has become a major focus of national and international economic and financial policy. The principal management issues are their size, their lack of transparency, their potential to disrupt financial markets and the risk that political objectives might influence their management.

A Sovereign Investment Fund invests public funds in a range of assets on behalf of a sovereign country. Sovereign Investment Funds are of two kinds: sovereign wealth funds (SWFs) and sovereign pension funds (SPFs). Funds can be sourced from mineral resources, foreign trade surpluses or from various 'new money' sources such as petrodollars and/or hedge funds.

SWFs are equity investment vehicles, established by and under the control of sovereign states: pools of assets owned and/or managed directly or indirectly by governments. They can be set up for various reasons – for instance, to improve the return on foreign exchange transactions and to smooth variations in commodity prices. In these situations SWFs can be seen as a source of economic strength in that they provide a source of capital for global investment. Alternatively they can take the form of SPFs. The pioneer SWF is generally held to be Government of Singapore Investment Corporation (GIC) (1981), since it was the first of the government-owned portfolio investment funds. In 1953 Kuwait established the Kuwait Investment Board. Since 2005 at least 12 SWFs have been established: estimates put their rate of growth at around $1 trillion a year.

The recent growth and expansion of SWFs have exposed two tensions in international economic and financial relations. First, the growth of SWFs reflects a dramatic redistribution of international wealth from traditional industrial countries like the USA to countries that historically have not been major players in international finance. Second, governments own or control a significant share of the new international wealth. This redistribution of wealth from private to public hands brings with it dramatic changes in decision-making practices that are often at variance with the traditional private sector, market-oriented viewpoints.

In recent years governments have formed pools of capital for various reasons, for instance, an obligation to finance public pension schemes (Public Pension Reserve Schemes), and the total of funds has risen accordingly. In 2006/7 the total of SWF pools was circa $2.6 trillion, by the end of 2007 it was $3 trillion (IMF), and the figure continues to rise (Butt et al., 2008). However, more recently many funds have suffered losses caused by the ongoing global financial crisis. Even in these circumstances SWFs continue to have their uses: they can inject capital where necessary; they can reduce volatility in markets, thereby contributing to market efficiency. But as they invest more of their assets in private financial markets considerable concerns have arisen as to the extent to which, or whether, they should follow the practices of private investors and pension funds (Sun and Hesse, 2009). It is also worth noting that many SWFs did not rebalance their portfolios in the wake of the financial crisis, suggesting that their role as pension providers has lost its importance (Global Pensions, 1 October 2009).

Much of the expansion of SWFs in recent years has been driven by the huge growth in East Asian reserves, and also by the need for oil-rich countries to provide income to replace income lost from diminishing oil reserves. SWFs may also take long-term strategic positions, thereby contributing to stability in the international economy. However, the 'credit crunch' has introduced a degree of uncertainty into the international financial system that has resulted in a number of SWFs sustaining significant losses. At the same time the asset base of the SWFs is expanding and the size of their offshore investment is increasing. Morgan Stanley has forecast that SWF assets will increase from a figure of $2–3 trillion to $12 trillion by 2015. SWFs are increasing and are now emerging in economies known to have geopolitical ambitions.

During the first quarter of 2009 SWF expenditure was lower than in any quarter since the end quarter of 2005. This was due to the adverse effects of falling oil prices and contracting global trade. Attempts to deal in 2009 were affected by perceptions of risk and the effects of market losses on investments in public companies (Monitor and FEEM, 2009). However, in the first quarter of 2009 funds once again began to look for investment opportunities abroad as opposed to looking for opportunities at home.

The spread of SWFs across national borders has triggered concerns in various quarters concerning a range of issues. These include the likelihood of economies being directed by 'outsiders', the possibility of SWFs wielding political influence, the effects of large flows into or out of money markets and of substantial shifts of funds from bonds to equities. Some of the interest in SWFs and some of the surrounding anxieties arise from the fact that governments are now acquiring stakes in what were hitherto private entities – in other words, there is a marked increase in the extent of government ownership and management of national assets (Gilson and Milhaupt, 2008). Countries which hitherto invested their surpluses in US Treasury securities are now seeking higher returns from equities or corporate holdings. (On 2 June 2009 China Investment Corp (CIC) announced that it had decided to buy US$ common stocks in Morgan Stanley's portfolio.)

Several governments have announced their intention to shift portfolio holdings to a broader arena. Although there is thus some considerable concern about strategic and political objectives of SWFs, transparency and governance are becoming equally important. As the banking crisis deepened media attention focused on the size and role of SWFs, and on the extent to which they might or were likely to play a role in the bailout of Western banks. Ironically the size of these funds increased as rising energy prices and trade surpluses swelled the coffers of exporting nations. The increase in size of these funds was, according to the BBC, 'simply a shift in the balance of power from Western industrialized countries to new emerging market giants such as China and the Middle East'.

7.2   SWFS, TRANSPARENCY AND ACCOUNTABILITY

Until recently few people knew what a SWF was, even though some of these funds have been in existence for decades. A SWF doesn't always look or act like other investment vehicles. These funds are owned by foreign governments whose policies and practices may differ from the policies of countries where they invest so that SWFs may generate controversy.

To help ensure general acceptance of the activities of SWFs, representatives of 26 countries gathered together to create a voluntary agreement which they called the 'Generally Accepted Principles and Practices (GAPP) for SWFs', commonly referred to as the 'Santiago Principles'. On 11 October 2008 the International Working Group (IWG) of the International Monetary Fund (IMF) on Sovereign Wealth Funds presented the Santiago Principles to the IMF's policy-guiding

International Monetary and Financial Committee (IMFC), which met in Washington, DC to consult about global economic developments and to take stock of the IWG's efforts. Finance Ministers, IWG representatives, the Organisation for Economic Co-operation and Development (OECD) and the European Commission (EC) also took the opportunity to discuss the Principles and SWF issues in a separate meeting. The IWG has made public the set of 24 voluntary Principles and related explanatory material (at http://www.iwg-swf.org) and announced that it has established a Formation Committee to explore the creation of a permanent international SWF body.

On 6 April 2009 the IWG met in Kuwait City to announce the establishment of the International Forum of Sovereign Wealth Funds (Forum). The Kuwait Declaration established that the Forum (a voluntary group of SWFs) will meet at least once a year to exchange views and facilitate an understanding of the GAPP and SWF activities.

In presenting the Santiago Principles to the IMFC members, Mr Hamad Al Suwaidi, Undersecretary of the Abu Dhabi Department of Finance and a director of the Abu Dhabi Investment Authority, said

> We believe that this document will in both home and recipient countries improve the understanding of the objectives, structures, and governance arrangements of SWFs; enhance the understanding of SWFs as economically and financially oriented entities; and help maintain an open and stable investment climate. Through the implementation of the Santiago Principles, we seek to ensure that the international investment environment will remain open. This is a very significant achievement given the diversity of the institutions involved, complexity of the subject matter, comprehensiveness of the document and the short time taken to reach an agreement.

If these Principles had worked as intended they would have gone a long way to achieving another important goal of the Santiago meeting – maintaining a stable global financial system and the free flow of capital and investment. A robust implementation of the GAPP should have helped to solve issues of transparency, accountability and questions related to the operations of SWFs. However, this did not happen.

Just one year later (13 October 2009) a report commissioned by the Investor Responsibility Research Center Institute (IRRCi) and conducted by RiskMetrics Group found evidence of a wide variety of aims and practices among funds (Mehrpouya et al., 2009).

For instance:

There has been little analysis of the actual influence of the SWFs on the companies in their portfolios and the related risks and opportunities. Progress appears to have been patchy.

Engagement practices were not disclosed by the SWFs: researchers had to glean information from alternative sources. There is a wide variety of aims and practices among funds.

There does not appear to be sufficient participation in governance by independent boards and management.

There does not appear to be enough interest by funds in environmental, social and governance (ESG) issues.

It would appear that public disclosure levels have clearly not yet met the standards demanded by the IRRCi.

7.3 SWFS, UK INVESTORS AND GOOD GOVERNANCE

In June 2009 UK pension funds and insurance companies made a startling announcement – they declared that they were now seeking to build an international network of investors and SWFs with an interest in long-term value, so as to put some major weight behind their lobbying of companies on important issues such as governance and their subsequent voting at annual general meetings.[1] Plans were drawn up to allow this venture to proceed.

The UK Institutional Shareholders' Committee (ISC) announced that its chairman, Keith Skeoch, chief executive officer at Standard Life would initiate discussions with senior practitioners from the global investment industry to plan ways to build the proposed network. The ISC is run jointly by the UK's four big institutional investor bodies: the Association of British Insurers, the Association of Investment Companies, the Investment Management Association and the National Association of Pension Funds. It was created in the wake of the 2001 Myners Review on institutional investment, although it recently came under fire from Paul Myners himself, who apparently dubbed it a 'rather low profile entity'. However, the ISC is a body with some muscle: it announced that its report would aim to beef up investor engagement and that its conclusions would feed into the forthcoming review on corporate governance in banks.

On 16 July 2009 Sir David Walker, former chairman of Morgan Stanley and the UK Financial Reporting Council (FRC), published his review of corporate governance in UK banks and other financial institutions. This review was to form the bedrock of the collaboration between the investors and SWFs and their management.

The key proposals of the review concerned

- Risk management: this should be undertaken by a board (that is, a risk committee).

- The role of non-executive directors (NEDs) was to be defined.
- Board, shareholder and regulatory engagement was to form the basis of collaboration.
- Remuneration policy was to be defined.

The key objective in building an international investor network was apparently to create a simple, non-bureaucratic system that would enable and encourage more institutions to participate in corporate lobbying and form a 'critical mass' on controversial company issues. The main focus would be 'dialogue' with companies to assist them to resolve their difficulties, but warned that it could instruct members to vote down resolutions and 'follow-up afterwards' if investors believe the company's response to investor concerns falls short. The review continued: '*The ISC considers that investors have on occasion been too reluctant to act in this way*' (Walker, 2009, p. 119, emphasis added). However, the ISC said it also needed regulatory certainty that rules on 'acting in concert and insider dealing' would not be a deterrent to building the network: 'The authorities should make it clear that collective dialogue is permitted. Also the authorities should make it clear that it is possible for individuals to receive price sensitive information in the course of dialogue provided there is appropriate ring-fencing (Walker, 2009, p. 119).

Amongst its other recommendations, the ISC said that asset owners should specify in tough mandates to fund managers exactly what type of commitment to corporate engagement, if any, they expect. It added 'where shareholders delegate responsibility for such dialogue to third parties, they should agree a policy, and, where appropriate, publish it and take steps to ensure that it is followed' (Walker, 2009, p. 118). However, investors appear to have had concerns that matters they had raised with boards were sometimes not discussed – in other words, that the process of dialogue was not always working as it should.

David Walker of the FRC points out that the aim should be to maintain control, and in particular, to maintain balance in investor engagement as over against adherence to the rules.

The UK Financial Services Authority (FSA) has given the green light to institutional investors to start ramping up collective lobbying of companies on corporate governance issues. In a letter sent to UK investor associations, which followed the concerns expressed by ISC, the FSA said that its rules did not prevent what it called 'legitimate activity' on joint engagements to strengthen investor influence over company policies such as pay and bonuses.

Alexander Justham, FSA director of markets, said: 'There is nothing under FSA rules that prevents investors discussing matters when it is for a legitimate purpose. Our letter provides clarity to investors that they are free to engage with the boards of companies as Sir David Walker envisaged.' The FSA said its market abuse rules did not prevent investors from engaging collectively with company management, although it warned that trading on the basis of knowing another investor's intentions or working jointly to avoid disclosure of shareholdings could constitute market abuse. Disclosure rules, which usually require investors with the same long-term voting strategy to aggregate their shareholdings if they breach the threshold for disclosure (3 per cent of a company's shares), would be unlikely to be triggered by ad hoc discussions between investors on corporate governance issues. Lastly, the FSA letter noted that its 'Acting in concert' rules, which would normally require investors to seek FSA approval if they reach a controlling shareholding (10 per cent or more of a company's shares) also did not cover ad hoc discussions or engagements that aim to promote 'generally accepted principles' of good corporate governance. Furthermore the FSA introduced a new code requiring large banks, building societies and broker dealers in the UK to align remuneration policies with effective risk management. Clarifying the rules round shareholder dialogue will make it easier for investors to take a collective approach to boards (BGN Entrepreneur, 2009).

Investment and cooperation arrangements are now beginning to develop in various directions:

- CIC have entered into agreement with the Noble Group (worldwide supply chain management and distribution related to agricultural activities).
- UK Canary Wharf is obtaining debt finance from Qatar Holdings.
- Prior to the 2011 conflict in that country, the Libyan SWF Libyan Investment Authority (LIA) (created primarily to manage the oil revenues of that country) had entered into a binding memorandum of understanding with Verenex Energy Inc. concerning the sale of its shares. The assumption was that LIA would buy remaining shares and distribute working capital to Verenex shareholders.

It is clear that arrangements between investors, companies and SWFs are only beginning to explore new and fruitful possibilities.

According to David Walker, SWFs own more than 10 per cent of the UK stock market. This makes them a powerful new shareholding bloc with an important role in corporate governance. The Association of British Insurers and the National Association of Pension Funds are urged to collaborate with SWFs.

7.4   RESOURCE WEALTH AND THE ETHICS OF GLOBAL INVESTMENT

On 30 August 2009 Norges Sovereign Wealth Fund sacked its entire team as a result of record losses. Norway had invested its oil wealth in a fund with a current market value of more than $400 billion. This fund was known as the 'Government Pension Fund'. The Finance Minister is responsible for the management of the Pension Fund-Global (Gjessing and Syse, 2007), but the operational management of the Pension Fund-Norway is carried out by Folketrygdfondet. However, it should be recognized that Norway's wealth fund has been unique in both its accountability and in the transparency with which it has conducted its affairs. (This approach is to be contrasted with that of the explanation for the cloak of secrecy behind which Singapore's SWFs conduct their affairs.)

Norway's $400 billion sovereign wealth fund is the world's second largest SWF: it has now reformulated its investment strategy to increase its exposure to environmentally responsible companies. The Norwegian Government Pension Fund has directed about 1 per cent of its funds, or $4 billion, into 'green shares' targeting investments in the developing world. As part of the shift, Norway has invested $1.2 billion into 232 Indian companies that support environmental sustainability and clean energy.

The Pension Fund-Global (SWF) has a dual ethical commitment; to engage with companies applying best-practice principles, and to avoid involvement with companies where there is a perceived risk to justice and/ or to human rights (Clark and Monk, 2010).

Norges Bank Investment Management (NBIM), which manages the assets for the Norwegian Pension Fund, has now added water to the existing five environmental target foci. The aim is to concentrate on projects where transparency buys legitimacy as seen by domestic audiences.

These funds are supposed to perform in such a way that future generations benefit. However, pressure by existing voters for short-term returns is bound to reduce the intergenerational benefits for which Norway's strategy has hitherto been praised. Are SWFs behaving ethically in tailoring their activities so as to please those who want short-term gains?

7.4.1   Sovereign Wealth Funds in the EU

Europe is the world's largest exporter of international investments and at the same time both imports and exports capital. Capital flows have hitherto been regarded liberally. However, the increases in SWF dealings in the EU and US banking sectors have raised concerns as to the degree of influence that might be wielded by these funds, and as a possible (if somewhat far-fetched) 'threat to the sovereignty of the nations in whose corporations they invest' (Gilson and Milhaupt, 2008, p. 1).

Another fear is voiced regarding the potential political influence of Russia and/or China stemming from the leverage of their investments. SWFs can be pools of assets banks, they can be private companies without revealing the identity of the owner or they may be funds channelled through existing projects. A recent IMF survey has shown that about half of SWFs are legal entities separate from the state or central bank, whereas the other half are a diverse group of assets not legally separate from the state.

In the USA there is a specific mechanism that ensures the national control of SWF investments. The Committee on Foreign Investment in the US (CFIUS) takes responsibility for monitoring overseas acquisitions of 10 per cent or more of a domestic company's total ownership.

The first SWF fund was established in 1953 by the Kuwait Investment Authority. The next wave of funds was associated with the oil price rises of the 1970/80s. Recent increases have been associated with high oil prices, globalization and the accumulation of foreign assets by emerging market economies. Since 2000 about 20 new funds have been created, and the IMF estimates that SWF assets could grow to about $6–10 trillion by 2012. However, at this point in time these funds still only account for about one-twentieth of those held by private sector participants. It is also the case that over the last months the credit difficulties experienced by EU and US banks have been eased by injections of capital from SWFs, thereby providing much needed market liquidity. Increasingly, however, SWFs are diversifying their portfolios.

In 2007 China declared its intention to invest $3 billion of its fund reserves in private holding companies. Concerns about financial stability, governance and political interference became rife (Gugler and Chaisse, 2009).

One of the issues of concern is the lack of transparency relating to the activities of SWFs – little is known about their management, assets, liabilities or investment strategies. There are some suspicions that some of their activities may be driven by the exigencies of their own national aims and objectives. On the other hand, these are merely suspicions, and the EU is an open market and the largest importer and exporter of foreign investment.

The EU has taken a coordinated stance on SWFs

In a document issued on 27 February 2008 the European Commission emphasized the importance of a coordinated and balanced approach on SWFs (Commission of the European Communities, 2008).

It calls on SWFs to demonstrate good governance, accountability and a sufficient level of transparency. In particular it emphasizes the need for a clear division of rights and responsibilities between managers and their governments, as well as an effective system of checks and balances when it comes to investment decisions.

The European Commission emphasized the importance of SWFs in the international financial system, and as such it will collaborate with the IMF in developing a code of conduct for SWFs. It also supports the OECD in identifying best practice guidelines for recipient countries.

The European Council of 13 and 14 March 2008 welcomed the Commission's proposals and invited it to continue its work in this field (European Union, 2008).

Following the EU's communication, Freshfields Bruckhaus Deringer welcomed the constructive approach taken by the EU Council in supporting a coordinated international approach to future guidelines.

> The EU has signalled that it will remain open to investment and will not be pressurised into a protectionist stance. Freshfields is particularly pleased that the EU has recognised that there is need for a Code of Conduct for SWFs, given that they have become a valuable source of capital for financial markets. Good governance and investment transparency will be central planks of any new measures. (Freshfields Bruckhaus Deringer, 2008)

What Europe and indeed global markets do not need is a fragmented policy towards SWFs which could deter future investment. Thus the European Council's recognition that a coordinated European and international approach is the best way to address any individual national concerns about SWFs is important.

In this perspective, with regard to the GAPP for SWFs, Joaquín Almunia, EU Commissioner for economic and monetary affairs, has declared the Santiago Principles a 'public global good' that can help to foster trust and confidence between SWFs and their originating and recipient countries (see also Almunia, 2008).

However, not all Europeans feel this way. The Italian Foreign Minister and his government fear that the outcome may be hostile takeovers, and has set up its own rules about the behaviour of SWFs.

The French President has called for the creation of European SWFs so that they can take a stake in European companies rather than allowing foreigners to enter the market.

Germany, however, welcomes the advent of SWFs.

7.5   CONCLUSIONS

The main features of SWFs can be summarized as follows.

SWFs globally significant economic issues

1. Seventy per cent of SWFs have their basis in oil and gas. High fuel prices mean current account surpluses in producer countries (for example, China, Singapore, Russia, Middle Eastern and Asian countries).
2. Many of these funds are used to buy stakes in Western companies, given the low returns on US Treasury bonds.
3. There is a worrying lack of transparency in the operations of many of these funds: this raises concerns – in the USA in particular – about effects in labour markets, protectionism and other effects on trade.
4. In many cases (for example, Kuwait, Singapore and others), there are legal restrictions on revealing information about assets.
5. The banking crisis focused attention on the role and size of SWFs, particularly those that played a major role in bailing out some of the most prestigious Western banks (Citigroup, UBS and so on).
6. The IMF predicts that by 2012 global SWFs will have a total value of around $10 trillion as opposed to the value of $3 trillion at the end of 2007. Other comments included that of the BBC which sees these changes as signs of the shift in the balance of power in the world economy from Western countries to emerging ones (China, Middle Eastern countries).

Issues relating to the ethical policy of the Norwegian Government Pension Fund

7. The Norwegian Government Pension Fund-Global, with a total value of NOK 2.85 trillion, is one of the largest investors in the world – a well-governed and remarkably transparent fund. However, Oxford researchers (Clark and Monk, 2010) have criticized the inflexible governance and management decision-taking system. Nevertheless, in October 2009, Norges Bank Investment Management, the Manager of the Pension Fund, has announced a major corporate governance campaign that will challenge four major US companies to split the roles of chairman and chief executive.
8. In the UK market – as owner of £32 billion UK listed shares – it is throwing its weight behind moves to get all UK corporate directors to be re-elected every year – a more demanding position than that required by the Walker Report.

SWFs and corporate responsibility

9. The emergence of SWFs raises the issue of their relation to corporate responsibility (Bendell et al., 2009). As SWFs become investors and owners of companies, firms with whom they do business will assess the ways in which they undertake their responsibilities in these roles. Furthermore as asset owners they have responsibilities to their ultimate beneficiaries (that is, their national governments). It may also be the case that institutional investors who maintain strong positions on excluding companies doing business with countries that have poor human rights records will have no dealings with companies that are tainted by non-committal attitudes to human rights.

10. UK institutional investors (in particular the Co-op Bank) pointed out that only four of the largest SWFs are from countries with democratically elected governments. This precludes participation in those countries by investors that care about the ethics of their investments (Hosking, 2008). Until now there has in general been a laissez-faire approach to the role of SWFs – for instance, the OECD argues that the world economy benefits from the growth of SWFs since they recycle trade surpluses (oil products and manufacturing exports) back into the world economy (OECD Investment Committee, 2008).

The Principles for Responsible Investment (PRI)

11. In 2005 the then UN Secretary-General (Kofi Annan) invited a group of the world's largest investors to become part of a process to develop these Principles. Representatives of 20 institutional investors from 12 countries agreed to participate and were supported by a 70-strong multi-stakeholder group. The process was coordinated by the United Nations Environment Programme Finance Initiative (UNEP FI) and by the UN Global Compact. The Principles were launched in 2006.

Integrating ESG into mainstream portfolios

12. Major investors see it as their duty to act in the best interests of their beneficiaries.

13. In this fiduciary role environmental, social and corporate governance (ESG) issues will affect the performance of investment portfolios in both the short and longer term (Freshfields Bruckhaus Deringer, 2005; Mansley and Dlugolecki, 2001; Mercer and IFC, 2009; UN Global Compact, PRI and UNEP FI, 2009).

NOTE

1. On this topic see also Hawley and Williams (2005).

REFERENCES

Almunia, J. (2008), 'The EU response to the rise of Sovereign Wealth Funds', Crans Montana Forum, Brussels, Belgium, 2 April, accessed at http://europa. eu/rapid/pressReleasesAction.do?reference=SPEECH/08/165&format=HTML &aged=1&language=EN&guiLanguage=en.

BBC (n.d.), http://www.bbc.co.uk/.

Bendell, J., N. Alam, S. Lin et al. (2009), 'The Eastern Turn in Responsible Enterprise: A Yearly Review of Corporate Responsibility from Lifeworth', Lifeworth, Manila, Philippines, accessed 19 December 2010 at http://lifeworth. com/lifeworth2008/2009/05/sovereign-wealth-fund-responsibility.

BGN Entrepreneur (2009), 'Watchdog spells out shareholder rules', 20 August, accessed at http://bgnentrepreneur.net/watchdog-spells-out-shareholder-rules/.

Butt, S., A. Shivdasani, C. Stendevad and A. Wyman (2008), 'Sovereign wealth funds: a growing global force in corporate finance', *Journal of Applied Corporate Finance*, **20** (1), 73–83.

Clark, G.L. and A.H.B. Monk (2010), 'The Norwegian Government Pension Fund: ethics over efficiency', *Rotman International Journal of Pension Management*, **3** (1), Spring, 14–9, accessed at http://ssrn.com/abstract=1618834.

Commission of the European Communities (2008), *A Common European Approach to Sovereign Wealth Funds*, COM(2008) 115 provisional, 27 February, Brussels.

European Union (2008), 'A common European approach to Sovereign Wealth Funds', 8 October, accessed at http://europa.eu/legislation_summaries/internal_market/single_market_capital/mi0003_en.htm.

Freshfields Bruckhaus Deringer (2005), *A Legal Framework for the Integration of Environmental, Social and Governance Issues into Institutional Investment*, Geneva, Switzerland: United Nations Environment Programme Finance Initiative (UNEP FI), accessed at www.unepfi.org/fileadmin/documents/fresh-fields_legal_resp_20051123.pdf.

Freshfields Bruckhaus Deringer (2008), 'Financial Services Daily News', accessed at www.freshfields.com/microsites/fsdn/logon.asp.

Gilson, R.J. and C.J. Milhaupt (2008), 'Sovereign wealth funds and corporate governance: a minimalist response to the new merchantilism', Stanford Law and Economics Olin working paper, no. 355; Columbia Law and Economics working paper, no 328; Rock Center for Corporate Governance working paper, no. 26, accessed at http://ssrn.com/abstract=1095023.

Gjessing, O.P.K. and H. Syse (2007), 'Norwegian petroleum wealth and universal ownership', *Corporate Governance: An International Review*, **15** (3), 427–37.

Global Pensions (n.d.), www.globalpensions.com/.

Gugler, P. and J. Chaisse (2009), 'Sovereign wealth funds in the European Union: general trust despite concerns', NCCR Trade Regulation working paper, 2009/4, Swiss National Centre of Competence in Research, accessed at http://ssrn.com/abstract=1372014.

Hawley J.P. and A.T. Williams (2005), 'Shifting ground: emerging global corporate-governance standards and the rise of fiduciary capitalism', *Environment and Planning A*, **37** (11), 1995–2013.

Hosking, P. (2008), 'Co-operative Bank boycotts funds over human rights', *The Times*, 21 May, accessed at http://business.timesonline.co.uk/tol/business/industry_sectors/banking_and_finance/article3972375.ece.

IFSWF (International Forum of Sovereign Wealth Funds) (n.d.), accessed at www.ifswf.org/.

IMF (International Monetary Fund) (n.d.), accessed at www.imf.org/.

IWG (International Working Group of Sovereign Wealth Funds), accessed at www.iwg-swf.org.

Mansley, M. and A. Dlugolecki (2001), 'Climate change – a risk management challenge for institutional investors', discussion paper no. 1, Universities Superannuation Scheme (USS), London.

Mehrpouya, A., C. Huang and T. Barnett (2009), *An Analysis of Proxy Voting and Engagement Policies and Practices of the Sovereign Wealth Funds*, New York: IRRCi (Investor Responsibility Research Center Institute) and RiskMetrics Group, 13 October, accessed at www.irrcinstitute.org/pdf/Sovereign_Wealth_Funds_Report-October_2009.pdf.

Mercer (Mercer LLC) and IFC (International Finance Corporation) (2009), *Gaining Ground: Integrating Environmental, Social and Governance (ESG) Factors into Investment Processes in Emerging Markets*, Australia: Mercer, March, accessed at www.ifc.org/ifcext/sustainability.nsf/AttachmentsByTitle/p_SI_GainingGround_Mercer/$FILE/270309MIC9080_IFC+Report_WEB+secured.pdf.

Monitor and FEEM (Fondazione Eni Enrico Mattei) (2009), *Weathering the Storm: Sovereign Wealth Funds in the Global Economic Crisis of 2008. SWF Annual Report 2008*, April, accessed at www.monitor.com/Portals/0/MonitorContent/imported/MonitorUnitedStates/Articles/PDFs/Monitor-FEEM_SWF_Weathering_the_Storm_04_2009.pdf.

Morgan Stanley (n.d.), http://www.morganstanley.com/.

OECD (Organisation for Economic Co-operation and Development) Investment Committee (2008), *Sovereign Wealth Funds and Recipient Country Policies*, Paris, France: OECD, 4 April, accessed at www.oecd.org/dataoecd/34/9/40408735.pdf.

PRI (Principles for Responsible Investment) (n.d.), http://www.unpri.org/principles/.

Sun T. and H. Hesse (2009), 'Sovereign wealth funds and financial stability', 30 March, accessed at www.voxeu.org/index.php?q=node/3360.

UN Global Compact, PRI (Principles for Responsible Investment) and UNEP FI (United Nations Environment Programme Finance Initiative) (2009), *Investor Leadership on Climate Change: An Analysis of the Investment Community's Role on Climate Change, and Snapshot of Recent Investor Activity*, New York: UN Global Compact, May, accessed at www.unpri.org/files/climate.pdf.

Walker, D. (2009), 'A review of corporate governance in UK banks and other financial industry entities', 16 July, accessed at http://webarchive.nationalarchives.gov.uk/+/http://www.hm-treasury.gov.uk/d/walker_review_consultation_160709.pdf.

8. What is long-term wealth creation and investing?

Georges Enderle

8.1 INTRODUCTION: THE COURAGE (OR NEED) FOR SETTING LONG-TERM GOALS

At the Hokkaido Toyako Summit in July 2008, the Group of Eight,[1] along with Indonesia, the Republic of Korea and Australia, agreed to achieve at least 50 per cent reduction of global greenhouse gas emissions by the year 2050. One year later, at the L'Aquila Summit in Italy, G8 leaders reconfirmed this goal, adding, as part of this, an 80 per cent or more reduction goal for developed countries by 2050. However, despite their commitment made in Toyako to seek to share and adopt this goal of 50 per cent reduction with all Parties to the United Nations Framework Convention on Climate Change (UNFCCC), they were not able in L'Aquila, and later in Copenhagen, to win over the developing countries of China, India, Brazil, Mexico and South Africa. But, at least, in the broader session of the Major Economies Forum on Energy and Climate, the 16 leaders of all major emitting countries[2] reiterated the importance of keeping the increase in average global temperature below 2 degrees Celsius above pre-industrial levels, as recognized by the G8, and decided to work together to identify a long-term global goal for substantially reducing global emissions by 2050 (G8 Summit, 2009).

Despite many uncertainties, this is a remarkable leap of 41 years into the future with a fairly precise goal to be achieved by all nations on the planet Earth. Such a global vision, still to be adopted by UNFCCC, has never been proposed to humanity before. Imagine the situation 41 years ago in 1969. No nation would have dared to set such a clearly defined goal for humanity to achieve by 2010.

It is astonishing that for the first time in human history we, the human family, are about to set common long-term environmental goals. For sure, this is not the result of an idealistic commitment, but is forced upon us by the likely long-term environmental consequences of current human behaviour. Certainly, it is not at all obvious that we will actually live up to this enormous environmental, social and political challenge and fulfil our ethical responsibility towards future generations.

The need for clear thinking about the human-made long-term consequences of human behaviour has dramatically increased with the power of modern technology; this raises the question of responsibility in a new and urgent manner. In an outstanding example, Hans Jonas has addressed this question, relatively early on and with extraordinary perspicacity, in his work *The Imperative of Responsibility: Foundations of an Ethics for the Technological Age* (1984). However, what was meant by long-term consequences remained relatively abstract. It has been the combination of the power of modern technology with the power of business and economics that has made the long-term consequences, accumulated by decisions made every day, much more concrete and compelling. Therefore, 'sustainability' – defined by the World Commission on Environment and Development 'to meet the needs of the present without compromising the ability of the future generations to meet their own needs' (WCED, 1987, p. 8) – requires adopting a very long-term perspective based on innumerable short-term decisions.

Given the crucial relevance of the long-term perspective and the 2050 goal, how does this matter for long-term wealth creation and investing? Specifically, are our economic and financial institutions prepared to make sure that we move towards sustainability and will achieve the greenhouse gas reduction of 50 per cent by 2050? This challenge is all the more daunting because it is aggravated on multiple fronts. The world population of 6.8 billion people as of 2009 is estimated to grow to 13 billion by 2050 (at constant growth rate). The real value of wealth has to account for inflation worldwide, and numerous social and environmental risks affecting the creation of wealth also have to be factored in.

Against this backdrop, the chapter focuses on the understanding of long-term wealth creation and investing. First, it outlines a new concept of wealth creation that provides a broad foundation for the subsequent discussion of long-term investment. Second, it presents the Principles for Responsible Investment as an interesting and promising example of a definition of long-term investment that takes into account also environmental, social and corporate governance (ESG) criteria. Third, it attempts to substantiate these criteria with the help of the elaborated metric of the Global Reporting Initiative. Fourth, it compares this conceptual framework with a practical business approach; that is, how KLD Research and Analytics, Inc. uses its 'FTSE KLD Global Sustainability Index'. Finally, it explores the potential and limitations of ESG criteria for determining long-term wealth creation and investing.

8.2   CONCEPTUALIZING WEALTH CREATION

Although wealth is a fundamental concept in economics – 'perhaps the conceptual starting point for the discipline' (Heilbroner, 1987, p. 880) – the current discussions on globalization, poverty and corporate responsibilities rarely articulate the implied assumptions about 'wealth'. Even less often, attempts are made to develop a firm and comprehensive concept of wealth that also accounts for crucial aspects like sustainability and social capital, considered indispensable today. Having developed such a concept elsewhere (see Enderle, 2009), I only highlight its main features here.

'Wealth' includes physical (i.e. natural or produced), financial, human and social capital, encompasses private and public wealth, accounts for its production and distribution, recognizes its material and spiritual side, and places wealth in the time horizon of sustainability. Moreover, possessing and acquiring wealth should be distinguished from creating wealth, which means a process of making something new and better and involves both a productive and a distributive dimension. As for the motivations that drive wealth creation, it does not suffice to point to the common answers in the economic and sociological literature such as self-interest, greed, the will to survive, the glory, honour and wellbeing of nations. When economic activities clearly focus on wealth creation, other motivations like the entrepreneurial spirit, the desire to serve others and 'the joy of finding' become more important, as suggested by David Landes in his powerful economic history (1999, p. 58).

To illustrate some features of this conceptual framework, we may refer to the examples of Medtronic Inc. and the Grameen Bank. Medtronic Inc. is proud to be 'the world's leading medical technology company, providing lifelong solutions to chronic disease' (http://www.medtronic. com/). In its over 50-year history, it has developed a wide range of medical devices, from heart pacemakers to devices to alleviate neurological and spinal disorders and to manage diabetes, and it continues to be in the forefront of the industry. Inspired to serve the customers, its innovative spirit has revolutionized not only its products and services but also its production processes, organization, culture and identity, while yielding continuous financial success. As this company illustrates, while wealth creation has a lot to do with technological innovation, it is more than that, since the innovation is made feasible and successful in economic and financial terms. Aiming at material improvement for the benefit of human lives, wealth creation includes both a material and a spiritual side and goes beyond the mere acquisition and accumulation of wealth.

The second example, the Grameen Bank originally from Bangladesh, has been an early driving force in the micro-credit movement and gained worldwide fame and recognition with the Nobel Prize for his founder Muhammad Yunus in 2006 (see http://www.grameen-info.org/). The core of its wealth-creating business model consists in putting trust in poor people, providing them with tiny loans to use them for productive purposes, and setting up an appropriate organizational structure and culture that helps the poor to move out of poverty. What has been achieved is getting necessary money into the hands of poor people who have used it, increased it and paid back the bank with interest while still retaining a reserve for themselves and their families. This steady income increase has had an enormous impact on the standard of living for the Grameen families. Children have received better education. Child mortality has been reduced dramatically. Women have voiced their concerns and engaged in political elections. The more than 30-year history of the Grameen family clearly shows what wealth creation under extreme conditions of poverty can be and achieve. Trust and organizational support enable the poor to take care of themselves with creativity and ingenuity. In Yunus' words: 'All that we give at Grameen is a support system which is not charity but rather a business program which aspires to create a mutually beneficial environment for a poor person legitimately to engage in traditional business transactions which materially improve his condition, thereby raising his dignity' (Arruda and Enderle, 2004, p. 33).

To conclude this short summary, it is suggested that this rich concept of wealth creation can provide guidance for companies and economies at the national and international levels as well. It can also offer a foundation for the understanding of long-term investing explored in the following sections.

8.3 PRINCIPLES FOR RESPONSIBLE INVESTMENT

Launched in April 2006 by the UN Secretary-General Kofi Annan, the Principles for Responsible Investment (PRI) provide a framework to assist investors in incorporating ESG criteria into their investment decision making and ownership practices. They were developed by an international group of individuals representing 20 institutional investors from 12 countries and 70 experts from the investment industry, intergovernmental and governmental organizations, civil society and academia, coordinated by the United Nations Environment Programme Finance Initiative (UNEP FI) and the UN Global Compact. According to the Annual Report of the PRI Initiative 2009 (PRI, 2009b), the initiative is now supported by 500 signatories, representing US$18 trillion assets and 36 countries (see also PRI, 2009a).

Although the term 'responsibility' is not explained directly, its meaning is described in the preamble:

> As institutional investors, we have a duty to act in the best long-term interests of our beneficiaries. In this fiduciary role, we believe that environmental, social, and corporate governance (ESG) issues can affect the performance of investment portfolios . . . . We also recognise that applying these Principles may better align investors with broader objectives of society. Therefore, where consistent with our fiduciary responsibilities, we commit to the following [six principles].

The moral foundation of 'responsible' investment lies in the fiduciary role of the institutional investors. They have been put in a position of trust by their beneficiaries, and thus are expected to act in the interest of those beneficiaries without gaining any material benefit, except when with the knowledge and consent of them (Boatright, 2008, p. 39). The fiduciary responsibilities, moreover, require taking a long-term perspective and acting in the beneficiaries' best long-term interests. This means institutional investors must consider that not only common financial and economic but also environmental, social and corporate governance issues can affect the performance of investment portfolios, and thus should be taken seriously. Furthermore, by accounting for these issues and following the six principles, broader objectives of society can be achieved. Hence, 'responsible' investment consists in acting in the beneficiaries' long-term best interests, which takes ESG factors into account, and, by doing so, in better aligning these interests with society's broader objectives. It is assumed that the institutional investors bear these moral responsibilities and are accountable to their beneficiaries. These responsibilities supposedly hold as long as they are consistent with the institutional investors' other fiduciary responsibilities. It is also noteworthy that the preamble does not mention a responsibility towards society (that is, in addition to the beneficiaries).

Based on this understanding of responsible investment, the signatories express their moral commitment to follow six principles and, at the end of the statement, encourage other investors to make the same commitment. These Principles define a whole policy packet for responsible investment and suggest a great number of possible actions for implementation (see PRI website). For the purpose of this chapter, I concentrate on the Principle #1 that states: 'We will incorporate ESG issues into investment analysis and decision-making processes.'

8.4 SUSTAINABILITY REPORTING GUIDELINES FOR ECONOMIC, ENVIRONMENTAL AND SOCIAL PERFORMANCE OF AN ORGANIZATION

There are countless ways of defining ESG issues, and it seems highly unlikely to find a worldwide consensus on common standards that would apply globally. Nevertheless, the process of globalization creates tremendous pressure to compare a variety of reporting standards of corporate performance and to move them towards more compatibility, if not convergence. An example of this trend is the statement of the International Accounting Standards Board and the US Financial Accounting Standards Board (issued on 11 September 2008) to accelerate the convergence timeline and set 2011 as the goal for completion of their major joint projects.

Another example is the Global Reporting Initiative (GRI) (http://www.globalreporting.org/Home) that was launched in 1997 and that released, in October 2006, the third generation of Sustainability Reporting Guidelines (RG). Developed in a broad multi-stakeholder dialogue, the Guidelines, a document of 44 pages, offer a thoroughly elaborated metric to capture comprehensively the economic, environmental and social performance of business and other organizations (such as NGOs and cities). At this point in time the RG with their global reach are the most widely recognized standards of sustainability reporting and therefore particularly apt to help define ESG issues.

Of particular interest for the purpose of this chapter is the way in which the RG define report content and quality and how they operationalize economic, environmental and social performance with the help of 9, 30 and 40 indicators, respectively. The Reporting Principles describe the outcomes to be achieved by a report and guide decisions throughout the reporting process (such as selecting which topics and indicators to report on and how to report on them).

Four principles define the report content: materiality, stakeholder inclusiveness, sustainability context and completeness (see RG, 8–13); and six principles determine the report quality: balance, comparability, accuracy, timeliness, clarity and reliability (see RG, 13–17).

While these principles guide the input of a report, the performance indicators (along with the profile and management approach of the reporting organization) show its output.

8.4.1   Sustainability Performance Indicators

Indicators are organized by economic, environmental and social categories. Each category includes a Disclosure on Management Approach and a corresponding set of core and additional performance indicators (see RG, 24–36). Because of the large number of indicators, only a selected set of them are presented here while the full list can be found on the GRI website.

Economic performance indicators
These include the aspect of 'economic performance' with four core indicators (EC1–EC4), the aspect of 'market presence' with one additional and two core indicators (EC5–EC7), and the aspect of 'indirect economic impacts' with one core and one additional indicator (EC8, EC9).

Several features are noteworthy: EC1 asks not only for the aggregate direct economic value generated but also for the distributional pattern of this aggregate, accounting for the fact that the productive and the distributive sides of wealth creation are interrelated and equally important (see Enderle, 2009). Hence one should report the economic value flows to key stakeholders such as employees (including executives), communities, capital providers and governments (taxes and so on). EC2 specifically mentions the climate change with its financial implications and other risks and opportunities for the organization's activities. EC3 looks at another long-term perspective, that is, how the organization covers its defined benefit plan obligations. And EC4 concerns the other side of the organization's relationship with government, namely, what the former receives from the latter in terms of significant financial assistance.

The market presence indicators cover the organization's relations with its local environments (of significant operations): comparing its entry level wage with local minimum wage (EC5); showing its involvement with locally based suppliers (EC6); and documenting procedures for local hiring proportion of senior management hired from the local community (EC7).

Finally, the aspect of indirect economic impacts draws attention to the organization's contributions to economic public goods: how and to what extent commercial, in kind or pro bono engagement help to develop and shape the impact of infrastructure investments and services provided for public benefit. It asks how the organization understands and describes significant indirect economic impacts (including negative ones).

Environmental performance indicators
These express an organization's impacts on living and non-living natural systems, including ecosystems, land, air and water, and cover performance as related to inputs (for example, material, energy, water) and outputs (for example, emissions, effluents, waste), biodiversity, environmental compliance, and other relevant information such as environmental expenditure and the impacts of products and services (27). Compared to economic and, even more, to social performance indicators, they are easier to quantify. The core indicators of the aspect 'materials' measure materials used by weight or volume (EN1) and the percentage of materials used that are recycled input materials (EN2). The core indicators of the aspect 'energy' capture direct (EN3) and indirect (EN4) energy consumption by the primary energy source, while the additional three indicators concern energy saved due to conservation and efficiency improvements (EN5) and the initiatives (and their results) of providing energy-efficient or renewable energy-based products and services (EN6) and of reducing indirect energy consumption (EN7). As for the aspect 'water', the indicators cover total water withdrawal by source (EN8), water sources that are significantly affected by that withdrawal (EN9), and the percentage and total volume of water recycled and reused (EN10).

The core indicators of the aspect 'biodiversity' concern the location and size of land owned, leased, managed in, or adjacent to, protected areas and other areas of high biodiversity value (EN11) and describe significant impacts of activities, products and services on biodiversity (EN12). The additional indicators relate to habitats protected or restored (EN13) and listed species (EN15) and specify strategies, current actions and future plans for managing impacts on biodiversity (EN14).

The aspect 'emissions, effluents, and waste' includes seven core and three additional indicators: direct and indirect greenhouse gas (GHG) emissions (EN16), other relevant indirect GHG emissions (EN17), initiatives and results of GHG emission reductions (EN18), emission of ozone-depleting substances (EN19), NO, SO and other significant air emissions (EN20), total water discharge (EN21), total weight of waste (EN22), total number and volume of significant spills (EN23), hazardous waste (according to the Basel Convention) transported, imported, exported and treated (EN24), and significantly affected water bodies and related habitats (EN25).

Further aspects cover 'products and services' (EN26, EN27), 'compliance' with environmental laws and regulations (EN28), 'transport' (EN29) and 'overall,' that is, total environmental protection expenditures and investments by type (EN30).

The social performance indicators
These are by far the most numerous with the following social categories: labour, human rights, society and product responsibility. Each of them has several 'aspects' with their corresponding indicators. A summary overview may suffice here (for more information see GRI website):

- Labour practices and decent work:
    Employment (LA1–LA3)
    Labour/management relations (LA4, LA5)
    Occupational health and safety (LA6–LA9)
    Training and education (LA10–LA12)
    Diversity and equal opportunity (LA13, LA14)
- Human rights:
    Investment and procurement practices (HR1–HR3)
    Non-discrimination (HR4)
    Freedom of association and collective bargaining (HR5)
    Child labour (HR6)
    Forced and compulsory labour (HR7)
    Security practices (HR8)
    Indigenous rights (HR9)
- Society:
    Community (SO1)
    Corruption (SO2–SO4)
    Public policy (SO5, SO6)
    Anti-competitive behaviour (SO7)
    Compliance (SO8)
- Product responsibility:
    Customer health and safety (PR1, PR2)
    Product and service labelling (PR3–PR5)
    Marketing communications (PR6, PR7)
    Customer privacy (PR8)
    Compliance (PR9)

8.4.2   Sector Supplements

In addition to the universally applicable core Guidelines with the sustainability performance indicators, GRI developed 'Sector Supplements' because some sectors face unique needs that require specialized guidance, for instance, the Financial Services Sector Supplement (FSSS). Due to the limited scope of this chapter, the Sector Supplements are not discussed further.

8.5 SUSTAINABILITY REPORTING GUIDELINES AND LONG-TERM PERFORMANCE AND INVESTMENT

As the discussion of the RG principles and indicators shows, the coverage of the potential 'footprint' of an organization is fairly comprehensive. It is not simply defined in the way that the organization understands its own performance and its narrowly circumscribed impact. Rather, the definition of the materiality of report content also depends on the inclusion of the relevant stakeholders and the broader 'sustainability' context. Admittedly, this requirement adds some vagueness and relies on sound judgement. But it seems there is no other way of defining materiality that transcends the traditional financial reporting which is highly questionable from the sustainability standpoint. Moreover, this broadening and sound judgement is not left to secret decision making in the organization but has to stand the test of transparency. As the RG state, 'transparency [is] a value and a goal that underlies all aspects of sustainability reporting. Transparency can be defined as the complete disclosure of information on the topics and indicators required to reflect impacts and enable stakeholders to make decisions, and the processes, procedures, and assumptions used to prepare those disclosures' (RG, 6). Obviously, this emphasis on transparency is consistent with the third principle of PRI: 'We will seek appropriate disclosure on ESG issues by the entities in which we invest.'

What do the RG require implicitly and explicitly with regard to the time horizon? To what extent do they help define and strengthen the long-term perspective for corporate performance and investment?

Obviously, they do not allow any short-termism in quarterly terms since they require annual reporting. Moreover, they engage the organization in a process that extends beyond a few years. To the extent that the organization, through the reporting process, is becoming more aware of its footprint, it is likely to expand its time horizon for planning, strategy, performance and control. Applying the principles of defining report content and quality and striving for more transparency will certainly enforce this tendency towards a longer time horizon.

However, it is more difficult to assess to what extent the RG are instrumental in strengthening a long-term perspective of, say, up to 2025 or

Table 8.1   Significance levels of sustainability indicators for long-term performance

	Group A	Group B	Group C
Economic performance indicators	EC2, EC3	EC6–EC9	EC1, EC4, EC5
Environmental performance indicators	EN9, EN11–15, EN25	EN5–EN7, EN10, EN23	EN1–EN4, EN8, EN16–EN22, EN24, EN25
Social performance indicators:			
Labour practices, decent work		LA8, LA9, LA11	LA1–LA7, LA10, LA12–LA14
Human rights		HR5–HR7	HR1–HR4, HR8, HR9
Society		SO1, SO4	SO2, SO3, SO6–SO8
Product responsibility		PR1, PR3, PR5, PR6	PR2, PR4, PR7–PR9

2050. In order to characterize the significance level for long-term performance, the sustainability performance indicators can be divided into three groups:

- Group A which clearly requires a long-term perspective (of 20 and more years);
- Group B which indirectly implies but does not explicitly require a long-term perspective;
- Group C which, in itself, only indicates the current performance situation and whose long-term impact depends on the amount of the quantitative indicators.

Tentatively, the 79 indicators may be grouped as shown in Table 8.1.

As Table 8.1 shows, only a few indicators clearly require adopting a long-term perspective: financial implications and other risks and opportunities due to climate change; defined benefit plan obligations; water sources significantly affected by withdrawal of water; impacts on biodiversity; and discharges of water and runoff significantly affecting water bodies and related habitats. Social performance indicators apparently do not clearly require a long-term perspective.

Group B, which indirectly implies but does not explicitly require a long-term perspective, includes multiple indicators of the economic, environmental and social categories. They concern the organization's policies, practices and procedures affecting its market presence and also its impacts on and understanding of public goods (such as infrastructure investments and services provided primarily for public benefit). Environmental performance indicators are energy savings and efficiencies, water recycled and reused, and significant spills. Social performance indicators cover programmes for occupational health and safety as well as for training and education. They also include significant organizational risks involved in using child labour, forced and compulsory labour, and in disregarding the freedom of association and collective bargaining. Moreover, they account for multiple impacts on communities and for actions taken in response to incidents of corruption. Finally, they concern the improvement of health and safety impacts of products and services on customers, required product and service information, practices related to customer satisfaction, and programmes for adherence to laws, standards, and voluntary codes related to marketing communications.

Most indicators in Group C are of a quantitative nature and need a threshold of significance in order to define materiality and possibly point to long-term relevance. Such thresholds might be determined through the organization's dialogue with the relevant stakeholders or by law or self-regulation of the industry. Regarding global challenges like climate change, worldwide agreements on global standards are necessary. It goes without saying that the determination of those thresholds in terms of sustainability raises many difficult problems.

As for the issues of governance, they are covered in the reporting on the organization's profile in ten points (RG, 20–21). In particular, the organization is asked to indicate any direct responsibility for economic, social and environmental performance assigned to a committee under the highest governance body (4.1). The governance provisions can be attributed to Group B.

8.6   FTSE KLD GLOBAL SUSTAINABILITY INDEX

KLD Research & Analytics, Inc. ('KLD'), founded by P.D. Kinder, S. Lydenberg and A.L. Domini in 1988 and recently acquired by RiskMetrics Group, is a private US company specializing in 'socially responsible investing', claiming to be an industry leader in analysis of environmental, social and governance factors (http://www.kld.com/). It has developed Socrates, a web-based database of quality research and analysis on the ESG performance of companies worldwide, and offers a family of domestic and global indexes for evaluating corporate performance.

Based on the largest 3,000 US publicly traded companies by market capitalization, KLD evaluates corporations for ESG performance on more than 280 data points using a proprietary ratings system. With Socrates that covers ESG and controversial (faith-based) business issues, clients can do the following: review individual company performance; screen portfolios for ESG performance and controversial business involvement; create buy lists and restricted lists for portfolio screening and benchmarks; query the database for key words or phrases; and monitor shareholder resolutions and company responses.

In the family of indexes, the FTSE KLD Global Sustainability Index (GSIN), launched in 2007, is of particular interest here (for the following, see http://www.kld.com/indexes/gsindex/ on GSIN Home, Methodology, Performance, Fact Sheet and Index Changes). GSIN is a broadly diversified global benchmark on ESG rankings. Applying a 'best of class' methodology, the GSIN holds companies with the highest sustainability rankings in each sector in each region, with a target of being sector-neutral and region-neutral. In line with the Brundtland definition (WCED, 1987), sustainability refers to the degree to which companies address the social and environmental needs of the present without compromising the quality of life of future generations. KLD rates a company's sustainability performance by analysing key ESG factors: environment, community and society, employees and supply chain, customers, governance and ethics (see Methodology). The GSIN series includes the FTSE KLD Global Sustainability Index (GSIN), four regional indexes (covering North America, Europe, Asia Pacific and Europe Asia Pacific), and the global ex-US index.

KLD constructs the FTSE KLD GSIN Series as follows:

1. Selection of eligible universe. The eligible universe for the GSIN includes companies that comprise the top 75 per cent of the market capitalization of each sector in each country of the S&P Developed BMI, the most complete index in the S&P Developed Global Equity Index series. There are 630 companies from 23 developed market countries (see Fact Sheet).
2. Evaluation. KLD evaluates the ESG performance of companies in the eligible universe. The analysis is based on a global sustainability ratings framework (see Methodology).
3. Ranking. KLD ranks companies by regional sector peer group according to ESG performance. Analysts identify key ESG performance indicators for each sector. They weight the key performance indicators accordingly to generate comparative rankings.

4. Selection. KLD selects the highest ranked companies comprising 50 per cent of the eligible universe in each regional sector, as measured by market capitalization.
5. Aggregation. KLD aggregates the regional indexes to create the benchmark global index.

The two-year performance (1 October 2007–30 September 2009) shows that the FTSE KLD GSIN follows the FTSE All World Developed Index very closely (see Fact Sheet and Performance).

As was true of the GRI sustainability reporting guidelines (RG), the question arises to what extent the GSIN may help to capture the long-term perspective of corporate performance and investment. In order to answer this question, one might first compare the different settings of the RG and the GSIN. The RG are designed for self-reporting and require stakeholder inclusion whereas the GSIN is set up by KLD and its research partners and managed by the GSIN Committee. The RG cover all types of organizational assets and are applicable to all kinds of organizations in any country around the globe. In contrast, the GSIN is closely connected to the equity index of S&P Developed BMI and includes companies only from developed market countries and of large capitalization (with an average of approximately US$11 billion). With regard to the sustainability performance indicators, the GSIN is by far less developed than the RG, which are fairly comprehensive and detailed. In sum, the RG and the GSIN clearly differ in the ways they define the materiality of the ESG factors. However, this does not imply that the contents of materiality are necessarily very different. Moreover, both approaches require a high level of transparency, which allows the users of the reports to make their own judgements.

Now, to what extent does the GSIN help capture the long-term perspective of corporate performance and investment? Using the above classification of significance level of sustainability indicators for long-term performance, it seems more difficult, in the case of GSIN, to attribute the indicators to Group A, B or C because the indicators are less specified and the GSIN depends, to a large extent, on the judgement of the GSIN Committee. With this caveat, one might not attribute the GSIN either to Group A, which clearly requires a long-term perspective (of 20 and more years), or to Group C, which only indicates the current performance situation. Consequently, the GSIN reflects the significance level of Group B, which indirectly implies but does not explicitly require a long-term perspective. Furthermore, it is noteworthy that the index change seems to follow a precautionary principle in that new companies can join the GSIN only annually while GSIN companies can be removed from the index quarterly.

8.7   POTENTIAL AND LIMITATIONS OF ESG CRITERIA FOR DETERMINING LONG-TERM WEALTH CREATION AND INVESTING

In search of a better understanding of long-term wealth creation and investing, several approaches have been explored: the Principles for Responsible Investment with its ESG criteria; the principles and indicators of the Global Reporting Initiative; and the KLD methodology for socially responsible investing. In this concluding section, the extent to which these approaches may help determine long-term wealth creation and investing is examined.

8.7.1   An Important Step to Move Away from Short-termism

As recent publications on investment analysis have shown,[3] short-termism in investing and evaluating corporate performance has become a considerable problem partially caused by the current functioning of the stock exchanges. So it is fair to say that the incorporation of ESG issues into investment analysis and decision-making processes is an important step in the move away from short-termism. Grappling with ESG issues certainly raises the awareness of the full impact of corporate performance in economic, environmental and social terms not only for investors and owners but also for the management of invested companies and society at large. To the extent that ESG expectations are increased, social pressure is generated that helps to hold companies and investors accountable in those terms. Moreover, the integration of ESG issues is likely not only to raise their awareness but also to improve their performance and to enhance longer-term thinking with time horizons of three to five years or more (though hardly of 40 to 50 years as suggested in the introduction).

8.7.2   Advantages and Insufficiencies of Voluntary Initiatives

All the initiatives discussed in this chapter are based on voluntary engagement, be it of institutional investors, various types of organizations or a private company specializing in socially responsible investing. One can jump to the conclusion, as many dissatisfied with the present situation actually do, that voluntary initiatives are by definition incapable of solving the problems of long-term wealth creation and investing, distracting from, rather than leading to, timely and adequate solutions. However, such an either-or choice between voluntary and mandatory approaches appears to be too simple and would undervalue the significance of voluntary initiatives. In fact, they can result in a number of advantages. On a voluntary basis, one can more easily experiment with new investment strategies, develop best practices, improve design and quality of investment indexes, clarify and strengthen the motivations furthering the interests of both the investors and society, enhance transparency, and gather and share experiences made in this process.

Of course, these advantages cannot undo the insufficiencies. Because of their voluntary nature, these initiatives only cover a limited number of organizations and likely fail to include those organizations that would need improvement the most. Moreover, the definition of materiality of ESG issues and the determination of thresholds have no binding force and thus are left to arbitrary interpretations, lack of clarity and misuse. Finally, there is no system in place that is able and willing to enforce and monitor the long-term requirements for wealth creation and investing.

8.7.3   Need for Institutional Frameworks

As important as voluntary initiatives are, they cannot replace appropriate institutional frameworks at the national and global levels. When challenges concern the whole society, individual organizations and even strong alliances of organizations are not able to address those challenges adequately. What is needed is a systemic approach that deals with the issues in their systemic complexity. As a case in point, we may refer to the financial and economic crisis in 2008–09. Institutions such as the US Treasury and the Federal Reserve and even the governments have to step up to make sure that the public interest prevails over private interests. It would be naive to expect that the good companies could save the system. Like rocks, they might be able to defy the storms of the financial crisis (at least for a certain time). But it lies beyond their power to rein them in. As Dominique Strauss-Kahn, managing director of the International Monetary Fund, states, 'A systemic crisis demands systemic solutions' (*Financial Times*, 23 September 2008). It goes without saying that systemic solutions are not readily available, but require thorough understanding of the problems, clear and persistent guidance and strong political will.

Fortunately, we do not have 'to reinvent the wheel' in terms of corporate reporting. The tools developed by GRI and PRI are valuable instruments that deserve, in one way or another, global adoption. In its Amsterdam Declaration on Transparency and Reporting (March 2009), the Board of GRI calls on all governments 'to extend and strengthen the global regime of sustainability reporting. In particular, assumptions about the adequacy of voluntary reporting must be reexamined' (http://www.globalreporting.org). It advances three major reasons for this call: first, such a regime could have moderated the root causes of the current economic crises. Second, it can best address the profound loss of trust in key institutions. And third, in order to sustain a revitalized and resilient economic system, it is necessary to account for the full costs and value of ESG activity.

We began this chapter by pointing to the astonishing fact that we, the human family, are about to set a common long-term environmental goal, that is, to keep the increase in average global temperature below 2 degrees Celsius above pre-industrial levels. Long-term thinking and acting accordingly are indispensable, if the human family wants to survive and flourish without major disruptions. An essential part of this endeavour is genuine wealth creation and investing. That means to overcome the fixation about 'making money', to engage in sustainable development and create wealth in the long run. Public and private wealth reinforce each other. Innovative growth and fair distribution are complementary, not substitutive. And wealth creation as human activity cannot be merely material, but is necessarily of spiritual significance as well.

Obviously the PRI and the GRI metric of Sustainability Reporting Guidelines cannot fully satisfy this rich understanding of wealth creation. Numerous questions remain unanswered: the perseverance of political will for sustainable global goals over decades; the continued flourishing of an innovative spirit; global justice between and among generations; the proper balance of public and private choices; and the vindication of spirituality in economic life. But it is suggested that the integration of ESG factors into business and economics constitutes an important move towards this overarching goal. It goes without saying that long-term wealth creation and investing are challenges for the long term.

NOTES

1. Canada, France, Germany, Italy, Japan, the Russian Federation, the UK and the USA.
2. G8 plus China, India, Brazil, Mexico and South Africa plus Australia, the Republic of Korea and Indonesia. Moreover, the European Commission, Sweden, Denmark and the UN Secretary-General.
3. See Lydenberg (2007), Juravle and Lewis (2008), CFA (2006, 2008) and http://www.aspeninstitute.org/publications.

REFERENCES

Arruda, M.C. and G. Enderle (eds) (2004), *Improving Globalization*, Rio de Janeiro, Brazil: Editora FGV.

Aspen Institute Business and Society Program (2007), 'Long-term value creation: guiding principles for corporations and investors', accessed 1 December 2010 at www.aspeninstitute.org/publications.

Boatright, J.R. (2008), *Ethics in Finance*, 2nd edn, Malden, MA: Blackwell.

CFA Institute Center for Financial Market Integrity/Business Roundtable Institute for Corporate Ethics (2006), 'Breaking the short-term cycle', accessed 1 December 2010 at www.cfapubs.org/doi/pdf/10.2469/ccb.v2006.n1.4194.

CFA Institute Center for Financial Market Integrity (2008), 'Short-termism survey. Practices and preferences of investment professionals. Earnings & other guidance, communications & incentives', 28 May, accessed 1 December 2010 at www.cfainstitute.org/Survey/short_termism_survey_report_may_2008.pdf.

Enderle, G. (2009), 'A rich concept of wealth creation beyond profit maximization and adding value', *Journal of Business Ethics*, **84** (Supplement 3), 281–95.

G8 Summit (2009), Documents: 'Chair's Summary'; 'Declaration of the Leaders of the Major Economies Forum on Energy and Climate', accessed 1 December 2010 at www.g8italia2009.it/G8/Home.

GRI (Global Reporting Initiative) (n.d.) accessed 1 December 2010 at www.globalreporting.org.

Heilbroner, R.L. (1987), 'Wealth', in J. Eatwell, M. Milgate and P. Newman (eds), *The New Palgrave: A Dictionary of Economics*, vol. 4, London: Macmillan, pp. 880–3.

Jonas, H. (1984), *The Imperative of Responsibility: Foundations of an Ethics for the Technological Age*, Chicago, IL: University of Chicago Press.

Juravle, C. and A. Lewis (2008), 'Identifying impediments to SRI in Europe: a review of the practitioner and academic literature', *Business Ethics: A European Review*, **17** (3), 285–310.

KLD Research & Analytics, Inc. (n.d.) accessed 1 December 2010 at www.kld.com.

Landes, D.S. (1999), *The Wealth and Poverty of Nations: Why Some Are So Rich and Some Are So Poor*, New York: Norton.

Lydenberg, S. (2007), 'Long-term investing. A proposal for how to define and implement long-term investing', in A. White and M. Kelly (eds), *2007 Summit on the Future of the Corporation*, paper no. 5, pp. 47–57.

PRI (United Nations Principles for Responsible Investment) (2009a), *PRI Report on Progress 2009*, accessed 1 December 2010 at www.unpri.org.

PRI (United Nations Principles for Responsible Investment) (2009b), *Annual Report of the PRI Initiative 2009*, accessed 1 December 2010 at www.unpri.org.

UNFCCC (United Nations Framework Convention on Climate Change) (2008), *Report of the Conference of the Parties on its thirteenth session, held in Bali from 3–15 December 2007. Addendum: Part Two: action taken by the Conference of the Parties at its thirteenth session*, 1F4C CMCa/rCchP /22000087 /6/Add.1*.

World Commission on Environment and Development (WCED) (1987), *Our Common Future*, New York: Oxford University Press.

9. Corporate social performance and cost of capital: a meaningful relationship?

Antonello Di Giulio, Paolo Migliavacca and Antonio Tencati*

9.1 INTRODUCTION

In the last decades, in a seemingly endless debate, researchers and practitioners have questioned the existence of a nexus between corporate social responsibility (CSR) and value-creation processes. Most of the efforts and publications have addressed the linkage between corporate social performance (CSP)[1] and corporate financial performance (CFP). Even though any univocal conclusion about this linkage is not possible, many authors claim there is a positive relationship between CSP and CFP (Devinney, 2009; Griffin and Mahon, 1997; Margolis and Walsh, 2003; Margolis et al., 2007; Orlitzky et al., 2003; Salzmann et al., 2005). So, different and more operational approaches, and further studies, are decidedly needed to understand how companies create value by engaging, involving and partnering with stakeholders (Perrini et al., 2009). In more detail, it is important to underline that the value-generating capability of a company depends on two crucial factors: the risk, defined as the distribution of possible outcomes in a firm's performance over a given time horizon due to changes in key underlying variables (Deloach, 2000, p. 48), and the ability to create, maintain and reinforce relationships with critical stakeholders. Risk is intrinsic to the company's activity and may arise at any stage of interaction with stakeholders. The stakeholder management literature (for example, Post et al., 2002) states that by strategically managing stakeholder relationships a firm is able to generate consistent and sustainable value for itself, and for the stakeholders that contribute to the process of value creation, by enhancing firm performance, reducing risks and seizing opportunities related to risks.

Although previous studies on the CSP-risk relationship, among which are those referenced in the meta-analytic study by Orlitzky and Benjamin

(2001), have provided a pivotal contribution to explain the CSP-risk linkage, the impact that the strategic management of stakeholder expectations has on the financial and non-financial risk of a company and on CSP still needs to be highlighted. This chapter addresses the issue by analysing the possible link between a reliable, robust and verifiable measure of CSP (Fowler and Hope, 2007), developed and provided by the SAM Group, and the weighted average cost of capital (WACC), a synthetic indicator that embodies the overall risk as perceived by stakeholders and especially by the financial ones.

9.2   THE STAKEHOLDER VIEW OF THE FIRM AND THE CONCEPT OF RISK

A well-known definition of 'stakeholder' is any group or individual who can affect or is affected by the achievement of the firm's objectives (Freeman, 1984, p. 46). Based upon the work of Freeman, Clarkson (1995) differentiates between primary and secondary stakeholders. Primary stakeholders are those groups, organizations or persons that/who continuously engage in the company activities and whose participation is essential for the survival of the firm. In this category we find employees, suppliers, customers, banks, and financial institutions, shareholders, the government and the local community. Secondary stakeholders are those groups that affect or are affected by, influence or are influenced by the corporation; however, they do not engage in transactions with the corporation and they are not essential for its survival. Media and various interest groups fall within this category.

In more recent years, Post et al. (2002) developed a new stakeholder view of the firm, also called 'extended enterprise', that emphasizes the importance of managing stakeholder relationships for the creation of organizational wealth. They state that 'the capacity of a firm to generate sustainable wealth over time, and hence its long-term value, is determined by its relationships with critical stakeholders' (Post et al., 2002, p. 9) and 'any stakeholder relationship may be the most critical one at a particular time or on a particular issue' (Post et al., 2002, p. 8). Therefore, a company can endure if it builds and maintains sustainable and durable relationships with its entire stakeholder network. 'These relationships are the essential assets that managers must manage, and they are the ultimate sources of organizational wealth' (Post et al., 2002, p. 8).

With the evolution of our society towards a network society, 'every stakeholder approach must refer to the way corporations position themselves and act within their network of relations as a process' (Lozano,

2005, p. 72). This can happen by setting formal contracts, which are therefore protected by law, or by establishing a mutually reinforcing and beneficial dialogue between the parties. The dialogue may reduce the uncertainty involved in planning the future, improve the firm's processes, reduce the costs, support sales growth and help to embrace opportunities arising from a fast-changing business environment (Stakeholder Research Associates Canada, United Nations Environment Programme and AccountAbility, 2005). Yet a further step is required, and this involves moving from dialogue with stakeholders to strategic partnerships: they help to build a more sustainable society by 'applying the complementary capabilities of the actors and eliminating the duplication of effort. Furthermore, new alliances can provide a constructive way to engage the energies of disparate societal actors, address the democratic deficit, and build trust' (Holliday and Pepper, 2001, p. 21). While partnering has some unquestionable benefits, it may entail the risk of knowledge spillover; a partnership will be successful only if 'the expected value of the combined inflows of knowledge from partners exceeds the expected loss/erosion of advantages due to knowledge spillovers to competitors' (Dyer and Singh, 1998, p. 675).

A more advanced stakeholder view of the firm, as proposed in this contribution, finds its fundaments in a relational view of the firm; however, it goes beyond the inside-out thinking, where a company sees the environment from a self-centred perspective (Lozano, 2005), to encompass all the relationships of the stakeholder network and the risk inherent in any relationship. Risk is important because it impacts the way the firm and several entities relate to each other and with the surrounding environment; risk evenly affects internal and external processes, corporate reputation and, as a major consequence, the cost of running business. In such a situation an analysis of risk becomes crucial to determining the long-term success or failure of a firm in an increasingly interconnected context. Moreover the awareness of risk should influence the nature, timing and extent of communications with stakeholders (COSO, 2004).

A sustainability oriented company faces the risk in a positive manner (Schaltegger and Burritt, 2005). It does not conceive risk as a negative externality, with solely downside implications, but it sees risk as an element that can contribute to enhancing the performance and stability of the organization by exploiting its potential upsides. The World Business Council for Sustainable Development (WBCSD), in the 2004 report *Running the Risk*, suggests companies take a holistic approach to risk and sustainability in order to overcome the amplified impact of traditional and non-traditional risks. According to the WBCSD, companies and stakeholders are encouraged by mutual benefits to work hand in hand in order to assess, manage and share risks (WBCSD, 2004).

Nowadays value-creation processes call for being attentive to the welfare of stakeholders (Ehrhardt, 1994). Hence, a firm must define an overall strategy that addresses the needs of different constituencies in order to strengthen the social consensus and the perceived licence to operate (Tencati and Perrini, 2006).

9.3   THE CSP-RISK RELATIONSHIP

Many scholars investigating the CSP-risk relationship have supported the argument for the positive impact of a high level of CSP on business risk. Orlitzky and Benjamin (2001) are among these researchers. In their meta-analytic study they point out that the higher the level of a firm's CSP, the lower the financial risk. By reviewing the results of earlier works they found that the CSP-risk relationship is of reciprocal causality; in particular, CSP appears to more strongly correlate with measures of market risk, such as total market risk and systematic risk (beta), than with measures of accounting risk. Moreover, of all CSP measures, social performance reputation correlates most negatively with risk.

The linkage between CSP and risk can be divided into two mainstream areas of research: the first analyses the relationship from a managerial perspective and the second from a financial or investment perspective. For the purposes of this work, all the literature on performance and risk associated with socially responsible investments (SRI) has been excluded from the latter category.

9.3.1   CSP and Risk: A Managerial Perspective

Although performance and risk are two sides of the same coin, researchers have focused alternately on one side or the other. In today's unstable business environment it is erroneous to concentrate only on the absolute level of financial performance, from a managerial perspective; managers have to also focus on the variability of financial performance. In such an environment the ability to avoid, minimize or exploit risk opportunities determines the conditions for the long-term survival and the sustainability of the organization.

According to some authors (Waddock and Graves, 1997), social responsibility improves the company's goodwill and provides strategic flexibility, leading to financial outperformance. A positive goodwill also derives from improved relations with employees and customers (Davis, 1975; Solomon and Hanson, 1985). It manifests itself through fewer labour problems and an increased willingness by customers to buy products or services from companies with a high social performance. Another benefit may come from improved relations with bankers, investors and government officials (McGuire et al., 1988). Companies may take advantage of a facilitated access to different sources of capital, and there may be a reduction in the number of lawsuits filed against them or fines levied by public authorities.

In most of the studies the interests of stakeholders are considered within the concept of CSP. Consistent with the good-management theory (Waddock and Graves, 1997), which derives primarily from the instrumental stakeholder theory, good management practices correlate positively with CSP. In fact, investing in CSP enables relationships with primary stakeholders to improve with positively cascading effects on financial performance and reduced risk. Good human resource management reduces labour absenteeism while increasing morale, satisfaction and productivity.

CSP and the modern view of stakeholder theory (Cornell and Shapiro, 1987) are intertwined. According to the latter theory the value of a firm not only depends on the cost of explicit claims but also on implicit claims. Companies that act irresponsibly might assist stakeholders' attempts to transform their implicit contracts into explicit agreements, thereby incurring higher costs. For instance, a firm with little or no concern for its contributions to pollution and environmental damages may become the object of a government intervention imposing a more stringent regulatory framework that raises the cost of compliance with law.

Stakeholder sympathy calls for a proactive strategy of relations building, moving from dialogue to strategic partnership with multiple constituencies (Holliday and Pepper, 2001). Partnering with NGOs, for instance, may benefit companies since they can leverage NGOs' assets to gain a competitive advantage (Yaziji, 2004). As the author further states, they facilitate the process of innovation; they are better able to foresee shifts in demand; they have extraordinary lobbying capabilities to shape legislation; and finally, given their far-reaching audiences and technical expertise, they help corporations reshape industry standards.

Disdain of stakeholder claims leads to higher risks than if the claims were afforded consideration in the firm's strategic decision-making process from the outset (McGuire et al., 1988). Chemical, pharmaceutical and tobacco companies, for example, have incurred heavy legal sanctions by acting irresponsibly.

9.3.2   CSP and Risk: A Financial Perspective

Another theoretical argument is the relationship between CSP and investment risk. Investors consider low-level CSP firms as riskier investments. They perceive poor CSP as a lack of management skills and thereby judge these companies as riskier investments because of the higher likelihood of incurring explicit costs through stakeholders (Alexander and Buchholz, 1978; Spicer, 1978). These risks arise from the possibility of adverse judicial decisions, consumer retaliation, and adverse regulatory or legislative consequences. Therefore, the odds of such actions induce investors to revise the probability distribution of future costs and revenues (Shane and Spicer, 1983). Positive social performance improves a company's financial and non-financial risk positions because of the increasingly stable relationships with stakeholders. Highly responsible firms may also be characterized as having a low percentage of total debt to total assets (McGuire et al., 1988). Since debt is low and decreases as a consequence of good social performance, the firm can address the resources it saves to better satisfy the implicit and explicit claims of stakeholders other than debt providers, creating the basis for a virtuous cycle.

Spicer (1978) notes that within the investment community there is a common vision about the existence of a moderate-to-strong association between the risk of a corporation and its attention to issues of social responsibility. From the theory-of-finance perspective (Markowitz, 1952), he continues, an investment in a company low in CSP could be inefficient because the company tends to show, by and large, higher financial risks. Based upon this theory, known as the portfolio theory, all decisions are made according to the mean-variance principle, in which the optimal investment choice is the one with the higher mean and lower risk. Thus, a company with low CSP has to guarantee a higher rate of return to investors to compensate for the higher risk. A similar request may come from stakeholders. Because of the higher cost of capital (WACC), stakeholders will try to raise the cost of explicit contracts and/or transform implicit contracts into explicit ones.

A second paradigm to assess the CSP-investment risk relationship focuses on net present value (NPV) of free cash flow (FCF). This is a relevant financial variable because it expresses the amount of cash generated by the business after meeting all its obligations for interest, tax and dividends and after all capital investment. Consistent with the efficient-market theory (Fama, 1970), investors consider the effect of publicly available information on both future cash and investment risk simultaneously. If a corporate social investment reduces the cash flow without reducing the risk,[2] the NPV of future cash flow will be negatively affected. If, instead, a firm makes the same investment, but it reduces the probability of explicit or implicit stakeholders' claims, then the risk-adjusted rate will decline making it possible to compensate, or even overcompensate, for the reduction in cash flow, leading to an increase in the NPV of an investment. CSP investments may also indirectly have a positive impact on cash flows. In conclusion, the NPV depends on the cash-generating capability of the CSP investment and the impact on the risk profile of the company. Therefore it is of extreme importance to establish a rigorous set of rules to carefully manage the capital allocation process (Mackey et al., 2007).

9.3.3   CSP and the Cost of Capital as a Measure of the Risk Perceived by Stakeholders

In financial terms, the cost of capital is the minimum risk-adjusted return required by stakeholders to deal with the firm. In this respect the use of the WACC permits consideration of all risks and, in particular, the variability of the costs arising from implicit and explicit contracts that the firm establishes with its stakeholders. For this reason, any firm needs to invest time and resources to establish close and easy to manage relationships with stakeholders in order to reduce the costs of doing business and the risks implicit in the company's activity.

A company with a high financial and non-financial risk is more likely to have neglected sound CSR practices and policies aligned with the principle of sustainable development. In these circumstances non-financial stakeholders will be less willing, all else being equal, to work with the company – or they will only do it at a higher cost to the company. The bad reputation circulating in the market negatively affects relationships with customers, employees, competitors, suppliers and the community. There may be spillover costs imposed on non-financial stakeholders when a firm is financially distressed (Grinblatt and Titman, 2001). Customers will not be willing to pay a lot for products or services from a risky firm, or they will simply not purchase them at all. In fact, if a company is at risk of going out of business, customers rightly calculate that it may later be more difficult for them to find spare parts. At the same time, the two authors assert, employees and suppliers are both exposed to risk since they can lose the job or the contract; for this reason, they will demand higher wages and charge higher prices. Since a risky company usually receives bad ratings, a high level of risk also affects the ability to raise funds. Suppliers of capital, in fact, will raise the price of financing such a company. The final result of being financially distressed is that companies need to find investment options that generate consistent returns to face the higher cost of capital.

Risk also impacts the ability to sustain the growth of revenues over time. *Ceteris paribus*, lower revenues reduce profit margins and this phenomenon affects another stakeholder – that is, the government – since it translates into lower tax revenues and higher unemployment. Shareholders, however, will suffer from a drop in the share price as well as in the distribution of dividends as a result of a reduction in the level of earnings from operations and free cash flow.

9.3.4   Hypothesis

Therefore, on the basis of the previous literature review and the related theoretical framework, we advance the following hypothesis:

Prior CSP is negatively related to subsequent cost of capital (WACC).

9.4   METHODOLOGY

In order to test this hypothesis we developed a research methodology that takes into account some referential research papers (for example, McGuire et al., 1988; Waddock and Graves, 1997) on the relationship between CSP and a set of one or more financial variables.

In more detail, the CSP-WACC relationship was investigated through correlation and regression analyses.

9.4.1   Population

The research population included all companies listed in the Dow Jones Sustainability World Index (DJSWI).

9.4.2   Sample Data and Selection

The data sample used to perform this study encompassed all companies listed in the DJSWI from 2000 to 2005. For each company we selected the CSP scores released every year by the SAM Group and the yearly financial performance at the end of December. Given the worldwide dimension of the index, all data from the income and financial statements were converted into US dollars at the historical exchange rate for each year.

The initial data set comprised 473 companies, which were part of the index for at least three years, from 2000 to 2005. In fact three years comprises the minimum acceptable timeframe to assess the evolution of the relationship between WACC and the other variables. For the companies that satisfied the condition ($N = 283$), we took all CSP scores available and related financial and economic variable performance. Then all the financial companies marked as banks, insurance, real estate and financial services were excluded. Therefore only the industrial companies were accepted for inclusion in the sample. Finally, when the financial variables were entered, missing or unusable values led to a final sample of 181 companies.

9.4.3   Analysis and Time Periods

In the statistical analysis performed for this study, the WACC was selected as the dependent variable, CSP as the main independent variable, and firm risk, size and performance indicators as the control variables. A further step enabled us to control all variables for the effects of sector and country through two dummy variables.

Given an historical series of six years' data and the need for a rigorous statistical analysis, for each variable the average value over three years was calculated. In our case of prior CSP-subsequent WACC, a one-year lag between the variables was considered since the investments on CSP produce durable effects on the company's risk in the medium to long term. Therefore, to continue the analysis, we used the average CSP scores and control variable values for the period 2000–02 and the average WACC for the period 2003–05.

9.4.4   Weighted Average Cost of Capital and Control Variables

The WACC was calculated by taking data from the COMPUSTAT database, Bloomberg and KPMG tax research (KPMG, 2001, 2003, 2005).

All data on control variables were obtained from the COMPUSTAT database.

9.5   DISCUSSION

The correlation and regression results clearly show the existence of a negative relationship between prior CSP and subsequent WACC.[3]

In line with the theoretical framework presented in the first part of this chapter, companies that adopt good management practices – that is, those which are perceived as less risky – receive higher social performance scores (Waddock and Graves, 1997). Results also contribute to confirming the perspective adopted by McGuire et al. (1988), which states that setting positive relations with stakeholders reduces the probability that lawsuits will be filed against the company or that the firm will be fined by public authorities. Moreover, it improves access to different sources of capital and, as a consequence, lowers the overall cost of funding.

Being a good corporate citizen pays off (Orlitzky et al., 2003), since highly responsible companies have, on average, better financial performance than their low-CSP counterparts. Improved CSP has a relevant impact on financial as well as non-financial risks. The WACC represents both the overall cost of funding weighted for the components of debt and equity and the hurdle rate in capital investment decisions that involve choosing among several investment options. Since resources are scarce and valuable, managers, consistently with the mean-variance principle (Markowitz, 1952, 1987), select the investment options that guarantee the higher rate of return for a given amount of risk. Our results give evidence that improved social performance lowers the investment risk, as previously asserted by Spicer (1978). Therefore, since CSP investments lower the risk of an organization, managers should consider this kind of investment as a strategic lever for the long-term competitiveness and sustainability of the company.

Evidence shows that the strength of the cause-and-effect relationship mentioned above is influenced by the sector. In particular, for companies operating in sectors such as communications technology, semiconductors, software, computer services and the Internet, telecommunications and basic industries (that is, mining, aluminium, steel and forestry), the impact of CSP investment on the level of WACC is reduced. This could be related to the roles and the perceptions of the final consumers for these sectors. In addition it emerged that belonging to a certain country per se does not influence the overall cost of capital.

Furthermore, it seems also that, in the medium-long term, the financial markets are able to appreciate the increment of value created through CSP investment. This suggests that managers should establish a structured communication and invest in it in order to spread value. In addition it is important that, according to a relational-state perspective (Albareda, et al., 2008), firms, public authorities and civil society collaborate and develop joint efforts towards the adoption of common, comparable and understandable reporting standards and reliable measures of CSP (Tencati et al., 2004). In particular, in order to highlight and control the dynamics of the relationships with the different constituencies and better support strategic decision-making processes, new evaluation and reporting methodologies should overcome the traditional triple bottom line (TBL) agenda (Elkington, 1997; Global Reporting Initiative, 2006) and embrace a multiple bottom line thinking, based on a stakeholder framework (Perrini and Tencati, 2006; Tencati and Zsolnai, 2009).

If prior CSP is a good predictor of WACC at a later stage, as the regression models and the related explanatory power (R^2) confirm, this also supports the idea that by strategically managing stakeholders' expectations and investing in CSP the overall risk profile of a firm decreases. Thus, by moving from a logic of dialogue with stakeholders to a logic of strategic partnership, companies could benefit in terms of risk reduction, improved reputation in the market, new business opportunities, higher financial performance and eventually a lowered cost of capital.

Ceteris paribus, CSP investments – when social responsibility is an integral component of the strategic company's objectives – are preferable to other investment options because they tend to show higher NPV. Furthermore, since a high level of CSP implies lower financial and non-financial risks, investors can use social performance as screening criteria for portfolio diversification.

This study, to some extent, also provides further support to the growing body of literature that recognizes SRI as financial instruments that assure a better risk/return profile and, above all, a pivotal linkage between private investors and sustainable development (Perrini et al., 2006, pp. 78–84).

9.6 LIMITATIONS AND IMPLICATIONS FOR FUTURE RESEARCH

As with all empirical studies, this work has many limitations. It was mainly intended as a first attempt to introduce a different and innovative perspective in the analysis of the CSP-CFP relationship. By using a robust set of CSP scores, developed and provided by the SAM Group, and the WACC – that is, a representative indicator of the overall risk profile of a firm as perceived by stakeholders – we aimed at investigating the financial impact of CSR strategies in a more operational and reliable way. Therefore, we started by focusing our attention on the prior CSP-subsequent WACC relationship. It is clear that if we really want to understand the issue, we need to go deeper into the analysis of the topic by considering other linkages. For example, in order to better clarify the causal relationship a future work could examine how prior WACC is related to subsequent CSP, using WACC as the main independent variable. Furthermore, a different timeframe could also be assumed by investigating the contemporaneous (that is, cross-sectional) relationship between CSP and WACC.

Moreover, further quantitative analyses are needed. For instance, the data set could be homogenized by country to carry out a specific analysis of the national effect on the CSP-WACC relationship. While this chapter tries to shed a first light on the impact of the sector on that relationship, following works might better investigate the industry effect, for example, by identifying high-, medium- or low-impact sectors. In addition, studies could follow to investigate whether low-CSP companies, according to a financial perspective (Markowitz, 1952; Spicer, 1978), offer higher returns to stakeholders to offset the greater financial and non-financial risks.

Another avenue for future research may be to investigate the impact on a company – in terms of the volatility of its stock price, or beta, and on the WACC – of being listed in an ethical index. The institutional-ownership perspective (Graves and Waddock, 1994) and the development of the SRI industry, characterized by the long-term approach to investments, may offer an interesting departure point.

Finally, research on effective strategies and tools to implement the concept of CSR, and to improve the value generated by a company over the long term through stakeholder engagement processes, would be of extreme value in orienting firms towards a more holistic and integrative approach to business management. Throughout the chapter a special emphasis was put on the risks related to the relationships within the stakeholder network in which a firm is embedded and the benefits derived from a sound management of these relationships on the level of CSP and the cost of capital. The sustainability of a company is increasingly dependent on its ability to establish close linkages with stakeholders (Perrini and Tencati, 2007; Tencati and Zsolnai, 2010). It would be useful to conduct further managerial studies to offer advanced solutions and methods to control the risk and even seize opportunities to support leading positions in the market also thanks to strategic partnerships with stakeholders (Brugmann and Prahalad, 2007; Porter and Kramer, 2006).

NOTES

*   The authors thank the SAM Group (http://www.sam-group.com/htmle/main.cfm) for the availability of its data set. The views expressed in this chapter are those of the authors and do not necessarily represent those of the SAM Group. Any possible error in the interpretation or use of the data remains the sole responsibility of the authors.
1.   CSP can be defined as 'a business organization's configuration of principles of social responsibility, processes of social responsiveness, and policies, programs, and observable outcomes as they relate to the firm's societal relationships' (Wood, 1991, p. 693). For a provocative analysis of the concept of CSP, see Gond and Crane (2010).
2.   We refer to the total risk as perceived by stakeholders, measured as the WACC.
3.   Detailed results are available from the authors on request. For further information on findings and methodology, see also Di Giulio et al. (2007).

REFERENCES

Albareda, L., J.M. Lozano, A. Tencati, A. Midttun and F. Perrini (2008), 'The changing role of governments in corporate social responsibility: drivers and responses', *Business Ethics: A European Review*, **17** (4), 347–63.
Alexander, G.J. and R.A. Buchholz (1978), 'Corporate social responsibility and stock market performance', *Academy of Management Journal*, **21**, 479–86.

Brugmann, J. and C.K. Prahalad (2007), 'Cocreating business's new social compact', *Harvard Business Review*, **85** (2), 80–90.

Clarkson, M.B.E. (1995), 'A stakeholder framework for analyzing and evaluating corporate performance', *Academy of Management Review*, **20**, 92–117.

Cornell, B. and A.C. Shapiro (1987), 'Corporate stakeholders and corporate finance', *Financial Management*, **16**, 5–14.

COSO (Committee of Sponsoring Organizations of the Treadway Commission) (2004), *Enterprise Risk Management – Integrated Framework*, Jersey City, NJ: COSO.

Davis, L. (1975), 'Five propositions for social responsibility', *Business Horizons*, June, 19–24.

Deloach, J.W. (2000), *Enterprise-wide Risk Management: Strategies for Linking Risk and Opportunity*, London: Financial Times Prentice Hall.

Devinney, T.M. (2009), 'Is the socially responsible corporation a myth? The good, the bad, and the ugly of corporate social responsibility', *Academy of Management Perspectives*, **23** (2), 44–56.

Di Giulio, A., P.O. Migliavacca and A. Tencati (2007), 'What relationship between corporate social performance and the cost of capital?', Paper presented to the Academy of Management 2007 Annual Meeting, Philadelphia, PA, 3–8 August.

Dyer, J.H. and H. Singh (1998), 'The relational view: cooperative strategy and sources of interorganizational competitive advantage', *Academy of Management Review*, **23**, 660–79.

Ehrhardt, M.C. (1994), *The Search for Value: Measuring the Company's Cost of Capital*, Boston, MA: Harvard Business School Press.

Elkington, J. (1997), *Cannibal with Forks. The Triple Bottom Line of 21st Century Business*, Oxford: Capstone Publishing.

Fama, E.F. (1970), 'Efficient capital markets: a review of theory and empirical work', *Journal of Finance*, **25**, 383–417.

Fowler, S.J. and C. Hope (2007), 'A critical review of sustainable business indices and their impact', *Journal of Business Ethics*, **76**, 243–52.

Freeman, R.E. (1984), *Strategic Management: A Stakeholder Approach*, Boston, MA: Pitman.

Global Reporting Initiative (GRI) (2006), 'G3 Guidelines', accessed June 2008 at www.globalreporting.org/.

Gond, J.-P. and A. Crane (2010), 'Corporate social performance disoriented: saving the lost paradigm?', *Business & Society*, **49** (4), 677–703.

Graves, S.B and S.A. Waddock (1994), 'Institutional owners and corporate social performance', *Academy of Management Journal*, **37**, 1034–46.

Griffin, J.J. and J.F. Mahon (1997), 'The corporate social performance and corporate financial performance debate: twenty-five years of incomparable research', *Business & Society*, **36** (1), 5–31.

Grinblatt, M. and S. Titman (2001), *Financial Markets and Corporate Strategy*, 2nd edn, New York: McGraw-Hill.

Holliday, C. and J. Pepper (2001), *Sustainability Through the Market: Seven Keys to Success*, Geneva, Switzerland: World Business Council for Sustainable Development.

KPMG (2001), 'Corporate Tax Rate Survey – January 2001', accessed September 2006 at www.kpmg.com/Global/en/Pages/default.aspx.

KPMG (2003), 'Corporate Tax Rate Survey – January 2003', accessed September 2006 at www.kpmg.com/Global/en/Pages/default.aspx.

KPMG (2005), 'Corporate Tax Rate Survey – January 2005', accessed September 2006 at www.kpmg.com/Global/en/Pages/default.aspx.

Lozano, J.M. (2005), 'Towards the relational corporation: from managing stakeholder relationships to building stakeholder relationships (waiting for Copernicus)', *Corporate Governance: The International Journal of Business in Society*, **5** (2), 60–77.

Mackey, A., T.B. Mackey and J.B. Barney (2007), 'Corporate social responsibility and firm performance: investor preferences and corporate strategies', *Academy of Management Review*, **32**, 817–35.

Margolis, J.D. and J.P. Walsh (2003), 'Misery loves companies: rethinking social initiatives by business', *Administrative Science Quarterly*, **48**, 268–305.

Margolis, J.D., H.A. Elfenbein and J.P. Walsh (2007), 'Does it pay to be good? A meta-analysis and redirection of research on the relationship between corporate social and financial performance', unpublished paper, July, accessed January 2010 at http://stakeholder.bu.edu/Docs/Walsh,%20Jim%20Does%20It%20Pay%20to%20Be%20Good.pdf.

Markowitz, H. (1952), 'Portfolio selection', *Journal of Finance*, **7**, 77–91.

Markowitz, H.M. (1987), *Mean-variance Analysis in Portfolio Choice and Capital Markets*, Oxford: Basil Blackwell.

McGuire, J.B., A. Sundgren and T. Schneeweis (1988), 'Corporate social responsibility and firm financial performance', *Academy of Management Journal*, **31**, 854–72.

Orlitzky, M. and J.D. Benjamin (2001), 'Corporate social performance and firm risk: a meta-analytic review', *Business & Society*, **40** (4), 369–96.

Orlitzky, M., F.L. Schmidt and S.L. Rynes (2003), 'Corporate social and financial performance: a meta-analysis', *Organization Studies*, **24** (3), 403–41.

Perrini, F. and A. Tencati (2006), 'Sustainability and stakeholder management: the need for new corporate performance evaluation and reporting systems', *Business Strategy and the Environment*, **15** (5), 296–308.

Perrini, F. and A. Tencati (2007), 'Stakeholder management and sustainability evaluation and reporting system (SERS): a new corporate performance management framework', in S. Sharma, M. Starik and B. Husted (eds), *Organizations and the Sustainability Mosaic: Crafting Long-term Ecological and Societal Solutions*, vol. 4 in Edward Elgar Series 'New Perspectives in Research on Corporate Sustainability', Cheltenham, UK and Northampton, MA, USA: Edward Elgar Publishing, pp. 168–92.

Perrini, F., S. Pogutz and A. Tencati (2006), *Developing Corporate Social Responsibility. A European Perspective*, Cheltenham, UK and Northampton, MA, USA: Edward Elgar.

Perrini, F., A. Russo, A. Tencati and C. Vurro (2009), 'Going beyond a long-lasting debate: what is behind the relationship between corporate social and financial performance?', 'Sustainable Value', EABIS research project working paper, accessed 20 July 2010 at www.investorvalue.org/.

Porter, M.E. and M.R. Kramer (2006), 'Strategy and society: the link between competitive advantage and corporate social responsibility', *Harvard Business Review*, **84** (12), 78–92.

Post, J.E., L.E. Preston and S. Sachs (2002), 'Managing the extended enterprise: the new stakeholder view', *California Management Review*, **45** (1), 6–28.

Salzmann, O., A. Ionescu-Somers and U. Steger (2005), 'The business case for corporate sustainability: literature review and research options', *European Management Journal*, **23** (1), 27–36.

Schaltegger, S. and R. Burritt (2005), 'Corporate sustainability', in H. Folmer and T. Tietenberg (eds), *The International Yearbook of Environmental and Resource Economics 2005/2006*, Cheltenham, UK and Northampton, MA, USA: Edward Elgar Publishing, pp. 185–222.

Shane, P.B. and B.H. Spicer (1983), 'Market response to environmental information produced outside the firm', *Accounting Review*, **58**, 521–38.

Solomon, R.C. and K. Hanson (1985), *It's Good Business*, New York: Atheneum.

Spicer, B.H. (1978), 'Investors, corporate social performance and information disclosure: an empirical study', *Accounting Review*, **53**, 94–111.

Stakeholder Research Associates Canada, United Nations Environment Programme and AccountAbility (2005), *The Stakeholder Engagement Manual*, vol. 1, Cobourg, ON: Stakeholder Research Associates Canada, accessed 20 November 2005 at www.uneptie.org.

Tencati, A. and F. Perrini (2006), 'The sustainability perspective: a new governance model', in A. Kakabadse and M. Morsing (eds), *Corporate Social Responsibility: Reconciling Aspiration with Application*, Houndmills and New York: Palgrave Macmillan, pp. 94–111.

Tencati, A. and L. Zsolnai (2009), 'The collaborative enterprise', *Journal of Business Ethics*, **85**, 367–76.

Tencati, A. and L. Zsolnai (eds) (2010), *The Collaborative Enterprise: Creating Values for a Sustainable World*, Oxford and Bern: Peter Lang AG – International Academic Publishers.

Tencati, A., F. Perrini and S. Pogutz (2004), 'New tools to foster corporate socially responsible behaviour', *Journal of Business Ethics*, **53**, 173–90.

Waddock, S.A. and S.B. Graves (1997), 'The corporate social performance-financial performance link', *Strategic Management Journal*, **18**, 303–19.

WBCSD (World Business Council for Sustainable Development) (2004), *Running the Risk – Risk and Sustainable Development: A Business Perspective*, Geneva, Switzerland: World Business Council for Sustainable Development, accessed June 2006 at www.wbcsd.org.

Wood, D.J. (1991), 'Corporate social performance revisited', *Academy of Management Review*, **16**, 691–718.

Yaziji, M. (2004), 'Turning gadflies into allies', *Harvard Business Review*, **82** (2), 110–15.

PART 3

Focusing on the relationships with
stakeholders and the community

10. Sustainability, business and human rights

Wesley Cragg

10.1 THE INTERSECTION OF HUMAN RIGHTS AND SUSTAINABLE DEVELOPMENT

The concepts of sustainability, or sustainable development, on the one hand, and human rights, on the other, lie at the foundations of two of the most influential frameworks for identifying and articulating the ethical responsibilities of the contemporary transnational corporation. This is true both at the level of theory and the level of practice. The language of human rights plays a central role in integrative social contract theory, to cite just one example (Donaldson and Dunfee, 1999). It also plays a central practical role in the articulation of codes of ethics on the part of corporations seeking to define their understanding of their ethical responsibilities,[1] and in discussions of those responsibilities by civil society as evidenced by such international standards as the OECD Guidelines[2] for International Enterprises, the Global Compact, the UN Draft Norms (Office of the United Nations High Commissioner for Human Rights, 2003) and the reports by John Ruggie, the UN Special Representative of the Secretary-General on Human Rights and Transnational Corporations (Ruggie, 2006, 2007, 2008).

The focus on human rights and business is hardly surprising. As Tom Campbell points out, rights are to be treasured because they are 'valuable possessions that enable us to exercise freedom of choice and protect our own interests and those of other people' (Campbell, 2006, p. 4). As such, human rights have become central to the work of the United Nations. Their protection is regarded as among the most important obligations of national and international law and they are a cornerstone of the constitutions of most democratic systems of government. That human rights and business has become a central topic of business ethics is equally unsurprising. The modern multinational corporation today drives economic development globally and locally. In many countries in the developing world, the decisions of corporations have an impact on the welfare of people that is equal to or greater than the government (Cragg, 2005). And as John Ruggie points out in his third report, 'there are few if any internationally recognized human rights that business cannot impact – or be perceived to impact – in some manner' (Ruggie, 2008, p. 15).

The language of sustainability is equally prominent both theoretically and practically. Since the publication of the Bruntland Report, the concept of sustainable development has anchored a powerful framework of ideas whose popularity would seem to derive at least in part from its capacity to adapt and give voice to a wide range of theoretical languages, including the languages of science and social science and, perhaps most significantly, business management. Sustainability is about human wellbeing, the wellbeing of those alive today and those who will inherit what today's generation will leave behind. Although originally focused on the natural environment and its protection, sustainability and sustainable development now covers a full range of economic and social values in additional to the domain of environmental protection. It is now a concept that like human rights is built into most international and corporate codes of ethics. It appears as the first principle under Part II of the OECD Guidelines: 'Contribute to economic, social, and environmental progress with a view to achieving sustainable development.'[3] It has also become a favourite framework for corporate social responsibility (CSR) reporting by corporations seeking to persuade a sceptical public of their commitment to meeting their social responsibilities.[4]

It is quite clear simply from the examples of ethics codes referred to in the previous paragraphs that the language of sustainability and the language of human rights are intertwined with what appears at first glance to be no apparent tension. This is intriguing for a number of reasons. First, the normative logic of the theoretical frameworks on which the concepts of human rights and sustainable development rest are incommensurable, the one building on the language of consequentialism and the other the language of deontology.

The focus of sustainability and sustainable development is ensuring that commercial activity does not cause harm or leave people worse off than would otherwise be the case and more positively contributes positively to human wellbeing present and future. The language of sustainability is good or bad, better or worse. In contrast, the language of human rights is the language of right and wrong. Its focus is whether or not a human rights value or principle has been respected. It is the language of yes or no. Where rights are at stake, either they are respected or they are not. What is equally significant, if one's framework is a human rights framework, human rights always trump outcome-oriented considerations. The claim that human welfare might be further advanced by actions that would override the rights of specific individuals impacted by those actions might well be true but can never win where human rights have moral status. It follows that human rights principles and values can clash with sustainable development principles.

At the level of practice, human rights and sustainable development rhetoric can also be seen to cohabit uneasily. There are many reasons for this. Looking at business through the eyes of management, corporations are reasonably comfortable measuring or having their performance measured against sustainability or sustainable development benchmarks. This is in part because sustainability benchmarks are both negotiable and measurable. Sustainability targets can be set, improvements over time promised and achieved and progress reported and evaluated. Where human rights are concerned, however, the picture is quite different. Human rights obligations, though sometimes contestable, are not negotiable. That is to say, there may not always be consensus about whether a particular activity or action is consistent with a respect for human rights. Equally, it might not always be clear what respect for human rights requires in specific situations. What is clear, however, is that, if it is agreed that respect for human rights requires or prohibits a particular action, then either the standard is met or it is not. Furthermore, once determined, the standard itself is not negotiable and does not change from setting to setting or industry to industry.

There are other problems as well. As Tom Campbell points out, under conditions of globalization, 'rights discourse is often seen as part of a basically western and therefore parochial culture ill-suited to the needs and aspirations of (the) majority of the world's population' (Campbell, 2006, p. 10). Further, even in the Western world, a focus on rights discourse has been greeted with scepticism faced with the knowledge that 'rights have not always served progressive purposes' (Campbell, 2006, p. 10).

Human rights standards therefore pose a significant challenge for corporations. This is disguised by the fact that, to a considerable degree, corporations are increasingly willing to embed human rights rhetoric into their ethics codes and their corporate vocabulary. Neither are they uncomfortable, for the most part, working in an environment in which setting human rights standards and the responsibility for ensuring they are respected is assumed by governments. For corporations, working within legal constraints is a fact of life. Indeed, stable legal environments enhance their capacity to do business. They allow corporations to sort out with some clarity the standards they must respect. However, any proposal to hold corporations directly accountable for human rights violations, for example, in an international court or law, as was proposed by the UN Draft Norms, is likely to be resisted.[5]

What we can conclude from this discussion is that, at a surface level, where corporations are concerned, the rhetoric of human rights and the rhetoric of sustainability and sustainable development appear to intersect and mingle with no apparent tension. However, if we probe below the surface, clarity about the nature of the intersection of these two ethical frameworks is less easy to find.

10.2   WHAT HUMAN RIGHTS ARE

Of the two frameworks, the human rights framework is the more complex. Understanding whether and how the two types of values intersect and can be integrated requires first understanding the structural characteristics of human rights frameworks.

10.2.1   Human Beings as Autonomous Moral Agents

The idea that human beings have rights by virtue of their status as human beings has its roots in early Christian and Stoic thought. It emerges clearly for the first time, however, in the twelfth and thirteenth centuries.[6] Evolving out of the medieval concept of natural law, human rights principles are grounded on three fundamental moral propositions. The first concerns the concept of moral agency. Human beings are rational agents uniquely capable of making decisions guided by moral deliberation. It is for this reason that human beings are justifiably held morally responsible for the choices they make and the actions in which they engage (Griffin, 2004, p. 32).

Moral agency confers moral autonomy, namely, the capacity to make decisions based on moral reflection. The exercise of moral agency, however, requires that human beings as individuals or persons have the freedom to make choices in accordance with values of their own choosing.[7] In the absence of the freedom that choice requires, the exercise of moral agency is blocked. Creating the space in which moral agency can be exercised is therefore a fundamental human interest and a core moral value of foundational importance. That is to say, ensuring that human beings as moral agents are freed of morally arbitrary constraints that block the exercise of moral agency is a fundamentally important human moral objective.

The second pillar on which the concept of human rights is built is human equality. Moral agency is a characteristic that is shared equally by all human beings. What human beings require for its exercise is also shared equally by all human beings. Human equality, then, is grounded first on the human capacity to engage in moral deliberation and, based on moral deliberation, to decide how to live, and second, on the equally shared need for the moral space required for the expression of that unique capacity. Failure to recognize that as moral agents all human beings are created equal opens the door to morally arbitrary constraints that block the capacity of those who are the target of discrimination to live self-directed lives.

Finally, moral agency confers dignity. Moral agency is of no value unless human beings as moral agents are granted the freedom that the expression of moral agency requires. To acknowledge and respect human moral autonomy is to treat those whose freedom and moral autonomy is respected with dignity. By virtue of their shared status as moral agents capable of directing their lives in accordance with values of their own choosing, all human beings are equally worthy of being treated with dignity and respect. Failure to treat human being equally constitutes discrimination. The effect of discrimination is to restrict in a morally arbitrary fashion the capacity of those discriminated against to guide their lives in accordance with values of their own choosing. That is to say, it is to limit the choices of those discriminated against based on characteristics that are unrelated to their capacity to exercise moral judgement as morally autonomous human beings.

10.2.2   The Function of Human Rights

Human rights are those rights required by human beings to secure the freedom they need to pursue goals and objectives of their own choosing. This need is a universal human need. It is shared equally by all human beings and when respected both confers and acknowledges human dignity. Human rights values and principles therefore define and are designed to protect interests that all human beings share with each other as human beings (Gewirth, 1996, p. 9). They are principles or values whose respect is required for the realization of human freedom, dignity and equality.

Where and when they are respected, human rights have both intrinsic and instrumental value. They are intrinsically valuable because they affirm that the bearers of human rights are persons equal in moral status to all other human beings and worthy, therefore, of equality of treatment on all matters impacting on their capacity to exercise moral judgement.

Human rights, however, are also of significant instrumental value. This is because their respect creates the freedom that allows human rights bearers to do things that otherwise they would not be able to do. Respect for human rights ensures equal and fairly shared access to the education and the medical care, the employment and the recreation opportunities a society makes available to its citizens. Human rights are designed to create a social, political, legal and economic environment in which people are able to live lives guided by values of their own choosing unimpeded by morally arbitrary barriers that block access to opportunities that would otherwise be available. Consequently, all human beings have an equal interest in ensuring that their human rights are protected and promoted.

10.2.3 Five Key Characteristics

Human rights as just described have a number of distinctive, interrelated characteristics of which the following are particularly important for this discussion.[8] First and most important, human rights are core or fundamental moral rights. They set the fundamental conditions for the moral treatment of human beings as human beings, or persons as persons (Campbell, 2006, p. 34).

Second, since moral agency and moral autonomy are intrinsic characteristics of human beings as human beings, all human beings are the bearers of human rights. This means, as Tom Campbell points out, that 'they apply to everyone whatever the existing societal and legal rights may be within particular states'. They are 'those rights that ought to be respected globally' (Campbell, 2006, p. 103).

Third, human rights are intimately related to human wellbeing in two ways. Respect for human rights communicates an acknowledgement of the inherent dignity and moral status of those so treated. To have one's moral status as a human rights bearer acknowledged is intrinsically valuable. This holds true whether or not any additional material benefits follow from that recognition. However, respect for human rights also opens the door to opportunities that might otherwise not be accessible. It allows individuals to direct their lives in the pursuit of the full range of possibilities available to others in the society in which they live. The range and nature of those possibilities will of necessity vary depending on the society in which one lives. However, respect for one's human rights will ensure that access to possibilities will not be arbitrarily blocked by such characteristics as race or religion or gender.

Fourth, because their purpose is to allow human beings to exercise moral agency, a defining human quality, human rights have an overriding character. That is to say, they trump or take precedence over all other moral and non-moral values and principles and the obligations they generate. Their function is to ensure that rights bearers are not arbitrarily prevented by other individuals, groups or their society from realizing their potential as human beings, as they understand it, and insofar as they so choose to do so.

For the purposes of this discussion, it is important to point out that human rights override other moral values because of their fundamental importance for building societies where exercising the full range of human capacities is a high social priority and where access to the range of possibilities available in a given society is equally shared by all members of that society.

Fifth, what Tom Campbell describes as a practicality requirement attaches to human rights. He interprets this to mean 'that it is possible or practicable to embody the right in actual societal or legal rules that promote the interests to which the right in question is directed (Campbell, 2006, p. 35). Respect for human rights does not require institutionalizing human rights as laws or formal rules backed up by formal instruments of enforcement. There is nothing incoherent about the suggestion that there might exist social settings where the values on which human rights are grounded, namely, freedom, equality and dignity, were embedded in social practice in ways that did not require their formalization and formal protection. It is where formal protection is required that the obligation to provide protection emerges. For this to happen, the right must be embedded in a system of formal rules. At this juncture of human history, it is widely assumed that those formal rules will take the form of laws enacted and enforced by the state for the purpose of ensuring that human rights bearers are able to exercise their rights in choosing how to live.

Because human rights are core and overriding moral values, institutionalizing their respect, protection and promotion becomes a high moral priority for any society where their respect is threatened. It follows that where the capacity to advance respect for human rights, but more particularly, where the capacity to secure or assist in securing their respect exists, there exists also an obligation to do so. Further, since institutionalizing respect for human rights is so fundamental, where the capacity to institutionalize that respect exists, exercising that capacity is also a fundamental moral obligation.

The function of human rights, then, is to instantiate conditions in which human dignity, freedom and equality are respected. The obligations flowing from the existence of human rights are not voluntary or matters of choice. To the contrary, respect for human rights is a moral obligation that human beings owe to each other. To be effective, where respect for them is threatened, human rights must be embedded in a formal system of rules that are binding and overriding in character.

10.2.4 The International Bill of Human Rights

It is interesting for the purposes of illustration to see all the characteristics set out above captured in the International Bill of Human Rights which consists of the Universal Declaration of Human Rights, the International

Covenant on Economic, Social and Cultural Rights, and the International Covenant on Civil and Political Rights.[9] The Universal Declaration of Human Rights is the overarching document and describes the nature and character of human rights. The preamble to the Universal Declaration of Human Rights makes it clear that:

> ... as a common standard of achievement for all peoples and all nations, to the end that *every individual and every organ of society*, keeping this Declaration constantly in mind, shall strive by teaching and education to promote respect for these rights and freedoms and by progressive measures, national and international, to secure their universal and effective recognition and observance ... (emphasis added)

The first Article affirms as fundamental values, freedom, equality and dignity. Articles 3 to 21 focus on civil and political freedoms whose purpose is to protect people from arbitrary interference in deciding the values by which to guide their lives. Articles 22 to 27 focus on the economic, social and cultural rights whose protection and respect is required if individuals are to acquire the education and the skills required to make meaningful choices in a complex world like our own. Finally, Articles 28 to 30 set out the need for the creation of systems of government that give full expression to human rights together with the obligations human beings owe to each other individually and collectively to build social systems in which respect for human rights is embedded.

10.3   HUMAN RIGHTS SUSTAINABILITY AND FUTURE GENERATIONS

An important consequence of this account is that the function of human rights is to order relations between and among people who are human rights bearers, which is to say people currently alive. The purpose of human rights is to ensure that everyone at any particular point in time is fairly treated and has an equal opportunity to avail him or herself of opportunities the society in which they are a part makes available. It follows equally that future persons are not human rights bearers.

Sustainability, on the other hand, revolves around understandings of the obligations of people today to ensure that the opportunities available to people not yet born to meet their needs and build their lives are not arbitrarily limited by economic activity (the use of natural resources, for example) designed to satisfy the needs and desires of people currently alive. The primary focus of sustainability is therefore the wellbeing or welfare of future generations.

Sustainability is about ensuring that future generations have as good access to the resources required to live lives of their own choosing as the present generation. Human rights are about ensuring equitable access to resources available for use by the generation of which one is a part. The function of human rights is to protect and ensure respect for the freedom, equality and dignity of existing rights bearers. The same is true of potential rights bearers but only when they become rights bearers. Human rights exist only in the present. Nonetheless, we know that respect for human rights will be of fundamental moral importance to future generations. We also know that what is true of the past and the present will also be true for future generations, namely, that respect for and protection of human rights will require embodiment in ongoing institutional structures in the future where human rights are threatened and need protection.

Looked at from this perspective, it makes perfect sense to suggest that those now alive have an obligation to ensure that their own pursuit of economic, social or political objectives does not undermine the capacity of future generations to create conditions required for the enjoyment of human rights in their own lifetime. Put more positively, we might say that those currently alive have an obligation to build and maintain institutions and practices that will ensure that future generations are able to protect and advance respect for human rights at a level at least equal to or greater than that enjoyed by people now alive.

10.4 BUSINESS, SUSTAINABILITY AND HUMAN RIGHTS

For reasons already set out, it is not hard to see how business, business ethics and sustainability intersect. The fact that so many firms have adopted a sustainability framework for the purpose of reporting on how they understand their social responsibilities is evidence of this fact. The discussion of business, business ethics and human rights, however, lies at a more tortured intersection.

It is not possible to engage in what is in fact a contentious issue, specifically, determining the scope and nature of the human rights obligations of business.[10] What we can say uncontroversially, however, is that a broad global consensus has formed around the view that the state, whatever form it takes, has a binding obligation to respect and protect the human rights of their subjects as their rights are laid out in the International Bill of Rights.[11] It is equally widely agreed that corporations have an obligation to obey the law. It follows uncontroversially that corporations have a responsibility to respect human rights as set out in national and international law.

Equally uncontroversially, a wide range and number of corporations have accepted that they have an obligation to respect human rights even in settings where governments do not require that they do so, or are uninterested or unwilling to enforce human rights laws. It follows that these corporations have human rights obligations.

Finally, as the United Nations Declaration of Human Rights proclaims, there is a widely shared obligation on everyone and all organs of society to respect, protect and advance respect for human rights where they have the capacity to do so.

Given this admittedly limited account, how then do human rights connect to sustainability and future generations?

I proposed earlier that the human rights obligations of the present to the future would appear to lie in fostering practices and institutions that protect and advance respect for human rights in a continuing present. Given that corporations have human rights obligations, a commitment to sustainable development will require that corporations contribute to the institutionalization of human rights principles and practices where they have the capacity to do so. There are two forums in which corporations, particularly multinational corporations, have this capacity.

(a)   One of the most striking social developments in the last century has been the growing power of the modern corporation to engage in and influence public debate around issues that impact their interests. This power is a function of their access to financial, economic, scientific and technological resources that frequently equal and increasingly exceed those available to the governments responsible for regulating their activities. It is also a function of the rights conferred by law, in this case specifically the right to participate in public debates in the form of advertising, legal challenges, political contributions and lobbying to name just a few of the obvious examples.

If we accept the principle that with power comes responsibility (Davis, 1960), then one of the ethical obligations of corporations is to use their power to engage in the shaping of public policy in ways that encourage governments to fulfil their obligations under international law and the International Bill of Human Rights particularly with regard to institutionalizing the protection of human rights. This obligation must of necessity mean support for embedding in institutional frameworks the requirement that corporations themselves respect and protect human rights wherever they engage in business.

This is not a discretionary obligation. The obligation exists whether acted on or not. However, it is clear that by its very nature the obligation must be self-imposed and in that sense voluntary. It is not an obligation that can be imposed by law though the law can be used to attempt to limit the power of corporations to influence public policy.[12] However, it is a primary obligation for many reasons. It is clear, for example, that in many parts of the world, particularly the developing and underdeveloped world, the activities of corporations have more direct impact on the wellbeing of people living in those countries than the government (Cragg, 2005). It is equally clear that even where strong, stable government is the order of the day, corporations, with their financial resources and their access to technology and science, are capable of producing products whose potential impacts governments do not have the resources to assess and regulate (Cragg, 2005). So too, in international counsels, corporate access to knowledge and information with its implications for economic development makes corporate involvement in shaping international policies and institutions virtually inescapable.

How corporations employ the power to influence and shape public policy and the institutions responsible for implementing public policy is therefore of enormous significance for meeting the obligation to pass to future generations the institutional frameworks that will make it possible for them to enjoy human rights protections similar to or greater than those that currently exist. It follows that corporations have an ethical responsibility to use their power to influence and shape public policy and public institutions, and to support responsibly the creation of institutions capable of protecting human rights when they are threatened.

(b) It is clear, however, that corporations have the capacity not simply to support the creation of public institutions capable of protecting human rights. They also have the capacity to institutionalize the protection of human rights in their own operations. The institutionalization of human rights protections requires several things. It must be possible in theory and practice to embed human rights protections in the form of rules or principles in corporate management systems. It must be possible to monitor the implementation of the rules to determine compliance and to communicate findings in publicly available reports. Finally, the reports must be subject to verification. Unless these conditions are satisfied, it will not be possible to determine whether respect for the rights in question has been institutionalized and whether a corporation's human rights obligations are being met.[13]

As it turns out, these conditions are all realizable. Management systems are being developed and refined that allow training, monitoring, reporting and auditing. These systems are now commonplace. The Global Reporting Initiative has taken great strides in developing transparent monitoring and reporting systems. AccountAbility, Social Accountability International, the CAUX Roundtable, Transparency International and a variety of other public, private and voluntary sector organizations are engaged in developing sophisticated management systems for embedding ethical standards in organizations, and monitoring, reporting and auditing the effective implementation of those standards throughout an organization's operations.[14] Access to these systems and training programmes means that corporations today are able to institutionalize the protection of human rights in their own operations.

For some, the fact that corporations today have the capacity to build respect for human rights and the protection of human rights into their management systems will provide little comfort. Expecting corporations to voluntarily take up their ethical obligations in this regard, it might be thought, is simply too idealistic. Realism in this regard has its merits. What it should point to, however, is a need to persuade or require domestic and international organizations, whose cooperation corporations need under conditions of globalization to do business efficiently, to add their voice and leverage to the task of persuading corporations to fulfil their human rights obligations. These organizations include domestic and international financial institutions, export development agencies and the World Bank to use just a few examples.

What needs to be added to the picture just sketched, therefore, is recognition that the obligation to institutionalize the protection of human rights extends well beyond for-profit corporations to the multitude of organizations and institutions that have a role in determining how business is done globally and locally. If the principle that power confers responsibility applies to private sector, for-profit corporations, the same must be true for others as well, including NGOs, industry associations, international institutions like the OECD and the United Nations, governments and the public, to give just a few examples.

10.5   CONCLUSIONS

Human rights frameworks, because of their focus on the present, pose a particular challenge when seeking to understand the obligations of those currently alive to future generations. The preceding discussion suggests that meeting that challenge requires understanding: (i) the value to individuals of living in a world in which human rights are respected and; (ii) the role institutions do and can play in linking the past, the present and the future. The focus of human rights obligations is the continuing present. Meeting those obligations in the continuous present requires embedding human rights protections in institutional frameworks that are capable of extending those protections evenly in a uniform and comprehensive manner where they are threatened.

Corporations, because of their capacity to impact the enjoyment of human rights where they do business, shape and influence public policy, and build human rights protections into their management systems, have an obligation to support and participate in the institutionalization of human rights in the settings in which they are active and where human rights are inadequately protected. Meeting this obligation could be expected to help stabilize and institutionalize ongoing respect for and protection of human rights. Where corporations fulfil these obligations, they are helping to lay the foundations for the protection and respect for human rights required for fair and equitable access on the part of future generations. We might describe the result as a commitment to moral sustainability.

NOTES

1. An interesting example, the case of Shell Oil, is cited and discussed by Donaldson and Dunfee (1999, p. 4). See also the Global Compact and the OECD Guidelines which are included in a 'Compendium of Ethics Codes' on the Canadian Business Ethics Research Network website (http://www.cbern.ca) at http://www.cbern.ca/Userfiles/Servers/Server_625664/File/Tools/Codes_Compendium_Jan_2007.pdf (accessed 6 December 2010).
2. The OECD Guidelines, for example, call on business enterprises to 'Respect the human rights of those affected by their activities . . .'. The first and second principles of the Global Compact both focus on the human rights obligations of corporations.
3. See http://www.cbern.ca referenced in note 1 for a compendium that includes the Guidelines and many other examples of business codes of ethics.
4. See the annual reports of virtually all large resource extraction companies like Shell Oil or Teck Cominco or retail companies like Body Shop or Nike.
5. For example, by the International Chamber of Commerce and the International Organization of Employers and a number of other industry associations.
6. For a useful overview of the philosophical and theological foundations and evolution of the idea of human rights, see chapter 4 entitled 'Natural law and natural rights' of Lloyd (1973).
7. Alan Gewirth develops this argument at length in chapters 1–3 of Gewirth (1978) and much more briefly in Gewirth (1996, pp. 16 ff.).
8. The discussion in this part of the chapter parallels closely my discussion of the same themes in Cragg (2009).

9. These three instruments can be obtained as 'Fact Sheet No. 2' from the United Nations Centre for Human Rights in both Geneva and New York.
10. Numerous discussions of this nature do of course exist. Two useful examples are Campbell and Miller (2004) and Addo (1999).
11. John Ruggie's first report (Ruggie, 2006) sets out conclusive evidence supporting this view.
12. Examples here would be by legislating controls on advertising and contributions to political parties and candidates.
13. This is implied by the institutionalization required as described in Section 10.2 above.
14. AccountAbility has recently concluded a broadly based consultation on Assurance Standards (http://www.accountability.org, accessed 6 December 2010) Social Accountability International, whose focus is more specifically labour standards, is also involved in developing assurance standards and methodologies. Its governing body draws its membership from business, academic and voluntary sector organizations. The CAUX Roundtable is an international business-oriented organization with connections to a number of different faith traditions.

REFERENCES

Addo, M.K. (ed.) (1999), *Human Rights Standards and the Responsibility of Transnational Corporations,* The Hague, The Netherlands: Kluwer Law International.

Campbell, T. (2006), *Rights: A Critical Introduction*, London and New York, NY: Routledge.

Campbell, T. and S. Miller (eds) (2004), *Human Rights and the Moral Responsibilities of Corporate and Public Sector Organisations*, Dordrecht, The Netherlands and Boston, MA: Kluwer Academic Publishers.

Cragg, W. (2005), 'Ethics, globalization and the phenomenon of self regulation: an introduction', in W. Cragg (ed.), *Ethics Codes, Corporations and the Challenge of Globalization*, Cheltenham, UK and Northampton, MA, USA: Edward Elgar, pp. 1–19.

Cragg, W. (2009), 'Business and human rights', in G.G. Brenkert and T.L. Beauchamp (eds), *The Oxford Handbook of Business Ethics*, New York: Oxford University Press, pp. 267–304.

Davis, K. (1960), 'Can business afford to ignore social responsibilities?', *California Management Review*, **2** (3), 70–6.

Donaldson, T. and T. Dunfee (1999), *Ties That Bind,* Boston, MA: Harvard Business School Press.

Gewirth, A. (1978), *Reasons and Morality*, Chicago, IL: University of Chicago Press.

Gewirth, A. (1996), *The Community of Rights*, Chicago, IL: University of Chicago Press.

Griffin, J. (2004), 'Human rights: whose duties?', in T. Campbell and S. Miller (eds), *Human Rights and the Moral Responsibilities of Corporate and Public Sector Organisations*, Dordrecht, The Netherlands, and Boston, MA: Kluwer Academic Publishers, pp. 31–43.

Lloyd, D. (1973), *The Idea of Law*, London: Penguin Books.

Office of the United Nations High Commissioner for Human Rights (2003), *Norms on the Responsibilities of Transnational Corporations and Other Business*

Enterprises with regard to Human Rights (E/CN.4/Sub.2/2003/12/Rev.2), accessed 14 August 2007 at http://ap.ohchr.org/documents/alldocs.aspx?doc_id=7440.

Ruggie, J. (2006), *Promotion and Protection of Human Rights: Interim Report of the Special Representative of the Secretary-General on the Issue of Human Rights and Transnational Corporations and Other Business Enterprises (E/CN.4/2006/97)*, Office of the United Nations High Commissioner for Human Rights, accessed 6 December 2010 at http://daccess-dds-ny.un.org/doc/UNDOC/GEN/GO6/110/27/PDF/G06611027.pdf?OpenElement.

Ruggie, J. (2007), *Business and Human Rights: Mapping International Standards of Responsibility and Accountability for Corporate Acts (A/HRC/4/035)*, Office of the United Nations High Commissioner for Human Rights, accessed 6 December 2010 at http://daccess-dds-ny.un.org/doc/UNDOC/GEN/GO7/108/85/PDF/G0710885.pdf?OpenElement.

Ruggie, J. (2008), *Promote, Respect and Remedy: A Framework for Business and Human Rights (A/HRC/8/5)*, Office of the United Nations High Commissioner for Human Rights, accessed 6 December, 2010 at http://daccess-dds-ny.un.org/doc/UNDOC/GEN/G08/128/61/PDF/G0812861.pdf?OpenElement.

11. Social responsibility in the supply chain: CSR or corporate social watchdogs?

Laura J. Spence and Michael Bourlakis*

11.1 INTRODUCTION

The way in which we are to understand the social role of the corporation has received renewed attention in the light of Matten and Crane's (2005) work on the corporation as the administrator of citizenship rights, taking on activities seen traditionally as the domain of governments. While their arguments have been criticized, most notably by Van Oosterhout (2005), and the form, limits on and consequences of corporate actions are far from homogeneous, the controlling and powerful position of large corporations is widely accepted (Nace, 2003).

This chapter contributes to understanding social responsibility from a supply chain perspective. We pose the question: 'What is the nature of social responsibility for large customers in the supply chain?' Supply chains are important because they are a means of achieving competitive advantage and enhancing organizational performance 'since competition is no longer between organizations, but among supply chains' (Li et al., 2006, p. 107). There are many examples of the importance of ethical issues in the supply chain in the sports apparel sector (Nike, Gap), but our thinking should not be restricted to these. For example, at the most fundamental level of food safety, two recent examples in the press include the retail sandwich chain Subway which experienced multiple cases of *Salmonella* poisoning linked to food coming from one of its suppliers, Dawn Farm Foods in Co. Kildare, Ireland (Hickman, 2008). Even those with strong ethical leanings such as Whole Foods are susceptible, suffering from an outbreak of infections with *E. coli* linked to one of its suppliers in Omaha, meatpacker Nebraska Beef (Mui and Shin, 2008). The point which we develop in this chapter is not around the actions and responsibilities of the corporation (traditionally understood to be its corporate social responsibility (CSR)), or indeed the actions and responsibilities of the supplier, but the fact that companies like Nike, Gap, Subway and Whole Foods know that they suffer the reputational impact of having suppliers with poor working practices or hygiene problems and hence become responsible for the actions of those suppliers. We argue that this puts the customer organization in the position of being a corporate social watchdog (CSW). We define the corporate social watchdog as a corporation which combines the role of regulator and policer of ethical standards in the supply chain, maintaining the power ultimately to delist and expose any organization not seen to be compliant with its requirements.

The chapter is organized as follows. First, a summary literature review of supply chains and traditional CSR is presented. Then, the case for the CSW as an important practical modus operandi for large corporations interested in social responsibility issues in the supply chain is discussed and contrasted to CSR. Finally, a more holistic approach of supply chain responsibility is recommended. We conclude with reflections for future research on social responsibility in the supply chain in the light of the discussion in the chapter.

11.2   LITERATURE REVIEW ON SUPPLY CHAINS AND CORPORATE SOCIAL RESPONSIBILITY

In this literature review we focus on the supply chain perspective in terms of social responsibility. The extant literature has been presented in more detail elsewhere (Spence, 2006), here we summarize the key perspectives and orientations in CSR in the supply chain.

We purposefully focus on the nature of CSR within the supply chain context rather than in a more general sense (that is, we do not here rehearse all the content and perspectives of CSR). While CSR in isolation from supply chains is also of interest, supply chain issues are usually then addressed by consideration of suppliers as an example of an organization's stakeholders. Here we want to go beyond this rather limiting approach and build on the majority of the literature pertaining to supply chains and CSR which focuses on the nature of the relationship between supplier and customer.

From the perspective of the supply chain management literature long-term stable partnerships are the ideal type of relationship and everything which fosters these seen as positive (Spekman et al., 1998). Van Tulder et al. (2009) suggest that CSR supply chain strategies might fall into a spectrum from chain liability for the customer organization to chain responsibility in which codes and standards are jointly negotiated through a process of dialogue. Cox (2004) in particular has sought to classify the implications of differing power balances on the customer-supplier relationship. His analysis ranges from an arm's length adversarial relationship to long-term mutual commitment to the relationship where commercial advantages are equally shared. In the latter case a trust-based and fair relationship is the preferable one in which any ethical dilemmas can be resolved readily and in which there is no abuse of power differentials. In this context honesty in supplier relationships in terms of not misleading a supplier or sharing confidential information with competitors is an important ethical issue (Carter and Jennings, 2002; Cooper et al., 1997). As relationships tighten, however, we encroach on the difficult area of over-familiarity, loss of objectivity, nepotism and in the worst cases potentially bribery and corruption in the supplier relationship, which clearly needs to be guarded against (Atkinson, 2003).

Recent initiatives in the UK to ensure supplier diversity note many of the same issues as employee diversity, with a tendency to focus on large, familiar well-established firms resulting in discrimination against small- and medium-sized enterprises (SMEs) and women and ethnic minority-owned businesses (Ram and Smallbone, 2003). For example, SMEs and women and ethnic minority-owned businesses can be disadvantaged in the supply chain by factors such as supplier rationalization, programmes of standardization, complex invitations to tender (Ram and Smallbone, 2003, p. 189), aggregation and compliance with voluntary standards requirements (for example, total quality management, environmental management, CSR) (Spence, 2006).

A final aspect evident in the CSR and supply chain literature is the notion of extended responsibility (Spekman and Davies, 2004) of the customer for the actions of its suppliers. This final perspective is important for this chapter and sets the context for our theoretical contribution. Preuss (2000, p. 152) is one of the few who engages with the appropriateness of extended responsibility and asks 'whether the whole process of a company imposing criteria on suppliers, even if they are socially responsible, can lay claim to a moral quality or whether it simply represents an extension of buyer power over suppliers'. Walgenbach (2001) notes specifically that the implementation of international quality standard ISO 9000 in a supply chain has been found to act as a mechanism for both enabling and coercion. Lamprecht (2000) argues that an organization should trust the craft and competence of the supplier, not interfering with their practices. Demands made, often by multiple customers, may be incommensurate with normal operating practices (Spence, 2006). Suppliers, especially small ones, might not use the same tools or language of ethics as large firms (Pedersen, 2009), and they often have perfectly laudable practices in ethical terms (Murillo and Lozano, 2006). Against this backdrop we reframe the – no doubt in part well-meaning – CSR activities of the large corporate customer as emulating a watchdog role over its suppliers.

11.3 EVOLUTION FROM CSR TO CORPORATE SOCIAL WATCHDOGS

To date there has been little satisfactory understanding of the nature of the relationship in the supply chain in terms of CSR. The most developed approach is that offered by Van Tulder et al. (2009) who have proposed a framework which outlines a range of possible CSR strategies for codes of conduct (Table 11.1), and advocate a more integrated partnership approach in order to maximize supply chain social performance. Their work focuses on the creation of codes of conduct for health and safety throughout the supply chain. Our version of CSR correlates with their category of in-active strategies to supply chain responsibility, with their pro/ inter-active approach corresponding broadly to our supply chain responsibility perspective. However Van Tulder et al.'s work is restricted to the development of codes of conduct and maintains the position of power being directed by the large corporate customer in the chain. Our work goes beyond this perspective to embrace action at the level of the chain rather than within dyadic relationships, and to consider CSR as more than a code of conduct. Here we begin by revisiting the classic CSR perspective, and develop the new description of corporate social watchdogs.

Table 11.1   CSR code of conduct strategy

IN-ACTIVE	**RE-ACTIVE**	**ACTIVE**	**PRO/INTER-ACTIVE**
Codes of conduct strategy:			
Internal codes	Specific supplier codes	General supplier codes	Joint codification initiatives: dialogues
Specificity: low	Specificity: medium/high	Specificity: medium/low	Specificity: high
Compliance: low	Compliance: medium/low	Compliance: medium/high	Compliance: high
Implementation likelihood: low	Implementation likelihood: medium/low	Implementation likelihood: medium/high	Implementation likelihood: low
Chain Liability ← — — — — — → *Chain Responsibility*			

Source: Van Tulder et al. (2009).

Where social responsibility issues have been made operational, the standard practice is the well-established one of CSR. While it is a contested concept (Lockett et al., 2006), a consensus of sorts has been reached on the core characteristics of CSR. These are that it is voluntary, involves internalizing or managing externalities, encompassing a multiple stakeholder orientation, with alignment of social and economic responsibilities, it includes both practices and values and goes beyond philanthropy (Crane et al., 2008, pp. 7–8).

While stakeholder engagement is part of the classic CSR approach, the focus is clearly on the corporation as an entity at the hub of its stakeholders, suggesting a rather egocentric view of the operating environment. Where the CSR approach is dominant, the organization views itself as having no closer a relationship to its supply chain partners than other stakeholders. This may be evidenced by adversarial relationships that are characterized by open market negotiations around price-based factors.

The classic CSR position could be illustrated by Nike in the 1990s, when they had social responsibility programmes and codes of conduct but did not consider the labour conditions in their supplier companies to be of concern to them. This is a view which they have radically changed in the subsequent decades (see Zadek, 2004).

The unilateral perspective of CSR would be reflected by an inward looking code of conduct in which emphasis is put on the organizational ethos (Van Tulder et al., 2009). In such an organization, in order to understand the perspective on social responsibility in the supply chain, we should look to the purchasing ethics of the buyers (Carter and Jennings, 2002) and their individual motivations (Bakker and Kamann, 2007).

As awareness of the corporation's embeddedness in the supply chain becomes clear, perhaps as a result of a public scandal relating to a problem supplier, the corporation's members are made aware of the impact which irresponsible behaviour by their suppliers can have on them. This matches a general approach which takes the corporation from the nodal point of its stakeholders in dyadic relationships to being the dominant organization in a supply chain network. Hence, the corporation moves to more cooperative stages aiming to coordinate the exchange of its values in the supply chain (as with Van Tulder et al., 2009; Table 11.1). An example of this process was sparked in the UK by the cockle picking disaster in which 23 illegal Chinese immigrants died at Morecambe Bay in February 2004, led by a Gang Master who was eventually sentenced to 14 years imprisonment for his poor treatment of the workers.[1] This case highlighted the problem of poor temporary labour conditions, resulting in the establishment of the Temporary Labour Working Group[2] by food retailers and large suppliers in the UK and ultimately the Gang Master Licensing Act 2004.

The Temporary Labour Working Group is a cross-sector agreement, its members including supermarkets, food manufacturers, food wholesalers and importers, trade unions, farmers, growers and the temporary labour providers. They have agreed a Code of Practice for Labour Providers to Agriculture and the Fresh Produce Trade, intended as a model of cooperative working. Labour providers are encouraged to register their intent to comply with the code and be audited accordingly. The code covers basic business requirements (for example, tax and national insurance payment), taking in workers' conditions of employment and treatment of workers. All temporary labour in the UK now has to be licensed and achieve acceptable minimum standards for labour provision. Here we see in action how activities of others in the supply chain become a risk to the reputation of the corporation. This risk is mitigated by extending responsibility throughout the chain (Faisal et al., 2006; Spekman and Davis, 2004).

This notion of extended responsibility evident in the actions of global corporations we call the corporate social watchdog (CSW) approach. We define the term 'watchdog' to mean an individual or organization (self-appointed or publicly appointed) which monitors the activities of others.

By way of comparison, examples of watchdogs outside of the supply chain context include entirely adversarial watchdogs, independent watchdogs and watchdogs with mixed motivations. Corporate Watch, a UK-based research and campaigning organization on the social and environmental impacts of large corporations, runs as a workers' cooperative. They have a normative stance in their aims which are to 'expose the mechanisms by which corporations function and the detrimental effects they have on society and the environment as an inevitable result of their current legal structure'.[3] This type of watchdog is entirely and explicitly partial and designed to undermine the activities of corporations wherever they don't meet the watchdog's agenda. A second example is the independent watchdog, which operates within the establishment, such as the Sustainable Development Commission (SDC). The SDC is the UK 'Government's independent watchdog on sustainable development'.[4] They advise on sustainable development issues at various ministerial levels and advocate the sustainable perspective in policy formulation. The third use of the watchdog idea is an example of the mixed motive watchdog and is the one, we argue, that is most enlightening for CSW, which is watchdog journalism (Jakubowicz, 1989/99).

Watchdog, or public, journalism puts the media in the role of representing the people and acting as adversaries to politicians and large corporations by revealing truth and striving for justice. This model of journalism incorporates the role of a 'watchdog in order to control the authorities' (Carpentier, 2007, p. 158.). Carpentier goes on to note the potential purposeful avoidance of objectivity in public (or civic) journalism, highlighting the 'area of tension between involvement and neutrality' (p. 160) which we similarly see in the account of the CSW approach presented here. Further supporting the evidence for parallels with CSW, in a typology of media effects, McQuail (1987, p. 85) notes the effect of ideological stances of the media as resulting in social control, socialization, reality definition and institutional change – all aspects of which we would also expect to see result from CSW activities.

The term 'watchdog' is drawn from reference to a canine which guards and warns others of some predefined wrong-doing (inefficiency, illegality, unethical or dangerous behaviour). A crucial point here is the definition of wrongdoing for the given watchdog. In a literal sense, cases exist where the trigger for a guard dog to react is morally unjustified – for example, in apartheid South Africa white land owners commonly trained their dogs to bark, even attack, when they saw a black man. This is an extreme case but highlights nicely the point that the activity focused on by the watchdog may not be universally understood as morally corrupt.

In Table 11.2 the case for corporations as watchdogs in their supply chains is illustrated.

Accordingly, the CSW, as we have argued, combines the role of regulator and policer of ethical standards in the supply chain, and maintains the power ultimately to delist and expose any organization not seen to be compliant with its requirements (that is, 'judge' to extend the analogy). At the extreme, it may be viewed that the corporation takes a paternalistic degree of moral responsibility for the suppliers, acting in *loco parentis*, almost as if they were subsidiaries of the corporation. Automotive manufacturer Toyota is renowned for such close relationships with its suppliers, for example (see Spence, 2006). This approach may be motivated by good will, but is also in the enlightened self-interest of the corporate customer.

The CSW approach is an important one because it identifies and highlights the social effects of the power and control held by large corporate customers over their suppliers. In the CSW approach the relationship between the corporation and its suppliers becomes a dominant focus of consideration. Cox (2004) has noted that despite a rhetoric of partnership and win-win situations, power differences remain an important issue. Indeed, SME suppliers can be very sceptical about partnership with large organizations (Morissey and Pittaway, 2004). However, there is some evidence that the power imbalance and inevitability of such stances is understood and accepted by small suppliers (Hingley, 2005).

There are also practical and moral implications for the CSW concept. While public outcry when there is a problem in the supply chain

Table 11.2   Understanding large corporate customers as watchdogs for their supply chain

1.	How has the watchdog received its mandate?	Mixed mandate: self-appointed, sustained by the power held over suppliers. Also appointed by proxy by societal expectations.
2.	What are the motivations for acting as a watchdog?	Varied, include possible combinations of: risk mitigation; enlightened self-interest; imperialist approaches assuming moral superiority; paternalism; commitment and resource availability to improve practices of self and others (that is, do the right thing).
3.	In whose interests are the risks identified?	In the interests of consumers and by association the public interest. Also strongly in the interests of the watchdog/corporation itself since any public identification of wrongdoing (that is, unethical/illegal behaviour) carries reputational risk for them.
4.	What is the activity being observed?	Likely to be activities relating to health and safety, working practices, freedom of association, supplier relationships, environmental practices.
5.	What standard is performance measured against?	Legal requirements, international standards (for example, International Labour Organization, ISO standards), trade standards (for example, British Retail Consortium), company codes (for example, UK retailer, John Lewis Partnership Responsible Sourcing Code of Practice).
6.	What sanctions does the watchdog have at its disposal?	Public/industry exposure; delisting; repeated auditing; facilitation of change; engagement and cooperation; dialogue and reassessment of requirements.

effectively gives large corporate customers extended social responsibility for the actions of their suppliers, this in practice is incredibly difficult to control for. In this chapter we have focused on first tier suppliers only. In practice compliance with CSR requirements may be expected for second, third, fourth or higher tier suppliers (that is, the supplier's suppliers). It would be extraordinarily resource-intensive to control suppliers beyond the first level in this way, so what practical approach might mitigate the wider risk? On the other hand, corporations might question their right and whether it is morally just to take the implicitly imperialist approach of the CSW. While this moral high ground could also be used as an excuse for not taking wider responsibility than in-house operations, it might also hold considerable truth. We return again to the question of on what moral basis one organization seeks to determine the social practices of another. Indeed, are corporate customers better equipped to determine social responsibility? Are they more ethical, in a sense, than their suppliers?

At a more conceptual level, there are parallels between CSW and the notion of cultural imperialism or homogenization, effectively regulating culture (Tomlinson, 1997, p. 119). This is especially pertinent where suppliers are located in a different cultural context. In this respect the requirement for locally determined social responsibility compliance by a corporate customer can be understood as a cultural imposition. While this point requires further consideration, CSW does incorporate a dominating element of consistent influence and control of the large corporate customer on its suppliers. Again this is particularly important in the context of globalization wherein, as Anthony Giddens reminds us, '[g]lobalisation is widely seen in the developing world as merely the latest stage in the exploitation of the third world by the West – a project from which the rich countries gain at the expense of the poor' (Giddens, 2003, p. xx). In this case, the large corporation acts as a social watchdog, imposing its own standards in part at least in order to protect its own reputation. Bannerjee (2007, pp. 66–93) points out in scathing terms the inequity and hypocrisy of Western corporate imposition of sustainability and CSR requirements on developing countries, when the Western context enjoyed a lack of these constraints in its developing phase.

11.4   THE NEXT STEP? SUPPLY CHAIN RESPONSIBILITY

In consequence of the dissatisfactory CSW approach, we are proposing an approach to responsibility which goes beyond both CSR and CSW to take a perspective from the whole of the supply chain called supply chain responsibility (SCR). SCR is the chain-wide consideration of, and response to, issues beyond the narrow economic, technical and legal requirements of the supply chain to accomplish social (and environmental) benefits along with the traditional economic gains which every member in that supply chain seeks.[5] The key features of SCR are:

- A chain-wide commitment to achieving social (and environmental) benefits.
- The legitimacy and possibility of all links in the chain to have a voice.

- Genuine partnership approach.
- Acknowledgement of different approaches to ethics by different organizational forms within the supply chain.

For a significant shift to be made from CSR to CSW to SCR, all members of the supply chain need to be committed to the achievement of social and environmental goals as well as economic ones. In many respects, the public mood has shifted, with an expectation of social responsibility across the private and public sectors.

CSR and CSW are both focused on the dominance of the individual corporation. The shift to SCR requires the expansion of activity to the whole supply chain. SCR involves taking responsibility beyond the extended enterprise (Spekman and Davis, 2004), and requires others than the dominant corporation to find their voice, and indeed have it heard. Where SCR is the approach taken, all members have a contribution to make in terms of how the responsibility should be played out. This might include individual suppliers, representative trade associations, trade unions and consumer bodies.

SCR also puts relationships and partnerships at the heart of tackling social responsibility issues, requiring more sophisticated management (Johnsen et al., 2008). This is the partnership approach that is based on collaboration where each member commits to that partnership. It allows the joint planning of goals, objectives and supply chain activities between individual firms aiming to achieve a highly committed, integrated partnership based on an open two-way flow of communication and information sharing.

Implicit in the CSR and CSW approaches is the privileging of the assumed standard of ethics of the corporation over the practices and actions of other organizations and groups in the supply chain. In SCR this is not the case. No single organization's ethics should dominate the chain. Accordingly, the social responsibility and ethical standards are determined via the partnerships along the chain. Understandably, achieving this would require sophisticated coordination and is an aspirational target, but should be a priority if SCR is to be achieved.

11.5 CONCLUDING REMARKS

In this chapter we have presented a new way of understanding the social responsibilities for the large customer in the supply chain. We argue that large firms engaged in social responsibility have gone beyond the isolated CSR approach towards the position of CSWs in which they set the standards and take responsibility for the activities of their first tier suppliers.

The concept of the CSW warrants considerable further investigation since this is the approach which we predominantly observe in contemporary business culture and which we claim is problematic. As things stand, we are unavoidably drawn back to Milton Friedman's (1970), now rather passé, adage that corporations and their managers are not qualified to make social and ethical decisions. While this perspective has been much critiqued, the extension of the reach and impact of the social and ethical opinions and decisions of a corporation's managers is much magnified where social responsibility compliance is applied through a supply chain. This brings us ultimately to the deeply ethical question of the appropriate moral reach and limits of the modern multinational corporation. It is in this context that we believe the CSW approach is of most significance.

We ultimately propose that the most desirable – though we concede aspirational – situation would be for a wider level of SCR in which the power and responsibility for activities is not held by one of the actors but shared across the supply chain. In this way large corporations might move from CSR to CSW to SCR.

NOTES

*   We thank the following for their comments on earlier versions of this chapter: seminar participants at Bath, Brunel and Cardiff Universities, the TransAtlantic Business Ethics Conference in Milan 2008 and Andrew Crane. We are also grateful to the Institute of Business Ethics who funded the research which led to this chapter. See Spence (2006) for the full research report.
1.   For an analysis of the Morecambe Bay disaster see Meadowcroft and Blundell (2004).
2.   For further details see htp://www.lpcode.co.uk (accessed 19 August 2009).
3.   http://www.corporatewatch.org.uk (accessed 19 August 2009).
4.   http://www.sd-commission.org.uk/index.php (accessed 19 August 2009).
5.   The definition builds on that by Aguilera et al. (2007).

REFERENCES

Aguilera, R., D. Rupp, C. Williams and J. Ganapathi (2007), 'Putting the S back in corporate social responsibility: a multi-level theory of social change in organizations', *Academy of Management Review*, **32** (3), 836–63.

Atkinson, W. (2003), 'Procurement ethics: new buying tools present different ethical challenges', *Purchasing*, **132** (4), 27–9.

Bakker, E. and D. Kamman (2007), 'Perception and social factors as influencing supply management: a research agenda', *Journal of Purchasing & Supply Management,* **13**, 304–16.

Bannerjee, S.B. (2007), *Corporate Social Responsibility: The Good, the Bad and the Ugly*, Cheltenham, UK and Northampton, MA, USA: Edward Elgar Publishing.

Carpentier, N. (2007), 'Journalism, media and democracy', in B. Cammaerts and N. Carpentier (eds), *Reclaiming the Media: Communication Rights and Democratic Media Roles*, Bristol: Intellect, pp. 151–216.

Carter C. and M. Jennings (2002), 'Social responsibility and supply chain relationships', *Transport Research Part E*, **38**, 37–52.

Cooper, R., G. Frank and R. Kemp (1997), 'Ethical issues, helps and challenges: perceptions of members of the Chartered Institute of Purchasing and Supply', *European Journal of Purchasing & Supply Management*, **3** (4), 189–98.

Cox, A. (2004), 'The art of the possible: relationship management in power regimes and supply chains', *Supply Chain Management: An International Journal*, **9** (5), 346–56.

Crane, A., D. Matten and L.J. Spence (eds) (2008), *Corporate Social Responsibility: Readings and Cases in a Global Context*, London: Routledge.

Faisal, M., D. Banwet and R. Shankar (2006), 'Supply chain risk mitigation: modelling the enablers', *Business Process Management Journal*, **12** (4), 535–52.

Friedman, M. (1970), 'The social responsibility of business is to increase its profits', *New York Times Magazine*, 13 September, 32–3, 122–6.

Giddens, A. (2003), *Runaway World: How Globalization is Reshaping our Lives*, New York: Routledge.

Hickman, M. (2008), 'Sandwich chain supplier linked to outbreak of salmonella', *Independent*, 9 August.

Hingley, M. (2005), 'Power imbalanced relationships: cases from UK fresh food supply', *International Journal of Retail & Distribution Management*, **33** (8/9), 551–69.

Jakubowicz, K. (1998/99), 'Normative models of media and journalism and broadcasting regulation in Central and Eastern Europe', *International Journal of Communications Law and Policy*, **2** (Winter), 1–32.

Johnsen, T., R. Johnsen and R. Lamming (2008), 'Supply relationship evaluation', *European Management Journal*, **26** (4), 274–87.

Lamprecht, J. (2000), *Quality and Power in the Supply Chain*, Oxford: Butterworth Heinemann.

Li, S., B. Ragu-Nathan, T.S. Ragu-Nathan and S. Subba Rao (2006), 'The impact of supply chain management practices on competitive advantage and organizational performance', *Omega*, **34** (2), April, 107–24.

Lockett, A., J. Moon and W. Visser (2006), 'Corporate social responsibility in management research: focus, nature, salience and sources of influence', *Journal of Management Studies*, **43** (1), 115–36.

Matten, D. and A. Crane (2005), 'Corporate citizenship: toward an extended theoretical conceptualization', *Academy of Management Review*, **30** (1), 166–79.

McQuail, D. (1987), 'Processes of media effects', in O. Boyd-Barrett and P. Braham (eds), *Media, Knowledge and Power*, London: Routledge, pp. 80–107.

Meadowcroft, J. and J. Blundell (2004), 'The Morecambe Bay cockle pickers: market failure or government disaster?', *Economic Affairs*, **24** (3), 69–71.

Morissey, B. and L. Pittaway (2004), 'Research note: a study of procurement behaviour in small firms', *Journal of Small Business and Enterprise Development*, **11** (2), 254–62.

Mui, Y.O. and A. Shin (2008), 'Grocer works to repair its image: Whole Foods tightens inspection rules after beef recall', *Washington Post*, 12 August, D01.

Murillo, D. and J. Lozano (2006), 'SMEs and CSR: an approach to CSR in their own words', *Journal of Business Ethics*, **67** (3), 227–40.

Nace, T. (2003), *Gangs of America: The Rise of Corporate Power and the Disabling of Democracy*, San Francisco, CA: Berrett-Koehler.

Pedersen, E.R. (2009), 'The many and the few: rounding up the SMEs that manage CSR in the supply chain', *Supply Chain Management: An International Journal*, **14** (2), 109–16.

Preuss, L. (2000), 'Should you buy your customer's values? On the transfer of moral values in industrial purchasing', *International Journal of Value-Based Management*, **13**, 141–58.

Ram, M. and D. Smallbone (2003), 'Supplier diversity initiatives and the diversification of ethnic minority business in the UK', *Policy Studies*, **24** (4), 187–204.

Spekman, R. and E. Davis (2004), 'Risky business: expanding the discussion on risk and the extended enterprise', *International Journal of Physical Distribution and Logistics Management*, **34** (5), 414–33.

Spekman R., J. Kamauff and N. Myhr (1998), 'An empirical investigation into supply chain management: a perspective on partnerships', *International Journal of Physical Distribution and Logistics Management*, **28** (8), 630–50.

Spence, L.J. (2006), *Supplier Relationships in the UK: Business Ethics and Procurement Practice*, London: Institute of Business Ethics.

Tomlinson, J. (1997), 'Internationalism, globalization and cultural imperialism', in K. Thompson (ed.), *Media and Cultural Regulation*, London: Sage, pp. 117–62.

Van Oosterhout, J. (2005), 'Corporate citizenship: an idea whose time has not yet come', *Academy of Management Review*, **30** (4), 677–84.

Van Tulder, R., J. van Wijk and A. Kolk (2009), 'From chain liability to chain responsibility: MNE approaches to implement safety and health codes in international supply chains', *Journal of Business Ethics*, **85** (Supplement 2), 399–412.

Walgenbach, P. (2001), 'The production of distrust by means of producing trust', *Organization Studies*, **22** (4), 693–714.

Zadek, S. (2004), 'The path to corporate responsibility at Nike', *Harvard Business Review*, **82** (December), 125–32.

12. Is multistakeholder dialogue really possible? Mutual resistance and bias in relationships between unions and NGOs

Josep M. Lozano and Daniel Arenas

12.1 INTRODUCTION

It has long been assumed that the development of corporate social responsibility (CSR) necessarily entails strong relationships with stakeholders. This may be an insufficient condition but is a necessary condition. These relations are often framed in terms of dialogue and sometimes reformulated as multistakeholder dialogue. If such multistakeholder dialogue is a requirement for dealing with companies individually, even greater emphasis is put on this aspect where sector-related agreements are involved (particularly when developing public policies). In this case, multistakeholder dialogue is presented as a necessity because it is associated with fostering consensus and building legitimacy. These public dialogues have often focused on two aspects: (1) the understanding (or definition) of CSR and (2) the establishment of a CSR agenda. However, the results have often either been unsatisfactory or have failed to live up to expectations. We believe that this is not deliberate on the part of participants but is rather due to the fact that insufficient attention is given to implicit aspects conditioning (and often blocking) dialogue. These aspects bear less on the stances struck by the various agents in relation to what is on the agenda and more on bias hindering confidence-building and a willingness to go beyond the 'politically correct' in CSR.

Spain is an ideal location for analysing these problems. That is because it strongly emphasizes the creation of multistakeholder institutional frameworks as a path towards CSR. For this reason we conducted a study with 60 of the most important players in the public dialogue on CSR in Spain. This took the form of personal interviews and focus groups. The research was less about canvassing players' views on CSR and more about discovering what each player thought of the roles played by other agents and their real interests in pursuing a CSR agenda.

While there is a consensus on the importance of developing CSR, each party suspects the others may have hidden interests in pursuing CSR. This is clearly seen in the analysis of the relations between the unions and NGOs. We believe this is where the strongest latent conflict over CSR lies. It arises from a lack of mutual recognition, a lack of perceived legitimacy and a certain degree of competition for companies' attention. This leads us to conclude that developing multistakeholder dialogue not only requires criteria, agendas and recommendations but also clarification of how stakeholders see each other. Although their perceptions are hurdles to mutual understanding, they are seldom taken into direct consideration.

12.2   A LOOK AT STAKEHOLDERS

CSR assumes that companies form part of a network of relations. These relations are not secondary but rather part and parcel of the company. Today, it is impossible to talk of CSR without mentioning its stakeholders. However, this approach may be used on the most micro level (stakeholder relations as an issue directly linked to business management) or the most macro level (stakeholder relations as an issue directly linked to public CSR dialogue) (Figure 12.1).

The commonest way of exploring the roles and responsibilities of companies in today's society has been to look at them as if they lay at the centre of a circle, surrounded by the players establishing relations with the company to the extent that they have stakes in its activities (Donaldson and Preston, 1995; Freeman, 1984). Stakeholder theory usually goes beyond a mere description of the various stakeholder groups and considers the normative and instrumental aspects of stakeholder management (Donaldson and Preston, 1995). A mix of normative and instrumental criteria can be found by defining the prominence of stakeholders in terms of their power, legitimacy and urgency (Mitchell et al., 1997). Some authors have also suggested a distinction between the power, legitimacy and urgency of requests made by a stakeholder group and the power, legitimacy and urgency of the group itself (Eesley and Lenox, 2006).

This diversity of interactions and approaches should lead to complementing a vision of stakeholders centred on the company (with all the stakeholders arrayed round it) with a multi-relational view. In other words, stakeholder theory can benefit from a less firm-centric view that focuses on the responsibilities, legitimacy and worldviews of the various

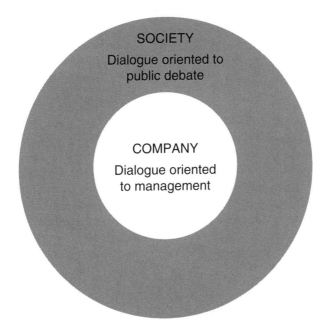

Figure 12.1   The micro and macro levels in the CSR dialogue

stakeholders as well as on relations between stakeholder groups. A more relational approach is needed (Goodstein and Wicks, 2007; Lozano, 2005, 2009). Typically, the relationship between companies and their stakeholders takes the form of a dialogue. Hence the need to pay more attention to the process, terms and assumptions of the dialogue than to the result. In this sense, who has and should have a voice in the dialogue becomes a central issue (Husted, 1998; Isaacs, 1999; Rasche and Esser, 2006; Scherer and Palazzo, 2007).

Considering stakeholders from a multi-relational perspective makes it easier to overcome the risk of forgetting national and regional contexts and their particular legal, social and political backgrounds. Indeed, several contributions encourage us to shift towards a more contextual and 'nationally contingent' approach to CSR (Matten and Moon, 2008). The engagement of a particular company with its stakeholders is part of a larger, ongoing conversation that shapes the role of business and the expectations of companies within a given society. Although this conversation is not immune to outside influences, it takes on different nuances in different national contexts (Antal and Sobczak, 2007).

The general CSR discourse results from the confluence of various players who attempt to find a point on which they agree and a common

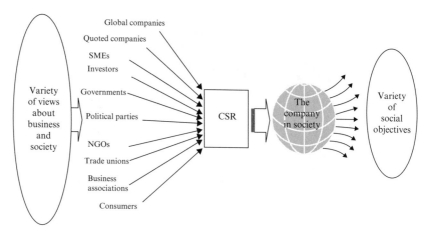

Figure 12.2   CSR – path or destination?

aim. The various players tend to agree on the importance given to CSR, but this is really a kind of consensus based on an overlap – something that is made clear in the definition set out in the Green Paper (Commission of the European Communities, 2001), which states that most CSR definitions consider this as companies' voluntary assumption of social and environmental concerns in their business operations and in their relations with other parties. The definition of CSR is thus basically one of overlapping consensus, to use John Rawls' phrase.

However, what is often forgotten when stressing that CSR is a meeting point for the various stakeholders is that each party considers CSR as a path rather than a destination (Figure 12.2). In other words, it is worth asking whether all the stakeholders agree on the importance of CSR because in the final analysis, they often expect companies to align their objectives with those of the stakeholders through CSR.

To call multistakeholder dialogue an essential element for developing CSR is a half-truth. Not only are CSR's meaning and agenda at stake, but also at stake are the legitimacy of the various players in society and their relations to the economic sphere. This is because there is a subtle interplay of assumptions in which each stakeholder seeks his own commitment to CSR, and this in turn gives rise to different views on the commitments of other stakeholders to CSR. In particular, the issue of legitimacy has been identified as an important one when discussing NGOs and their relationships with companies and other stakeholder groups (Baur, 2006; Burchell and Cook, 2006; Crane and Livesey, 2003; Jonker and Nijhof, 2006; Kaptein and Van Tulder, 2003).

12.3   CSR AS A DISCOURSE

To understand the dialogues between various stakeholders, one needs to know not only what they say but also what they propose and do. One also needs to know what mutual perceptions underlie their positions. For better or worse, the concept of CSR is not one that describes an objective reality. People negotiate meanings through CSR and thereby shape a social world and reality. Meanings are not fixed but are continuously built.

CSR can be understood as a discourse, and to do that one must understand the context within which it has been created. The concept 'field of discourse' refers to the notion that discourse comprises the different communications by different players on the issue in question. Thus, one can find opposite perspectives on the same issue within a discourse. It is therefore useful to view a given discourse as a field within which these players and perspectives relate to and reinforce or confront one another. One can say that each player strives to impose its own definitions and practices. These relationships and their outcomes constitute what we call the field of discourse. Naturally, not all players have the same power to negotiate or to impose on others their views, definitions, policies and actions.

Here, CSR is conceived as a discourse, a dynamic field within which reality is constructed as people communicate (and act in consequence). From a sense-making perspective (Weick, 1995), we can also define CSR as an interactive social process whereby companies create and recreate a shared frame of reference, both internally and externally, for their social objectives, activities and results.

Most theoretical approaches to the CSR discourse and its sense-making process do not explore emotional aspects, perceptions and assumptions. This neglect is surprising because individuals and organizations make sense of one another, of themselves and of what constitutes an appropriate relationship through emotions, perceptions and assumptions. This, in turn, helps everyone make sense of the activities of companies, and in particular, of their CSR outcomes (Basu and Palazzo, 2008). Mutual misrepresentations and mistrust among stakeholders are major obstacles in the implementation of CSR policies. It therefore seems reasonable to conclude that if one wants dialogue with given groups, one needs to understand the logic, background, expectations and even vocabularies of those groups. The problem is that understanding, trust and mutual perceptions are sometimes based on stereotypes and prejudices. Despite the importance of bringing stereotypes and prejudices to light, this is something that is seldom done.

Since the focus has so far been mainly on the relationship between corporations and stakeholders, little analysis has been made of how different stakeholders perceive one another. The perceptions that stakeholder groups have of one another and even the legitimacy they ascribe to others affect the trust between parties and scope for dialogue.

12.4   AN APPROACH TO THE SPANISH CASE

As we said before, national traditions are important in how the business sector interrelates with other social actors and how stakeholders perceive one another. In their study on the differences between Europe and the USA with regard to CSR development, Matten and Moon (2008) highlighted the decisive role played by the institutional context. In a comparative study of public CSR policies in Europe, Lozano et al. (2008) distinguished four major models: Partnership; Business in the Community; Sustainability and Citizenship; and Agora. The defining characteristic of the Agora CSR development model (which includes Spain) is that it gives priority to the creation of reflection groups and debating forums in which the various players take part. Within the Spanish context, there is a group of experts who meet again and again at conferences, political debates and entrepreneurial forums. These experts know one another and their respective positions and proposals well. One might say they form a certain 'CSR informal knowledge community'.

We are therefore interested in exploring the perceptions and discourses on CSR generated by this informal knowledge community. This term is an extrapolation of what in other contexts is called an 'epistemic community'. An epistemic community is a group of people who share certain suppositions, definitions of problems and a vocabulary. These common strands are not merely theoretical but also have practical consequences and are oriented towards decision making. Peter Haas' definition runs as follows: 'an epistemic community is a network of professionals with recognized expertise and competence in a particular domain and an authoritative claim to policy-relevant knowledge within that domain or issue-area' (Haas, 1992, p. 3).

The existence of a CSR informal knowledge community in Spain does not mean its members always agree. One of the things that characterize an informal knowledge community is that its members establish the field and common reference points for exploring what they agree and disagree on.

Reviewing the lists of members from various institutions fostering CSR in Spain, we concluded that there were between 60 and 80 prominent professionals present in most public CSR debates. Of these, 18 were selected for personal interviews, each lasting at least an hour and a half: four directors of CSR departments in companies; four representatives of employers' organizations; three members of parliament; three representatives from trade unions; and four representatives from NGOs or civil society organizations. Prior to the interviews, we also held six meetings with other representatives of the groups mentioned above, placing them each in one of five categories (business, business associations, politicians and representatives of public administration, NGOs and trade unions).

The sessions and interviews were taped and transcribed. The material, which ran to over 500 pages, was coded in several stages. We used the open coding method (Strauss and Corbin, 1998); that is, we established central categories or 'building blocks' with properties and sub-categories. Space precludes us from setting out all the research here. We will therefore focus on the salient points: the differences in the parties' perceptions as to what drives NGO and trade union involvement in CSR.

12.5   PERCEPTION OF NGOS' ROLE REGARDING CSR

This section briefly summarizes how NGOs are seen in relation to CSR. NGOs' relationship with trade unions is the one we consider to be most relevant.[1] Figure 12.3 summarizes this.

12.5.1   Perceptions of NGOs: An Overview

We consider these perceptions under three headings: how they are seen; how their legitimacy is valued and questioned; and how they see themselves.

NGOs: how they are seen

There is some recognition by the various stakeholders that NGOs have been one of the main players in CSR development, not only in Spain but also in a global context. However, there is considerable reticence about NGOs' way of getting involved.

Until recently, NGOs were seen as aid or social services organizations, particularly in Spain. Nevertheless, an ever-greater number of NGOs act as pressure groups. NGOs try to influence governments to adopt policies fostering equity and justice. This has led to strong growth in NGOs playing a denunciatory role and bringing social pressure to bear. Such NGOs are usually fairly large and are part of global networks.

Large NGOs in Spain (which used to be seen as mainly engaged in aid, emergency or environmental conservation matters) have thus acquired a new profile. Even so, this change of image is somewhat ambivalent. This

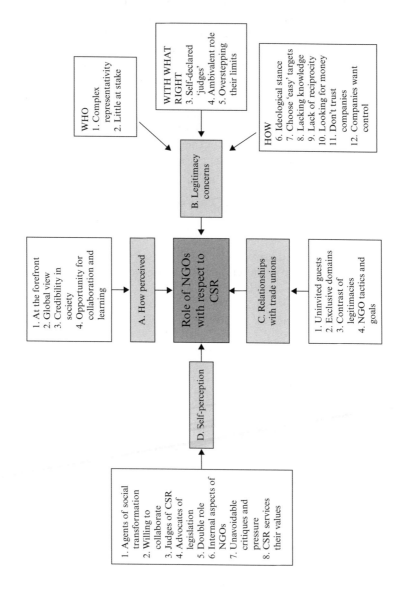

Figure 12.3   Perceptions of NGOs' role in relation to CSR

is because NGOs are seen as playing a double game – on the one hand, denouncing companies while, on the other, seeking corporate funding.

Adapting to this new relational framework and meeting the demands of civil society through NGOs has not come easily. Firms have had to make great conceptual and professional leaps to understand this new kind of relationship with social entities. Companies recognize that their traditional role vis-à-vis NGOs was to simply donate funds. As donors, the relationship was very superficial and did not affect the corporate structure. In this respect, a big change has taken place.

There is general agreement that NGOs enjoy the most credibility and best image with society. However, this masks a highly critical perception that NGOs use their media savvy to send messages that may be unfounded and/or fail to appreciate either the nature of business or the consequences of proposals. NGOs are also seen as using CSR to demand things of companies that they do not demand of themselves, particularly in the fields of governance, accountability, management and financial transparency.

NGOs: legitimacy challenges
There is a yawning gap between the way NGOs are seen by other stakeholders and how they see themselves. This is because NGOs see their CSR involvement as part of their commitment to social change but other players see it as an NGO ploy for getting corporate funding. Oddly enough, NGOs are possibly the players most critical of the confusion between CSR and philanthropy. The remaining players consider the main cause of this confusion lies in NGOs' financial interest in their relationship with companies.

The legitimacy of NGOs' dealings with companies is also disputed. There is less quarrel with NGOs' denunciatory role than with the legitimacy of NGOs' approach. These reservations concern NGOs' claim to represent the public interest and to act as judge and jury on the issue of corporate compliance with CSR guidelines. According to other players, NGOs are so diverse that it is hard to know whom they represent and what role each one plays. In short, it is hard for companies, business organizations, trade unions and public administration to know for whom NGOs really stand.

The other stakeholders therefore consider NGOs' approach to companies to be based on two misconceptions. The first is that NGOs do not always seem to understand the nature of companies and that this sometimes leads NGOs to make unrealistic and unreasonable demands. It is felt that many NGOs do not grasp how companies work and yet dare to criticize them without any knowledge or experience of the matter. Second,

NGOs are seen as having very little interest in firms themselves and consider them only in the context of the NGO's mission and aims. NGOs are perceived as being solely interested in wielding greater influence in order to achieve their ends. In some countries, NGOs directly pressure companies to make changes. In other cases, NGOs pressure governments to force companies to change their ways.

There is probably still a long way to go before NGOs and companies fully grasp the nature of one another's organizations. If progress is to be made, both companies and NGOs need to recognize their respective contributions to society and the intrinsic differences between the two kinds of organization.

How NGOs see themselves

NGOs see themselves as organizations fostering social change and the building of a better world, often by changing the economic ground rules. This colours their approach to CSR and provides the key to understanding their initiatives and proposals. NGOs also take it upon themselves to judge to what extent corporate commitment to CSR is borne out by the facts and whether companies adopt CSR for the right reasons.

Companies see the regulatory approach to CSR espoused by NGOs as a threat. Some major NGOs have argued the need for laws forcing companies to adopt CSR. A recurrent argument is the impact environmental legislation has had on firms. NGOs tend to believe that significant progress has been made only when legislation is enacted.

By contrast, it is significant that NGOs do little to question their self-appointed role and how they play it. The gap between NGOs' view of themselves and how others see them in relation to CSR could hardly be wider.

12.5.2 NGOs: Relations with Trade Unions (and Business Organizations)

Trade unions and business organizations stressed that NGOs lack certain legitimacy when it comes to pushing CSR.

Trade unions tend to see NGOs as jumping on the bandwagon and as latecomers to the social justice field. Unions point to their long history of fighting for workers' rights and note that their representatives are democratically elected. Unions also note they have very large memberships.

A view repeated by the trade unions is that NGOs played too great a role in the early stages of the debate on CSR in Spain. They also largely believe that NGOs want to supplant unions in defending workers. A generally held view among unions is that NGOs have a role to play but that they should not cast unions into the shade in the process.

The functions of each of the stakeholders would be much clearer if each party stuck more closely to its foundational purposes: in the case of unions, this means defending workers; in the case of NGOs, this means fostering international cooperation and development. Each kind of organization has its own specific functions, and the role played by each entity should be made crystal clear.

Here, union representatives stress the difference between what they term the company's internal CSR (that is, with internal stakeholders – basically the trade unions themselves) and the firm's external CSR, affecting external stakeholders, which include NGOs. Yet, unions argue that their own role in defending workers is sometimes arrogated by NGOs (usually in the developing world).

This latent tension between trade unions and NGOs is evidenced by the opinions and perceptions found in our study, but it seldom emerges in public debates on CSR. Hiding these differences tends to confirm prejudices and stereotypes and may hinder future CSR development. Contrary to popular belief, the big CSR debate still to be broached concerns NGOs and trade unions rather than companies. NGOs and trade unions need to talk frankly about the issues involved because failure to do so will make mutual recognition that much harder.

One of the key problems is that there are already negotiation mechanisms in place for regulating relations between companies and trade unions. Given that CSR does not form part of this traditional framework, the question is what these two players will do if NGOs use CSR to change the rules of the game.

As we shall see later, although CSR rhetoric repeatedly stresses 'multi-stakeholder dialogue', what the various stakeholders (including companies) seem to want is one-to-one dialogue with each stakeholder to discuss respective interests, values and missions. This necessarily implies a certain competition (in the name of defending and fostering CSR) for legitimacy and influence with companies and for public credibility.

12.6 PERCEPTION OF THE ROLE PLAYED BY UNIONS REGARDING CSR

We have grouped the themes affecting unions under three headings: how unions are seen; how unions see themselves and the legitimacy challenges this gives rise to; and some other considerations of special interest (Figure 12.4).

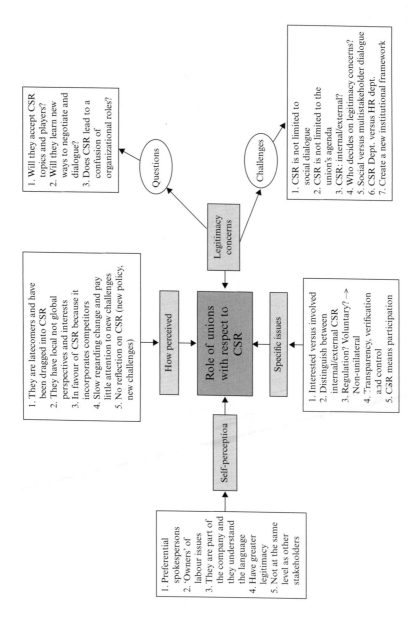

Figure 12.4   Perceptions of unions' role in relation to CSR

12.6.1   How Unions are Seen

There is a general view among companies and the various stakeholders that unions came late to the CSR debate, basically because the first stage of the process involved companies and global NGOs.

One of the commonest explanations for unions' tardy involvement in CSR is that unions failed to appreciate the scope of the economic and social changes taking place, possibly because unions are national in scope. There is a general belief that NGOs were the first to warn of the appalling conditions under which workers in the developing world toiled. As a result, it is as if the unions joined the CSR debate in order to make up for lost ground in their negotiations with companies and to put matters concerning labour relations on the CSR agenda.

It was felt that unions fear the CSR culture because it falls outside the labour negotiations framework and brings other players into the dialogue between companies and society. Hitherto, this dialogue was confined to collective negotiations. CSR has opened up a new forum for multilateral relations with new social players. Trade unions fear these developments may undermine their traditional role and purpose.

Both companies and other stakeholders think it fitting that trade unions play a big role in the CSR debate. The challenge is how unions can relate to companies and other stakeholders through multilateral dialogue and redefine their role, which is currently limited to what some call 'internal CSR'.

In particular, NGOs say that unions are guilty of double-talk when it comes to CSR. On the one hand, unions recognize the roles played by various interest groups – such as NGOs – but, on the other, they believe that social debate with companies should be confined to collective negotiation and that this is the sole preserve of unions.

Unions prefer to discuss CSR in the context of collective negotiation and give other forums a secondary role at best. When it comes to integrating the handicapped, reconciling work and family commitments, work, and health and safety at work, business organizations believe it is better to negotiate with unions than with NGOs and that the latter should not interfere using CSR as a pretext. Collective negotiation has a long history and an institutional framework has been developed for this purpose, giving rise to skills, a common language and various collaboration tools. NGOs, for their part, believe that CSR is not limited to collective negotiation and that unions are frightened of losing their traditional role.

This raises issues of an organizational nature: who should speak with unions when it comes to CSR matters? CSR departments need to be aware of the dangers of trying to hog relations with stakeholders and leaving other departments out in the cold – an issue of particular relevance to unions given that they already have someone to talk to in the company and that is the HR department, not the CSR one.

12.6.2 How the Unions See Themselves and the Legitimacy Challenges Posed as a Result

Some trade unionists are aware that other players continue to see unions as solely interested in conventional labour relations and as lukewarm to new social issues.

There is no single approach to CSR in the trade union movement. However, a growing number of unions feel that they cannot afford to ignore CSR given that it opens up new avenues for analysis and for relating to companies. This is why many sectors see CSR as something positive and are working to foster it.

There are three recurrent CSR issues in trade union circles. The first is the legitimacy of trade unions as workers' democratically elected representatives in contrast to other stakeholders forging relations with companies. Second, there is the distinction between the role of trade unions and those of other stakeholders, expressed in the difference between what unions term internal CSR and external CSR. Third, the unions are worried that HR policies will simply be subsumed in CSR policies and in the process change the way labour relations are handled. Trade unions also want to see frameworks for CSR verification, accreditation and control in companies and to take part in these processes.

Trade unions recognize that NGOs' denunciatory and lobbying roles have opened a new framework for dialogue with companies and that they have played an important role in CSR's development. However, they also think that NGOs analyse companies as outsiders and as such have no stake in firms' futures. Unlike NGOs, unions see themselves as forming a part of companies, as understanding their natures and feeling committed to their futures.

The distinction between internal and external CSR is crucial from the trade union standpoint; not only is it a way of assigning legitimacy between the various stakeholders but it is also a way of seeing and organizing CSR themes.

Once unions accepted their involvement in CSR themes, various objectives were set: first, to attempt to place CSR within the context of collective negotiation; second, to raise the quality and standards of companies' internal CSR policies by demanding verification and control mechanisms; third, to establish dialogue between companies and workers based upon participation.

Accordingly, unions now propose that CSR policies be verified and controlled by an independent body on which they are represented. They show some scepticism of the verification mechanisms provided by the consulting firms employed by large companies.

12.6.3   Other Themes of Special Interest

Unions' vision – especially regarding the distinction drawn between internal and external CSR – does not seem to be shared by any of the other stakeholders. On the other hand, the number of CSR themes linked to labour issues has risen over the last few years. While various players consider that unions are sitting on the fence, the unions believe that they have done sufficient to clarify their position.

Another key point concerns how trade unions see their approach to CSR. Unions consider worker participation to be of prime importance. This point is not reflected in other stakeholders' reflections on either CSR or on trade union aims. This stress on worker participation is one of the hallmarks of the union approach to CSR and sets them apart from the approaches taken by other stakeholders.

Trade unions are particularly sensitive when it comes to formalizing relations bearing on business matters. While formalization is sometimes seen as bureaucratic or inflexible, one of the limitations in CSR's development is the lack of a formal setting to discuss some of its aspects. In this respect, one of the key points in CSR development identified in this chapter (namely the latent conflict between unions and NGOs) requires frameworks in which it can be satisfactorily resolved.

One of the places in which the ambivalence of unions' stance on CSR is best reflected is in the relationship between CSR departments (where these exist) and HR departments. The way unions approach CSR is directly reflected by the position adopted by these departments. Here, unions rather than the company may provide the catalyst for change.

12.7   CONCLUSIONS

Some initial conclusions can be drawn from the study. Comparing these with other social contexts should prove worthwhile.

1. Legitimacy has become one of the central issues in multistakeholder dialogue. Legitimacy requires mutual recognition among the various stakeholders and an implicit commitment to CSR within a shared framework. However, it is hard to identify because it is masked by

apparent agreement (which is perhaps no more than a sop) on the value of CSR. Perhaps legitimacy and mutual recognition pose the biggest challenges for developing CSR (and not, as stressed so far, definitions, agendas and so on).

2. It seems that agreement on CSR is a kind of overlapping consensus that masks mutual distrust. Developing trust is probably needed more than agreement on definitions. This implies clarifying the relationships among the various stakeholders and their objectives.

3. Companies have been the focus and protagonists of CSR debates and confrontations. This research makes clear that there is latent conflict between unions and NGOs that is seldom voiced. There is deep-seated misunderstanding and mistrust among stakeholder groups (not only between particular firms and one of their stakeholders). This is especially true between unions and NGOs.

4. The development of public policies may slow or stop if the emphasis on multistakeholder agreement is not combined with the creation of an institutional framework that allows one to go beyond paying lip service to CSR.

5. More time and mutual experience are needed to develop a relational culture that goes beyond stereotypes and a simplistic, Manichean view of relationships where some parties feel used by others. In this respect, generalist multistakeholder dialogues can lead to endless reiterations (or, dead-ends), with no outcome other than their repetitive staging. Difficulties in managing CSR also stem from misperceptions and prejudices among stakeholders. Managers need to inspire greater stakeholder trust in the company and to foster trust among other groups (that is, by forming trust networks rather than just trust strings).

6. Finally, it is worth noting some of the more general issues that need to be borne in mind when developing CSR. The discourse on CSR is not sustainable over the long term. Multistakeholder dialogue also requires that a shared reference framework be built in which to embed diverse objectives and provide shared recognition of CSR's value. This is true at the micro level (how companies are perceived and how they are valued as social institutions) as well as at the macro level (what view of society is put forward and defended). The absence of this framework may explain why there is no link between macro and micro levels of multistakeholder dialogues.

NOTE

1. Lack of space precludes us from furnishing quotations to support our statements.

REFERENCES

Antal, A.B. and A. Sobczak (2007), 'Corporate social responsibility in France: a mix of national traditions and international influences', *Business & Society*, **46**, 9–32.

Basu, K. and G. Palazzo (2008), 'Corporate social responsibility: a process model of sensemaking', *Academy of Management Review*, **33**, 122–36.

Baur, D. (2006), 'What types of criteria help judge the legitimacy of NGOs as stakeholder of corporations?', working paper presented at the Master Class on Corporate Social Responsibility, Lausanne, Switzerland, 8–9 December.

Burchell, J. and J. Cook (2006), 'It's good to talk? Examining attitudes towards corporate social responsibility dialogue and engagement processes', *Business Ethics: A European Review*, **15**, 154–70.

Commission of the European Communities (2001), *Green Paper 'Promoting a European Framework for Social Responsibility'*, COM(2001) 366 final, Brussels, Belgium: Commission of the European Communities.

Crane, A. and D. Livesey (2003), 'Are you talking to me? – stakeholder communication and the risks and rewards of dialogue', in J. Andriof, S. Waddock, B. Husted and R.S. Sutherland (eds), *Unfolding Stakeholder Thinking 2: Relationships, Communication, Reporting and Performance*, Sheffield: Greenleaf, pp. 39–52.

Donaldson, T. and L.E. Preston (1995), 'The stakeholder theory of the corporation: concepts, evidence and implications', *Academy of Management Review*, **20**, 65–91.

Eesley, Ch. and M. Lenox (2006), 'Secondary stakeholders and firm self-regulation', *Strategic Management Journal*, **27**, 765–81.

Freeman, R.E. (1984), *Strategic Management: A Stakeholder Approach*, Boston, MA: Pitman.

Goodstein, J. and A.C. Wicks (2007), 'Corporate and stakeholder responsibility: making business ethics a two-way conversation', *Business Ethics Quarterly*, **17**, 375–98.

Haas, P. (1992), 'Introduction: epistemic communities and international policy coordination', *International Organization*, **46** (1), 1–35.

Husted, B.W. (1998), 'Organizational justice and the management of stakeholder relations', *Journal of Business Ethics*, **17**, 643–51.

Isaacs, W. (1999), *Dialogue and the Art of Thinking Together*, New York: Doubleday.

Jonker, J. and A. Nijhof (2006), 'Looking through the eyes of others: assessing mutual expectations and experiences in order to shape dialogue and collaboration between business and NGOs with respect to CSR', *Corporate Governance. An International Review*, **14**, 456–66.

Kaptein, M. and R. Van Tulder (2003), 'Toward effective stakeholder dialogue', *Business and Society Review*, **108**, 203–24.

Lozano, J.M. (2005), 'Towards the relational corporation: from managing stakeholder relationships to building stakeholder relationships (waiting for Copernicus)', *Corporate Governance: The International Journal of Business in Society*, **5** (2), 60–77.

Lozano, J.M. (2009), *The Relational Company. Responsibility, Sustainability, Citizenship*, Oxford: Peter Lang AG – International Academic Publishers.

Lozano, J.M., L. Albareda, T. Ysa, H. Rosche and M. Marcuccio (2008), *Government and Corporate Social Responsibility. Public Policies Beyond Regulation and Voluntary Compliance*, London: Palgrave Macmillan.

Matten, D. and J. Moon (2008), '"Implicit" and "Explicit" CSR: a conceptual framework for a comparative understanding of corporate social responsibility', *Academy of Management Review*, **33**, 404–24.

Mitchell, R.K., B.R. Agle and D.J. Wood (1997), 'Toward a theory of stakeholder identification and salience: defining the principle of who and what really counts', *Academy of Management Review*, **22**, 853–86.

Rasche, A. and D.E. Esser (2006), 'From stakeholder management to stakeholder accountability. Applying Habermasian discourse ethics to accountability research', *Journal of Business Ethics*, **65**, 251–67.

Scherer, A.G. and G. Palazzo (2007), 'Toward a political conception of corporate responsibility: business and society seen from a Habermasian perspective', *Academy of Management Review*, **32**, 1096–120.

Strauss, A.L. and J. Corbin (1998), *Basics of Qualitative Research: Techniques and Procedures for Developing Grounded Theory*, 2nd edn, London: Sage.

Weick, K.E. (1995), *Sensemaking in Organizations*, Thousands Oaks, CA: Sage.

13. Investigating the accountability dynamics underlying effective CSR disclosure

Clodia Vurro and Francesco Perrini

13.1 INTRODUCTION

Paralleling the renewed expectations of corporate conduct within a global stakeholder society, business outcomes are increasingly dependent on the ability of firms to act responsibly, integrating social and environmental concerns into business operations and the relationships with stakeholders on a voluntary basis and beyond legal prescriptions. Over the years, research and practice have progressively converged to advance the recognition that there is more to corporate success than the financial bottom line, and there are no reasons to believe that firms which spend their energies trying to be accountable for their wider economic, environmental and societal impacts will necessarily suffer for those efforts.

Accordingly, a variety of agents have pressured the private sector to go beyond financial measures as all-inclusive indicators of corporate performance. Sharing the same fundamental roots as corporate social responsibility (CSR) (Gond and Herrbach, 2006), non-financial disclosure and reporting have gathered momentum and are increasingly viewed as a way to codify, manage and communicate CSR commitment and stakeholder knowledge through inclusive data and information, similar to more traditional financial documents (Hummels and Timmer, 2004). Acquired from the so-called social accounting movement in the 1970s and aimed at broadening the scope of accounting from its traditional and legally defined focus on financial stakeholders to broader accountability with respect to various internal and external stakeholders, non-financial disclosure and reporting includes all tools firms commonly use to formalize their positions on CSR and to assist them in developing good business practices.[1]

Indeed, the mere act of pulling together information from business units with different priorities represents a step towards evaluating and measuring overall corporate responsibility performance. More importantly, that exercise also provides a concrete opportunity for the company to identify strengths and weaknesses across the whole corporate responsibility spectrum (Nitkin and Brooks, 1998) and improve its ability to manage the dialogue with stakeholders on a continuative basis. Put differently, non-financial disclosure and reporting may be viewed as a management process with the goal of improving performance by mapping, measuring, systematizing and communicating what firms do in stakeholder-related CSR areas. Non-financial disclosure exists to provide effective guidance for the progress of the firm, reporting its efforts to internal and external stakeholders. In other words, the process underlying social disclosure is depicted as a dialogue between the company and its stakeholders, or the means by which stakeholders can be effectively involved in the activities of the company (Greenwood, 2007).

Yet, notwithstanding an increasing interest in business practice, the dynamics of effective non-financial disclosure implementation are still largely unexplored. CSR disclosure represents the knowledge base for stakeholders and results from a set of internal procedures by which companies are held accountable to them. How can the accountability process behind CSR disclosure be structured most effectively?

In addressing this research question, we propose an in-depth qualitative analysis of the evolution in the accountability practices of an exemplary case study. Evidence suggests that benefits from disclosure, in terms of improved corporate social performance (CSP), are produced by integration of a corporate-wide orientation towards stakeholders into the whole set of accounting, auditing and reporting procedures. By means of stakeholder empowerment throughout the accountability process, disclosure becomes a means to leveraging relationships and supporting company-stakeholder reciprocal understanding.

The remainder of the chapter proceeds from background to methodology. Findings are next presented, showing the accountability processes underlying CSR disclosure. Finally, a theoretical model for stakeholder accountability is advanced, followed by a summary of the main conclusions.

13.2   BACKGROUND: CSR DISCLOSURE AND STAKEHOLDER DIALOGUE

Born of the so-called social accounting movement in the 1970s with the goal of broadening the scope of accountability to various internal and external stakeholders, CSR disclosure and reporting have become key in discussions of the relationship between business and society.

This tendency is the most direct outgrowth of the changing social ethos that has redefined the notion of a corporation's social responsibilities in a stakeholder society (Post et al., 2002). The related call for increasing stakeholder engagement in order to both enhance a company's sensitivity to its context of reference and the context's understanding of the dilemmas facing the organizations has generated a need for new methods of identifying, measuring and reporting on social and environmental impacts (Donaldson and Preston, 1995; Freeman, 1984; Mitchell et al., 1997). CSR disclosure and reporting practices have striven to accommodate company behaviour to the demands of the relevant stakeholders, while maximizing companies' chances for survival.

Over time, theoretical and empirical investigations have converged in identifying multiple underlying drivers of the impact of CSR disclosure on the ability of firms to manage their stakeholder networks. First of all, superior performers are expected to have an incentive to disclose their commitments and attainments in fields other than shareholder relationships. Disclosure through ad hoc reports acts as a signalling exercise to explicitly define the company to interested stakeholders, thus avoiding potential adverse selection risks and the exposure to future social costs (Dye, 1985; Verrecchia, 1983).

At the same time, within social contexts of changing, reciprocal expectations, companies will face social and political pressures to act in socially acceptable ways. Here disclosure and reporting shape stakeholder perceptions and expectations about actual changes in corporate behaviour, highlighting accomplishments in critical areas and justifying intentions, acts and omissions. In other words, CSR disclosure allows firms to control for potential legitimacy threats, thus improving CSP by means of its favourable impact on stakeholder perceptions. Since stakeholders will favour the company they view as legitimate, appropriate disclosure and reporting contribute to making stakeholders aware that corporate procedures are fair (Abbott and Monsen, 1979; Patten, 2002).

Finally, beyond cost-benefit analysis and legitimacy pressures coming from the context, the practices of CSR disclosure mirror certain adaptive managerial styles of dealing with an increasingly dynamic environment. Accordingly, reporting becomes a tool to improve managerial awareness of and control over the social impact of corporate activities – a vehicle for improving the ability to manage stakeholder relationships and thereby improve CSP (Bowman and Haire, 1975; Preston, 1981).

Despite emphasizing different aspects of the relationship between business and society, the perspectives presented converge on viewing disclosure as the locus of company-society dialogue aimed at strengthening the ability of companies to manage those informational needs of the network of relationships in which they are embedded (Maak and Pless, 2006; Waddock and Bodwell, 2004). It is by identifying, measuring, monitoring and reporting social, economic and environmental effects of their operations on the stakeholder society that companies are able to succeed as responsible players.

Yet, despite increasing theoretical recognition of the importance of investigating the impact of CSR reporting on the aggregate ability of an organization to respond to anticipated or existing social demands, empirical research lags far behind (Chatterji and Levine, 2006; Cormier et al., 2004; Roberts, 1992). In fact, a number of studies have described the content of CSR disclosure in order to determine the amount and type of social and environmental information companies provide (Deegan and Gordon, 1996; Gray et al., 1995; Jose and Lee, 2007). Analysis shows a general rise in the proportion of companies disclosing, with reporting practices encompassing a larger variety of themes over a broad spectrum of stakeholder-firm relationships. This tendency is paralleled by a growing reliance on third-party involvement in the disclosure process: from stakeholder panels at different stages to subject matter experts and professional assurance providers to strengthen credibility.

Research on the antecedents of CSR disclosure and reporting has also been conducted (Adams, 2002; Meek and Roberts, 1995; Patten, 2002; Roberts, 1992). Contextual factors such as stakeholder pressure or industry-specific characteristics have been identified as potential predictors of the level of disclosure. Others have relied on disclosure level as a mere proxy for CSR, thus threatening a comprehensive understanding of the difference between implementing CSR and structuring the dialogue with stakeholders about the appropriateness of CSR behaviour (Margolis and Walsh, 2003; Rowley and Berman, 2000). Finally, most of the existing research has treated disclosure as a univocal construct, one based on the implicit and simplistic assumption that the more firms disclose, the more accountable and responsible they become towards stakeholders, leaving the organizational dynamics aside (Clarkson et al., 2008).

In sum, despite recognizing the importance of disclosure to an ongoing stakeholder dialogue, the questions of whether stakeholder-related CSR disclosure contributes to improved stakeholder relationships and how best to structure the accountability processes behind CSR disclosure to improve performance both deserve further investigation.

13.3 METHOD

Empirical research so far has either analysed the content and structure of CSR-related reporting and disclosure per se or generally considered social and environmental reporting practices as resulting from a constellation of factors including regulatory requirements, competitive and economic pressures, evolving social demands and institutional norms.

Though rich, these explanations are incomplete because they fail to take account of the fact that firms operating under similar regulatory, competitive and social pressures can develop starkly different CSR-related practices. In other words, and in order to paint a more comprehensive picture, it is necessary to open organizational boundaries and look at what happens within the organization as the decision is taken to integrate new accountability models based on the voluntary disclosure of social and environmental information. In fact, providing information through social, environmental and sustainability reports is the most external result of a system of interrelated internal processes that inform companies how to provide an account of those actions for which they perceive themselves to be responsible. Inclusiveness, completeness and homogeneous coverage, as explained in the sections above, reflect organizational dynamics by which CSR disclosure procedures are designed and implemented, resulting in the release of CSR reports.

The processes that end up with CSR reporting are commonly referred to as social and ethical accounting, auditing and reporting (SEAAR), and they deal with the whole cycle of measurement, assessment and communication (that is, accounting, auditing and reporting) of a company's voluntary engagement in CSR (Gray, 2002). The empirical evidence that companies differ in their approaches to disclosure and reporting suggested to us the need to reconstruct the SEAAR paths leading to disclosure, in order to seize onto those processes that lead to superior reporting structures.

In order to investigate the dynamics underlying CSR reporting and disclosure, and in accordance with the explorative aim of the work, we searched for a context that could serve as an extreme case (Pettigrew, 1990) for longitudinal investigation. Extreme cases facilitate theory building because, by being unusual, they can illuminate both the unusual and the typical (Patton, 2002), making the dynamics being examined more visible than they might be in other contexts.

In order to select the case, we followed the procedure described below:

1. Identify an industry characterized by both the most critical social and environmental impacts and the highest relevance to CSR issues

and CSR pervasiveness. This step relied on the comparison between preliminary studies conducted by the authors on the content of social, environmental and sustainability documents publicly released by firms (Perrini and Vurro, 2007) and cross-industry reports published by CSR institutions and rating agencies (for example, KPMG, Business & Human Rights Research Center or AccountAbility, Global Reporting Initiative). CSR-based sectors were identified based on their association with a wide range of CSR issues, such as environmental impacts, product liability issues, community development, transparency and so on.

2. Identify cases having received third-party acknowledgements as outstanding cases of CSR and sustainability reporting implementation.

3. Select a case presenting the following characteristics:
    a. Information richness in terms of depth and scope of commitment to CSR in the following areas:
        i.   Governance and stakeholder engagement
        ii.   People
        iii. Environment
        iv.   Territory and local communities
        v.   Customers and suppliers
        vi.   Technological innovation for sustainability
        vii. Climate change
    b. Clearly identifiable stages in sustainability implementation. This is essential in order to provide both the opportunity to investigate threats of varying intensity to established ways of doing things and allow for comparison across different experiences even in the same empirical setting, thus improving the generalizability of observed results.
    c. Possibility to control for external, potentially confounding, driving factors, such as shocks, scandals, boycotts and so on.
    d. Ease of access to primary and secondary information.

Given the conditions above, the process resulted in the purposeful selection of AlphaOil – one of the top ten privately held integrated oil and gas companies, as indicated by the *Petroleum Intelligence Weekly* (2007) ranking of global oil companies.[2]

Then we investigated how its disclosure practices and related accountability processes evolved over time. Data and qualitative evidence were collected through a documental analysis of secondary data produced by the company and through in-depth, semi-structured interviews with managers in charge of CSR policies and disclosure.

13.4 BENEFITING FROM DISCLOSURE: THE BACKGROUND PROCESSES

13.4.1 Evolving CSR Disclosure and Reporting Practices

The change in AlphaOil's CSR disclosure and reporting practices was marked by a deeper evolution in key dispositional behaviour of the company with respect to stakeholder expectations, demands and criticisms. In other words, initial interpretations of CSR as an organizational orientation towards risk reduction and efficiency improvement have been progressively integrated into a broader view of CSR as a strategic option rooted in stakeholder engagement, dialogue and community development.

Such awareness of the potential competitive advantage of external acknowledgement, and participation in corporate commitment to CSR-related activities, was naturally mirrored in the typology of CSR reports released by the company, their structure and the functions associated with them.

Accordingly, formal and systematic information sharing with stakeholders in those areas beyond economic and financial results was, first, limited to the annual release of environmental reports and then to health, safety and environmental (HSE) reports. Such reports were characterized by an almost exclusive focus on the environmental management issues relevant to business operations and on the way companies managed to control and reduce risks associated with employees' health and safety at work. For this reason environment, human resources and local community (at least marginally) were the sole stakeholder categories addressed in depicting company responsibility. But in the final stages, HSE reports were completely integrated into sustainability reports and were characterized by a more comprehensive description of the company engagement with stakeholders beyond those areas in which impacts were most evident (that is, environment and employees). In other words, the traditional HSE reports were progressively extended, with AlphaOil broadening its disclosure attention to a diversified range of CSR-related themes: corporate governance and stakeholder engagement; people; the environment; territories and local communities; customers and suppliers; technological innovation for sustainability; and climate change.

Over time, reports have evolved towards methodological strictness, accuracy in data collection, traceability of data sources and completeness. Beyond traditional themes, such as the environment and worker safety, there has been a clear trend towards broadening the boundaries of the reports (for example, extending the report to the whole supply chain) and including a progressively wider range of stakeholders, such as customers, suppliers, governments and non-profits. CSR reports have moved away from mere compliance towards the development of a corporate citizenship strictly linked to multiple relations with stakeholders, environmental interest groups and communities in order to address important and shared social and environmental issues.

The evolution in company disclosure practices is even more evident in the functions associated with the reports over time. Early HSE reports were mainly viewed as monitoring tools, independent from economic balance sheets drawn up to prove compliance with above-average environmental and safety standards. As a result, such reports were scarcely integrated with annual reports and company-wide communications. They were based mostly on quantitative indicators directed more to experts in the field than to a broad audience of stakeholders, and primarily meant to support internal decision making. In other words, the reports seemed to be inside-oriented documents rather than tools for managing dialogue with stakeholders. Over time, the previously dominant view of reporting as a form of monitoring has been progressively replaced with a managerial approach. At some point, CSR reports began to be viewed as stakeholder-oriented tools, emerging from and addressed to firm-stakeholder dialogue, in order to provide effective guidance for company progress. Paralleling the perception of CSR as a strategic priority wielding an economic impact, integration with annual reports and other communication tools increased, with quantitative indicators made readable through qualitative descriptions and explanations of technicalities, all with a clear outside orientation.

13.4.2 Evolving Underlying CSR Accountability Approaches

The shift in the CSR disclosure practices resulted from a deeper, underlying evolution of AlphaOil's approach to SEAAR, with a growing recognition of the need for greater stakeholder inclusivity, reporting completeness and extensive stakeholder engagement throughout the process. Three stages can be identified in the evolution of AlphaOil's SEAAR practices. The company shifted from a predominantly reactive accountability approach, where CSR was practised in a mainly stagnant organizational context, to an accommodative one where the need for strengthening the visibility of CSR led to the adoption of acknowledgeable accountability procedures. Finally, the accommodative approach turned into a proactive one, with stakeholder dialogue becoming the precondition of renewal in CSR posture and behaviour.

The reactive SEAAR approach

Rooted in risk reduction and oriented towards efficiency improvement, the initial SEEAR accountability approach was addressed almost exclusively at the site and plant level, with a low level of integration across divisions and operating units. In other words, the leading criteria driving issue identification and the definition of an appropriate scope for accountability and disclosure were consistency and adaptability to each single unit's operating processes.

An overall inside orientation prevailed with ad hoc, reactive stakeholder engagement on pressing, specific issues but with localized benefits; in other words, SEAAR processes aimed at assuring stakeholders who were primarily affected by firm operations that the company was doing everything to keep risks and potential harms under control.

The accommodative SEAAR approach

Along with the increasing public visibility of the themes related to environmental protection and sustainable development, as well as the related interventions by public institutions and international organizations, a renewed need for stronger, acknowledgeable openness to the external world began to spread. The early risk-oriented approach to issue identification, measurement and communication yielded to the implementation of third-party standards and indicators enabling comparison over time and with competitors. The promotion of corporate-wide responses to HSE challenges became key, though still with an inside orientation and based on *ex post*, selective stakeholder consultation.

The onset of the accommodative stage marked a shift from a 'trust me' culture, in which stakeholders were assumed to have implicit faith that the company was acting in their best interest, to a 'tell me' culture, in which the need for stakeholder reassurance that the company was doing what they claimed became apparent. AlphaOil perceived its obligation to provide an external accounting and assessment of those actions for which it was held responsible.

As a result, internal mapping of corporate impacts on social and environmental contexts became associated with external scanning of the issues most relevant to stakeholders, together with the broadening of the CSR agenda.

Moreover, in an attempt to strengthen the visibility of engagement in CSR-related areas, AlphaOil plant certifications increased, together with a growing reliance on third-party accountability and reporting standards (for example, AccountAbility 1000 or the Global Reporting Initiative). SEAAR scope became broader, now requiring CSR-related statements and certifications from their suppliers (for example, ISO certifications, product quality certifications and certification of proper waste disposal). Codes of conduct and policies for human rights protection flourished.

Yet, despite the increase in the breadth and depth of involvement, the SEAAR approach at this stage was still accommodative, driven by pressing requests from stakeholders and based on one-way stakeholder mapping in which the company projected onto silent stakeholders its own interpretation of internal and external needs and requests.

The affirmative SEAAR accountability approach

The lack of internal coherence due to still locally bounded SEAAR processes (that is, site- or plant-based SEAAR accountability), combined with an increasingly demanding competitive environment, pushed the company towards renovation of its processes through the implementation of a brand new integrated model of CSR management. Compared to the previous two periods, in which CSR was considered as an addendum to corporate activities, the shift to a renewed interpretation of the corporate role in society as a way of being, rather than a theme to be managed, developed into an integrated, corporate-wide approach to managing processes affected by and affecting social and environmental performance.

As CSR became integrated and institutionalized from top to bottom and throughout business units, the adverse consequences of business activities yielded to the development of formal, boundary-spanning programmes aimed at anticipating and systematically managing potential social and environmental impacts.

In lieu of events that occurred in the accommodative stage, accountability efforts moved beyond the adoption of external standards and certifications, becoming both more tailored to internal processes and systematically attuned to evolving social concerns. In other words, the development of a systematic ability to interact with stakeholders became important not just to sharing possible solutions but also to perceptions of the relevant issues in order to shape transformation collaboratively (Figure 13.1).

The organization-wide orientation to stakeholder management, at the basis of the new CSR interpretation, started to inform accountability practices, with stakeholders involved in the generation of strategies, policies and programmes as well as associated indicators, targets and communication systems. In other words and contrary to previous stages, the company began to consider stakeholder empowerment as crucial throughout the different stages of the SEAAR process.

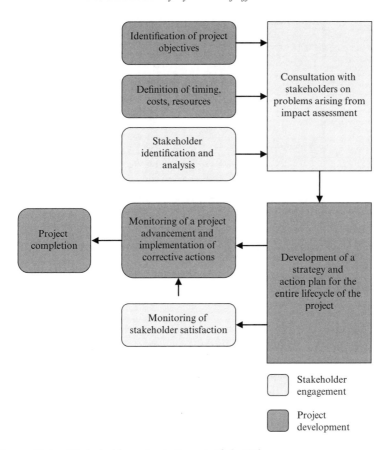

Figure 13.1   Stakeholder orientation at AlphaOil

13.5   STAKEHOLDER ORIENTATION AS KEY TO STAKEHOLDER ACCOUNTABILITY

We started the above qualitative investigation by asking ourselves what was behind the ability of firms to benefit from an inclusive, comprehensive and homogeneously distributed disclosure structure.

The evolution of CSR disclosure practices and underlying SEAAR approaches at AlphaOil are deeply rooted in underlying changes in company CSR interpretation. As the company moved towards both considering CSR issues more as ordinary managerial challenges than risks to be minimized and opening corporate boundaries to stakeholder dialogue and cooperation, renewed procedures and systems to support stakeholder

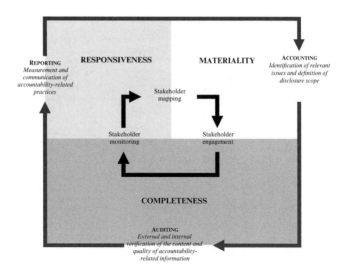

Figure 13.2   From stakeholder orientation to stakeholder accountability

empowerment were needed to manage multiple stakeholder-company interactions. Accordingly, the initial focus on stakeholder dialogue as the outcome of the overall accountability process, based on ad hoc interactions aimed at achieving local benefits, was progressively replaced by *ex ante* dialogue about the very scope and expected outcomes of company activities.

The above case points to the need for consistency between corporate attitude towards CSR and related SEAAR practices, which results in a certain disclosure structure (Chatterji and Levine, 2006). Once stakeholder orientation becomes paramount in managing the interaction between the company and its context of reference, beneficial CSR disclosure emerges from an accountability process whose stakeholder orientation is the founding principle (Waddock and Bodwell, 2004; Waddock et al., 2002).

Figure 13.2 generalizes the relationship between stakeholder orientation and stakeholder accountability, based on the findings from the case study.

Stakeholder orientation, defined here as an organization-wide disposition to integrating stakeholders into a company's strategic posture and ongoing operations, is the basis for the emergence of SEAAR processes able to sustain stakeholder dialogue and be transformed into an appropriate disclosure structure conducive to improved social performance.

Stakeholder orientation can be viewed as a recursive cycle of stakeholder identification, engagement and monitoring. It starts out by achieving an organizational understanding of who stakeholders are in their business and social contexts. Stakeholder identification and mapping are necessary prerequisites of the ability to engage in informed dialogue. This ability, in turn, allows a company to develop concrete, useful responses that are customized to the context and its specific players. Stakeholder monitoring makes stakeholder orientation an ongoing process, keeping company aligned with changing contexts.

In order for such a corporate disposition to become a concrete ability to answer stakeholder requests, consistent SEAAR procedures must be developed. The stakeholder orientation cycle and SEAAR cycle are intertwined, one mirroring and sustaining the other. In this way, company engagement in CSR moves away from simply specifying a check, towards clear, relevant and measurable goals with results monitored over time (Sharma and Vredenburg, 1998).

In greater detail, it is through stakeholder mapping and engagement that relevant CSR issues are identified and the depth of disclosure defined in a way that is material to both the company and stakeholders. In other words, the identification of and engagement with stakeholders inform the accountability stage of the SEAAR cycle, allowing the company both to derive indicators that are truly representative of company engagement in CSR and to define shared performance targets.

Once areas of reciprocal interest are identified, action programmes are defined and implemented on the basis of the priorities set in the stakeholder mapping stage. Stakeholder engagement shapes the auditing stage of the SEAAR cycle, cooperatively verifying the content and quality of information collected in the performance areas identified in the accountability phase. Moreover, verification of CSR-related activities and information through stakeholder engagement allows the company to produce a sufficiently wide-ranging document (that is, disclosure breadth), avoiding unexpected selectivity in stakeholder inclusion or disproportionate coverage of certain areas at the exclusion of others (that is, high disclosure concentration).

Finally, given the changing nature of stakeholders and the related expectations, monitoring becomes necessary to understand the extent to which reported data and information coherently and satisfactorily respond to stakeholders' concerns. Through stakeholder monitoring, reporting becomes more a strategic learning tool than a set of stand-alone practices (Gond and Herrbach, 2006). It is through monitoring that the company is able to tailor the whole set of communication and reporting practices to the specific needs of each stakeholder category and gather feedback necessary to improve the process, thereby maintaining alignment.

13.6 CONCLUSION

Based on the extensive evidence of company reliance on social, environmental and sustainability disclosure, our study investigated the dynamics through which CSR disclosure structure can impact the ability of companies to effectively manage their social context of reference, reflected in improved CSP.

Results showed that the better companies are at systematizing the processes underlying CSR disclosure, the stronger their abilities to manage their stakeholder network. Recognizing disclosure as the final step in the process by which companies are held accountable for the social and environmental impacts of their business activities, as well as their choices in CSR-related areas, we narrowed the focus to the underlying dynamics. The link between stakeholder orientation and stakeholder accountability emerged from the qualitative investigation of the evolution in SEAAR approaches adopted by an exemplary case in our sample.

Stakeholder empowerment through accountability, as rooted into corporate attitude towards stakeholders, emerged as key to superior disclosure practices, improving their relevance to both the company and its stakeholders, their comprehensive coverage and their accommodation to the information needs of relevant stakeholders.

The proliferation of CSR measures and standards, together with a growing attention by stakeholders to the effects of business activity on society, provide a progressively stronger incentive for managers to engage in the practices of measuring, monitoring and communicating their engagement in CSR. Our study suggests the need for cooperation and dialogue as the founding criteria conducive to more effective disclosure and reporting practices. It is through stakeholder engagement that information becomes relevant to decision making for the companies and stakeholders alike, causing multiple expectations to converge in shared goals.

Beyond providing quantitative and qualitative empirical evidence of the existence, relevance and dynamics of the relationship between CSR disclosure and CSP, our study suggests the need for a shift away from simplistic assumptions about the performance consequences of CSR-related tools and activities. The CSR phenomenon has achieved such a dimension and relevance in both corporate and political agendas that reorienting empirical and theoretical investigation towards a deeper understanding of what it means to succeed in CSR is increasingly stringent. In this regard, disentangling specific dimensions and tracing back underlying procedural dynamics can spearhead a cultural shift towards walking the walk of CSR.

NOTES

1. Non-financial disclosure includes social, environmental and sustainability disclosures.
2. Findings presented in this chapter are part of a larger research project conducted by the authors. For detailed information about methodology and results, refer to Vurro (2009) and Vurro and Perrini (2009).

REFERENCES

Abbott, W.F. and R.J. Monsen (1979), 'On the measurement of corporate social responsibility: self-reported disclosures as a method of measuring corporate social involvement', *Academy of Management Journal*, **22** (3), 501–15.

Adams, C.A. (2002), 'Internal organisational factors influencing corporate social and ethical reporting: beyond current theorising', *Accounting, Auditing & Accountability Journal*, **15** (2), 223–50.

Bowman, E.H. and M. Haire (1975), 'A strategic posture toward corporate social responsibility', *California Management Review*, **18** (2), 49–58.

Chatterji, A. and D. Levine (2006), 'Breaking down the wall of codes: evaluating non-financial performance measurement', *California Management Review*, **48** (2), 29–51.

Clarkson, P.M., Y. Li, G.D. Richardson and F.P. Vasvari (2008), 'Revisiting the relation between environmental performance and environmental disclosure', *Accounting, Organizations and Society*, **33** (4/5), 303–27.

Cormier, D., I.M. Gordon and M. Magnan (2004), 'Corporate environmental disclosure: contrasting management's perception with reality', *Journal of Business Ethics*, **49** (2), 143–65.

Deegan, C. and B. Gordon (1996), 'A study of the environmental disclosure practices of Australian corporations', *Accounting and Business Research*, **26** (3), 187–99.

Donaldson, T. and L.E. Preston (1995), 'The stakeholder theory of the corporation: concepts, evidence, and implications', *Academy of Management Review*, **20** (1), 65–91.

Dye, R.A. (1985), 'Disclosure of nonproprietary information', *Journal of Accounting Research*, **23** (1), 123–45.

Freeman, R.E. (1984), *Strategic Management: A Stakeholder Approach*, Boston, MA: Pitman.

Gond, J.-P. and O. Herrbach (2006), 'Social reporting as an organizational learning tool? A theoretical framework', *Journal of Business Ethics*, **65** (4), 359–71.

Gray, R. (2002), 'The social accounting project and accounting organizations and society: privileging engagement, imaginings, new accountings and pragmatism over critique?', *Accounting, Organizations and Society*, **27** (7), 687–708.

Gray, R., R. Kouhy and S. Lavers (1995), 'Corporate social and environmental reporting: a review of the literature and a longitudinal study of UK disclosure', *Accounting, Auditing & Accountability Journal*, **8** (2), 47–77.

Greenwood, M. (2007), 'Stakeholder engagement: beyond the myth of corporate responsibility', *Journal of Business Ethics*, **74** (4), 315–27.

Hummels, H. and D. Timmer (2004), 'Investors in need of social, ethical, and environmental information', *Journal of Business Ethics*, **52** (1), 73–84.

Jose, A. and S.-M. Lee (2007), 'Environmental reporting of global corporations: a content analysis based on website disclosure', *Journal of Business Ethics*, **72** (4), 307–21.

Maak, T. and N.M. Pless (2006), 'Responsible leadership in a stakeholder society – a relational perspective', *Journal of Business Ethics*, **66** (1), 99–115.

Margolis, J.D. and J.P. Walsh (2003), 'Misery loves companies: rethinking social initiatives by business', *Administrative Science Quarterly*, **48** (2), 268–305.

Meek, G.K. and C.B. Roberts (1995), 'Factors influencing voluntary annual report disclosures by U.S., U.K. and continental European multinational corporations', *Journal of International Business Studies*, **20** (3), 555–72.

Mitchell, R.K., B.R. Agle and D.J. Wood (1997), 'Toward a theory of stakeholder identification and salience: defining the principle of who and what really counts', *Academy of Management Review*, **22** (4), 853–86.

Nitkin, D. and L.J. Brooks (1998), 'Sustainability auditing and reporting: the Canadian experience', *Journal of Business Ethics*, **17** (13), 1499–507.

Patten, D.M. (2002), 'The relation between environmental performance and environmental disclosure: a research note', *Accounting, Organizations and Society*, **27** (8), 763–73.

Patton, M.Q. (2002), *Qualitative Research and Evaluation Methods*, 3rd edn, Thousand Oaks, CA: Sage.

Perrini, F. and C. Vurro (2007), 'CSR concern of corporations: a stakeholder-based analysis of Italian nonfinancial reports', paper presented at the Academy of Management Conference, Philadelphia, PA.

Pettigrew, A. (1990), 'Longitudinal field research on change: theory and practice', *Organization Science*, **1** (3), 267–92.

Post, J.E., L.E. Preston and S. Sachs (2002), *Redefining the Corporation: Stakeholder Management and Organizational Wealth*, Stanford, CA: Stanford University Press.

Preston, L.E. (1981), 'Research on corporate social reporting: directions for development', *Accounting, Organizations and Society*, **6** (3), 255–62.

Roberts, R.W. (1992), 'Determinants of corporate social responsibility disclosure: an application of stakeholder theory', *Accounting, Organizations and Society*, **17** (6), 595–612.

Rowley, T. and S. Berman (2000), 'A brand new brand of corporate social performance', *Business & Society*, **38** (4), 397–418.

Sharma, S. and H. Vredenburg (1998), 'Proactive corporate environmental strategy and the development of competitively valuable organizational capabilities', *Strategic Management Journal*, **19** (8), 729–53.

Verrecchia, R.E. (1983), 'Discretionary disclosure', *Journal of Accounting and Economics*, **5** (3), 179–94.

Vurro, C. (2009), 'Shaping the path to corporate social responsibility and sustainability: from nonfinancial disclosure to organizational learning dynamics', doctoral dissertation, Università Bocconi, Milan, Italy.

Vurro, C. and F. Perrini (2009), 'The impact of nonfinancial disclosure structure on corporate social performance', paper presented at the Academy of Management Annual Conference, Chicago, IL.

Waddock, S. and C. Bodwell (2004), 'Managing responsibility: what can be learned from the quality movement?', *California Management Review*, **47** (1), 25–37.

Waddock, S.A., C.B. Bodwell and S.B. Graves (2002), 'Responsibility: the new business imperative', *Academy of Management Executive*, **16** (2), 132–48.

PART 4

Fostering responsibility and sustainability

14. Deep authenticity – an essential phenomenon in the web of life

Knut J. Ims and Ove D. Jakobsen

14.1 INTRODUCTION

The concept of authenticity has received an increasing amount of attention recently. Taylor (1991) criticizes the increased degree of individualization in modern society, 'the malaise of modernity'. He claims that we have ignored the presence of an individual in a deeper sense, a 'self' that has ties to communities as well as a 'horizon of meaning'. For Taylor authenticity is the courage to be true to oneself within a horizon of important values, while traditional concepts of individuals are one-dimensional and instrumentalist and do not emphasize the importance of social and dialogical relations with others. Authenticity is often connected to the search for individual 'wellbeing', 'enjoyment of life' and 'quality of life'. People living in harmony with their own values and principles and experiencing meaning and purpose in their lives are supposed to be authentic. The fallacy is that individuals are not open to the horizon of significance. One consequence is loss of meaning. We suggest a conception of authenticity that interprets man as a part of a web of life.

Interesting contributions to a new conception of man are offered by Richard Niebuhr (Kaiser, 1995), who makes a phenomenological analysis of man's moral existence. Niebuhr's man is relational, and the self exists in a triadic relation to itself, to society and to nature. And the appropriate action is a fitting one within the context (Kaiser, 1995). This view has important consequences. It follows from here that the question 'Who am I?' is more important than 'What is real?' Niebuhr argues that we should reflect upon the former question because self-knowledge is an important avenue to the responsible life. And Niebuhr states that when we ask about responsibility, we ask about ourselves!

In another strand of literature, the 'deep ecology movement', the main norm is self-realization for all sentient beings (Næss, 1989). This means that all sentient beings have the right to self-unfolding on their own premises. The mature deep-ecological man has developed an ecological self, a self which is not impersonal but transpersonal and has the ability to identify with all other sentient beings. The ecological self negates the minimal self, which is self-centred, self-obsessed, attached to hedonistic pleasures and as a consequence alienated from itself, from other beings and nature. One consequence of being an ecological self is that if you hurt nature, you hurt your own interests and in a deep sense you hurt yourself (Drengson and Inoue, 1995; Næss, 1989; Sessions, 1995).

In accordance with deep-ecology thinking we argue that the interpretation of authenticity should be expanded or 'deepened' to encompass a holistic rather than individualistic context. This means that the individual's authenticity is richer and more meaningful because of its connection to the web of life. In other words, how we choose to live our lives is dependent upon our connections within the web of life. Both society and nature will have an impact on human authenticity, on both the individual and the collective levels.

Our argument is based on the presupposition that understanding is always guided by the interpretative framework used or our background assumptions. According to Rose, our interpretative framework is a continually evolving construction that functions to 'highlight or bring into focus certain features of experience, moving them from the background to the foreground of experimental awareness' (Rose, 2002, p. 11). This indicates that understanding starts from a set of ontological and epistemological presuppositions, which can be aggregated up to a worldview. In accordance with this view, we contend that authenticity depends on the interpreter's worldview. In the following paragraphs we will state some reasons for these assumptions and conclusions. More precisely we will draw a demarcation line between shallow and deep authenticity.

We will define shallow authenticity as a mode of being based upon a mechanic worldview, indicating that people might be authentic independent of their relations to other living organisms. Shallow authenticity is a characteristic of an individualistic mindset. In contrast we define deep authenticity as based upon an organic holistic worldview, indicating that authenticity is a relational concept. Deep authenticity is a characteristic of the individual strongly embedded in society and nature. To be deeply authentic implies being an integrated part of social and natural systems. In other words, deep authenticity is based upon organic interdependence as described in Næss' 'Ecosophy' (Drengson and Inoue, 1995; Næss, 1989) and in Whitehead's 'Philosophy of Organism' (Whitehead, 1925 [1967], 1929 [1985], 1933 [1967]).

From the statement that everything is intensively interconnected, it follows that a precondition for deep authenticity is cooperation between interrelated, self-realizing subjects. A deeply authentic person is simultaneously free and committed to society and nature. Shallow authenticity is possible within an atomized market based on a mechanic worldview where all entities are isolated atoms with a natural inclination to compete against each other. Deep authenticity is inseparably connected to communicative coexistence between human beings and nature. We will illustrate the discussion with some practical examples. First, we will examine and elaborate organic and mechanic worldviews as concepts in some detail. Next, we will discuss shallow and deep authenticity, respectively. The meaning of authenticity depends on the worldview being discussed.

14.2   ORGANIC AND MECHANIC WORLDVIEWS

Referring to Capra's (1982) definition, an organic worldview refers to a reality composed of living entities having a high degree of 'non-linear' interconnectedness. This means that individuals and communities simultaneously create and require each other. Thurow goes into more detail when he argues that societies are not merely statistical aggregations of individuals engaged in voluntary exchange but something much more subtle and complicated. 'A group or community cannot be understood if the unit of analysis is the individual taken by himself. A society is clearly something greater than the sum of its parts' (Daly and Cobb Jr, 1994, p. 7). According to Whitehead a society is self-sustaining and has its own reason for being. A society is more than a set of entities to which the same class-name applies. 'The self-identity of a society is founded upon the self-identity of its defining characteristics, and upon the mutual immanence of its occasions . . . and the creative advance into the future' (Whitehead, 1933 [1967], p. 204). Therefore it is important to ask questions about patterns, organization, rhythm and flow. We have contrasted some essential differences between organic and mechanic worldviews in Table 14.1.

We argue that organic thinking is based on the concept that culture is a collective phenomenon rather than a sum of individuals exclusively. Within this complex and dynamic framework, individual behaviour is both multifaceted and context-dependent; hence, accepting the organic worldview has far-reaching consequences for the interpretation of the individual as a self-realizing person in society.

In addition to holistic integration the organic worldview is based upon the concept of inherent values. The motivation for introducing values and purposes into nature is the acknowledgement that materialism cannot give an adequate account of the emergence and meaning of life. In accordance with this reasoning we argue that we have to rethink the status of life

Table 14.1   Mechanic and organic worldviews

Mechanic worldview	Organic worldview
Linear connectedness	Non-linear interconnectedness
Instrumental values	Inherent values
Deterministic	Co-creation
Physical laws	Creativity
Dualism	Holism
Isolated ego	Extended self
Purposelessness	Purposefulness

in nature and to accept that integrated organisms have inherent value. The term 'life' refers to the appreciation of things like 'self-enjoyment', 'freedom', 'creativity', 'purpose' and 'subjectivity', derived from the past and aimed at the future. The idea of including human nature as an element in ecosystems results in the notion that such variables as value and freedom can no longer be excluded from the descriptions of nature.

Within the organic worldview life and mind are interwoven with matter and motion. It is the essence of life that it exists for its own sake, as an intrinsic reaping of value. The point is that we can understand neither physical nature nor life unless we fuse them together as essential factors in the composition of the whole universe. Nothing in nature could be what it is, except as an integrated ingredient in nature as a dynamic whole.

In contrast to the organic worldview, mechanism presupposes that physical matter is identical with reality, and that everything can be explained in terms of imposed physical laws. From this perspective, the social sciences are characterized by the idea that bits of matter are isolated individuals (atomism), related to one another purely externally. 'The material universe, including the human organism, was a machine that could in principle be understood completely by analyzing it in terms of its smallest parts' (Capra, 1995, p. 21). Through natural laws, society represents no real unity in itself. Society is nothing more than a mere mechanism based on the interplay among egocentric individuals seeking their own ends ('the economic man').

As a consequence the explanations based upon the mechanic worldview claim that every biological or social event is a pattern of non-biological occurrences. This formulation cannot be interpreted as an assertion that all organisms are like machines. To avoid some of these problems we are using the term mechanism more broadly than machine. In other words, mechanism is a worldview claiming that physical matter is reality, complete and total. Everything in the universe can be explained in terms of physical laws.

Table 14.2   *Principles of coordination, in the context of different worldviews*

	Mechanic	Organic
Competition	1. Efficiency	3. Disintegration
Cooperation	2. Collusion	4. Responsible co- creation

The great forces of nature, such as gravitation, were entirely determined by the configurations of masses. Accepting that the whole universe is completely causal and deterministic has serious consequences concerning the possibilities of human creativity, freedom and self-fulfilment. Interpreted from a mechanic worldview, 'all that happened had a definite cause and gave rise to a definite effect, and . . . the future of any part of the system could – in principle – be predicted with absolute certainty if its state at any time was known in detail' (Capra, 1997, p. 120). A consequence of this logic is that 'dead' nature can provide no reasons, and it aims at nothing.

Today, the mechanical worldview still forms the basis of many scientific disciplines, including mainstream economics. In lifeless nature, problems can be solved within the framework of physical laws. It is, at least in principle, possible to arrive at unambiguous solutions to these kinds of convergent problems. Schumacher (1977) argues that convergent problems have nothing to do with self-consciousness or life functions. In accordance with Georgescu-Roegen (1971) and Daly and Cobb Jr (1994), we contend that this assertion still holds validity for modern mainstream economics.

The mechanic worldview is useful for describing and dealing with delimited physical phenomena encountered in our daily environment. We have argued (Ims and Jakobsen, 2006) that the ontological presuppositions are important for understanding appropriate market behaviour as indicated in Table 14.2. We maintain that a mechanic worldview implies competition among actors in the market as exhibited in cell 1 in Table 14.2. However we should be aware of the problems connected to using abstractions based on the limited worldview of mechanism. According to Whitehead we tend to forget that the mechanic worldview is an abstraction, and even worse, we tend to mistake the abstraction for the concrete actuality ('the fallacy of misplaced concreteness'). When emotions and values are missing, we lose the connectedness to living society (cell 3 in Table 14.2). Also cell 2 shows a constellation between the mechanic worldview and cooperation, which may be exemplified with different types of collusion. Collusion is illegal activity because it may lead to price fixing or the carving up of markets between different companies. In cells 3 and 4 we assume an organic worldview, and in these constellations the partners are perceived as integrated, through dialogical process, and they share common long-term values and interests. The organic paradigm presupposes cooperation (cell 4), which leads to responsible co-creation. The organic worldview involves cooperative communication processes among the partners as being essential, inherent parts of the market (network economy). We claim that market behaviour based on competition will often lead to disintegration and egocentric behaviour. Within an organic worldview use of one-sided power is destructive (cell 3).

Awareness of the ontological and ethical preconditions can help us to see the limitations of the mechanic worldview. To grasp the whole human being, as an individual and as a member of society, it is necessary to expand the perspective. The organic worldview is more fundamental, as the cosmos is seen as interrelated and connected manifestations of one inseparable reality – always in motion, alive, organic, spiritual and material at the same time (see cell 4 in Table 14.2).

14.3   REFLECTIONS ON AUTHENTICITY

For Taylor authenticity is a kind of self-fulfilment that is inseparable from a horizon of important values. And according to Taylor a self has an identity defined in terms of certain essential strong evaluations that provide the horizon. And humans have the capacity for second-order desires, that is, strong evaluations of desires, and they are responsible for their evaluations. However, the deepest evaluations are the most hidden and most subject to interplay with illusion. Thus the struggle for self-interpretation is not trivial. Taylor uses the term 'deep reflection' as a kind of radical evaluation, as 'a reflection which engages the self most wholly and deeply' (Taylor, 1985, p. 42).

The concept 'authenticity' has been described and discussed within philosophical existentialism for centuries. Soren Kierkegaard (1843/1978) maintains strongly that we are able to choose ourselves, and we have the ability to move from living a purely aesthetical life, in the sense of being an ego, to a stage of being which is called ethical. The aesthetic man lives in dread and despair because he cannot sense that he is meant for something higher. In contrast the ethical man truly chooses himself. Individuals who do not live authentically often lose the meaning of life and can be hit by chronic anxiety, boredom or despair. In our modern societies people avoiding the responsibility of living authentically, in the worst case, end up anaesthetizing themselves with alcohol or other drugs. For most people it is important to live as authentically as possible; however, in our globalized, complex world it is not easy to achieve this goal. In the Western world the

Table 14.3   Reflected self-understanding (inspired by Schumacher, 1977)

	Inner experience	Outer experience
Me	1. My inner world	3. Me in the eyes of others
Other beings	2. Other beings' inner world	4. The world in the eyes of other beings

advertising pressure oriented towards individuals, which is designed to delude the populace into believing that self-realization depends upon consumption habits, is very strong. The intriguing question is: what does it mean to live an authentic life? Some people choose to appreciate more of their own current approach to life, while others might choose to introduce new activities and lifestyles.

From an existentialistic point of view authentic persons must see themselves as fundamentally free, thereby acknowledging responsibility for their actions and lives. The only way to experience freedom is to regard and treat other people as free, since the acceptance of other people's authenticity is a condition of oneself being authentic. Some existentialists argue that authenticity is based upon intimate personal relations – love and friendship. To elaborate the concept of 'self-understanding' within an organic worldview, we distinguish between the following dimensions: 'inner' and 'outer' experience, and 'me' and 'other' beings, as shown in Table 14.3.

According to the organic worldview we are integrated parts of the web of life, embedded in human societies and nature. To understand our selves in this perspective requires a multidimensional perspective: first (cell 1 in Table 14.3), I have to know myself. This is the old Socratic imperative: 'Know Thyself!' It is a profound point of departure. Schumacher frames it thus: I have to 'feel what I feel like'. And the preconditions for understanding my inner self are self-awareness and self-confidence: 'Without self-awareness, the exploration and study of the inner man, i.e., one's interior world, is completely impossible' (Schumacher, 1977, p. 66). Without self-awareness and self-confidence we think and act mechanically, like a programmed computer. The result is that we have no freedom to act in accordance with our own ideas and intentions.

Second (cell 2), I have to be sensitive to the inner worlds of other people and 'feel what you feel like' (empathy). We believe that we may know something about the inner life of animals, but still more of what goes on inside other human beings. We do not believe that we are able to know much of a plant's inner life, and we know nothing about inanimate matter. Human society depends on 'our ability to understand others and their ability to understand us' (Schumacher, 1977, p. 81). According to a number of wise men in different traditions – Buddhists as well as Christians – it is impossible to understand others without first understanding ourselves.

Third (cell 3), in order to know myself it is necessary to know how I am known by others. Schumacher argues that the only source for knowing myself is my own inner feelings, and that I tend to understand myself as the centre of the universe. Having the ability 'to see ourselves as others see us . . . will help us to see our contradictions' (Schumacher, 1977, p. 97). Contradictions are not manifestations of error; instead, they are manifestations of truth. Opposites are a part of real life and we have to learn to keep opposites in mind simultaneously. The best way to gather knowledge about myself is by putting myself in other people's situations. This is possible because we are reflective social beings, living with others.

Fourth (cell 4), according to Schumacher this 'is the real homeland of every kind of behaviorism: only strictly observable behavior is of interest' (Schumacher, 1977, p. 100). Many people believe that this is the only field in which true knowledge can be obtained. The strange thing is that we in cell 4 have most knowledge concerning inanimate matter and least about the inner life of human beings. In cell 2 it is the other way round: we can know most about the higher levels of life and least about inanimate matter. In cell 4 we can observe movement and other kinds of changes in matter, but we cannot observe meaning, purpose, feelings or values through our physical senses. In terms of maturity we might say that 'the more mature the object of study, the less mature the science studying it' (Schumacher, 1977, p. 103). We argue that authenticity presupposes knowledge based upon all the four different cells.

Charles Taylor (1989, 1991) supports our reasoning by arguing that self-creation must be added to self-realization. Creativity is always reflexive and is exercised over and with respect to the self. Since the self is social, creativity is transactional and multidimensional. Therefore, creativity is both self-creative and co-creative. Taylor points out both the good and damaging aspects of the modern development of an authentic self, and he mentions the importance of some moral measurement system anchored in strong evaluations. To become authentic we have to take part in cooperative dialogues where we exchange our ideas with others and construct our values and beliefs in the course of communicative processes. In other words, to discover and be aware of our authenticity we have to converse with other people. Dialogue is essential if we want to develop our own authenticity, and according to Taylor authenticity is essential if we want to live a better life. This emphasis on dialogue is in accordance with Niebuhr, who argues that our thinking is an inner conversation where we deal with other concrete, particular selves (Kaiser, 1995).

Table 14.4   Shallow and deep authenticity

	Mechanic	Organic
Ego-centric	1. Shallow authenticity	3.
Eco-centric	2.	4. Deep authenticity

14.4   CONCLUDING COMMENTS

To penetrate authenticity we find it illuminating to draw a demarcation line between 'shallow' and 'deep'. By using these concepts we indicate our inspiration from 'the deep ecology movement' (Drengson and Inoue, 1995; Næss, 1989; Witoszek and Brennan, 1999). The difference between shallow and deep ecology concerns the willingness to go to the roots of problems and ask critical questions about oneself as well as modern society with its prevailing institutions. The danger is to confuse the 'self' with the 'ego-centric self'. Deep authenticity depends on our ability to flip to an organic worldview where awareness of an 'eco-centric self' becomes possible. We try to visualize the radical and necessary change in mindset in Table 14.4.

We argue that the organic worldview is more suitable than the mechanic for interpreting authenticity. Hidden and unintended consequences are very often connected to advanced technologies. The result is that what we do today will have consequences on many levels for ourselves, for others, for nature and for future generations. Once we discover that we as individual persons are always relating to other human beings, society and nature we have to clarify our positions in the web of life. A consequence of eco-centred awareness is that we become more responsible in the social and ecological worlds. To become more responsive, openness and dialogue are vital. We need courage to change our interpretative map to discover the interconnectedness in the social and environmental realities. The concept of deep authenticity is essential for grasping these new perspectives. In the context of deep authenticity we are free, and we are aware of the responsibility that is laid upon us. Freedom is a burden because we are called upon to act in response to the environment. But the single individual has to face the situation, and if necessary, break with the dominating norms. In our Western world the external pressure to become wealthy and outwardly successful is strong for each individual. To handle the individual, social and environmental challenges we are facing today we have to transition away from the idea of 'economic man' to that of 'ecological man'.

To be inauthentic is to choose the easiest way and thereby follow the avenue to self-deception – to circumvent and avoid facing up to the real problems in the world. It is to even ignore inconvenient truths, crucial facts about the state of the world in the hope that the problems will in the end be resolved by someone else.

In the perspective of marketing and management literature, assumptions about an organic worldview lead to new perspectives for all stakeholders and the relations between them. Responsibility towards all living beings illuminates the inherent value in the web of life. One important consequence is the shift from maximizing shareholder value to increasing the enjoyment of life for all stakeholders in the context of a long-term perspective.

REFERENCES

Capra, F. (1982), *The Turning Point – Science, Society and the Rising Culture*, London: Flamingo.
Capra, F. (1995), 'Deep ecology – a new paradigm', in G. Sessions (ed.), *Deep Ecology for the 21st Century*, London: Shambhala.
Capra, F. (1997), *The Web of Life – A New Synthesis of Mind and Matter*, London: Flaming.
Daly, H. and J.B. Cobb Jr (1994), *For the Common Good – Redirecting the Economy Toward Community, the Environment, and a Sustainable Future*, Boston, MA: Beacon Press.
Drengson, A. and Y. Inoue (eds) (1995), *The Deep Ecology Movement – An Introductory Anthology*, Berkeley, CA: North Atlantic Books.
Georgescu-Roegen, N. (1971), *The Entropy Law and the Economic Process*, Cambridge, MA: Harvard University Press.
Ims, K.J. and O. Jakobsen (2006), 'Cooperation and competition in the context of organic and mechanic worldview: a theoretical and case-based discussion', *Journal of Business Ethics*, **66** (1), 19–32.
Kaiser, R.M. (1995), *Roots of Relational Ethics: Responsibility in Origin and Maturity in H. Richard Niebuhr*, Atlanta, GA: Scholars Press.
Kierkegaard, S. (1843 [1978]), *Enten – Eller*, Samlede Værker, Bind 2 (*Either – Or*, collected work, vol. 2), Copenhagen: Gyldendal.
Næss, A. (1989), *Ecology, Community and Lifestyle: Outline of an Ecosophy*, translated and revised by D. Rothenberg, Cambridge: Cambridge University Press.
Rose, P. (2002), *On Whitehead*, Belmont, CA: Wadsworth Philosophers Series.
Schumacher, E.F. (1977), *A Guide for the Perplexed*, New York: Harper & Row.
Sessions, G. (ed.) (1995), *Deep Ecology for the 21st Century – Readings on the Philosophy and Practice of the New Environmentalism*, London: Shambhala.
Taylor, C. (1985), *Human Agency and Language: Philosophical Papers*, Cambridge: Cambridge University Press.
Taylor, C. (1989), *Sources of the Self: The Making of the Modern Identity*, Cambridge: Cambridge University Press.
Taylor, C. (1991), *The Ethics of Authenticity*, Cambridge, MA: Harvard University Press.

Whitehead, A.N. (1925), *Science and the Modern World*, Cambridge: Cambridge University Press, reprinted in 1967, New York: The Free Press.
Whitehead, A.N. (1929), *Process and Reality,* New York: The Macmillan Company, reprinted in 1985, New York: The Free Press.
Whitehead, A.N. (1933), *Adventures of Ideas,* New York: New American, reprinted in 1967, New York: The Free Press.
Witoszek, N. and A. Brennan (eds) (1999), *Philosophical Dialogues – Arne Næss and the Progress of Ecophilosophy*, Oxford: Rowman & Littlefield Publiners.

Index